Mary Isabella Bryson

Fred C. Roberts of Tientsin

Or for Christ and China

Mary Isabella Bryson

Fred C. Roberts of Tientsin
Or for Christ and China

ISBN/EAN: 9783337030285

Printed in Europe, USA, Canada, Australia, Japan

Cover: Foto ©ninafisch / pixelio.de

More available books at **www.hansebooks.com**

FRED. C. ROBERTS

OF TIENTSIN:

OR,

For Christ and China.

BY

MRS. BRYSON,
AUTHOR OF
"CHILD LIFE IN CHINESE HOMES," "THE STORY OF JAMES GILMOUR,"
"JOHN KENNETH MACKENZIE," ETC.

WITH AN INTRODUCTION BY THE

REV. F. B. MEYER, B.A.

LONDON:
H. R. ALLENSON,
30, PATERNOSTER ROW.
MDCCCXCV.

TO

THE FATHER AND MOTHER

WHOSE JOY IT WAS

TO LAY AT THE MASTER'S FEET,

A GIFT SO RARE,

FOR

THE CAUSE OF CHINA'S REDEMPTION

"All things he forsook, to give himself
To ministry among the poor and sad.
And now, still young, for many years his life
Had been among them; wheresoever need
Was bitterest, and the heart was pierced the most.
And mighty gifts of healing, and great power
For soul and body's aid and comforting,
Went with him in the toilsome way he trod.
Whenever called him the most hopeless cry,
Whenever want most sad and pain most sore,
Through the dark hours his constant watchings wore;
The touches of his tenderness were spent;
Till, from the saved, the succoured, the consoled,
One voice of blessing clung around his name."

E. HAMILTON KING.

PREFATORY WORDS

By Rev. F. B. MEYER, B.A.

———◆———

IT was my happy privilege to know Dr. Roberts intimately, and, as I write, sacred and lovely memories come trooping back from the past. He was a frequent visitor in the houses of his married sisters, who, with their husbands, were my loyal and generous fellow-labourers in the work of Christ connected with Melbourne Hall, Leicester.

He generally came during his vacations, and always left behind the savour of a sweet and strong soul. Glad and happy in spirit; courteous and sympathetic in manner; enthusiastic in devotion to his life-purpose; reverent and intense in his religious life,—his was a rare personality; and I am not surprised to learn that the Chinese Christians frequently remarked, that they never saw anyone so like the Lord Jesus as Dr. Roberts—" he dresses our wounds with his own hands; and the poorer a man is, the more care he lavishes upon him."

One of the most remarkable farewell meetings I ever attended, was that held at Melbourne Hall on the occasion of his departure for China in 1887. He, too, often referred to it in after years. It was a fresh anointing for service; not alone for him, but for others. We asked that he might have divine power, without realising that, as it passed through his slight frame, it might consume its energy prematurely. We asked that he might be long spared, without realising that God would give him length of days for ever and ever. We asked, as we read the ninety-first Psalm, that he might dwell in the secret place of the Most High, without realising that it might mean the innermost Presence of the King. Like the mother of the two apostles, we asked the Throne for our beloved friend, and our prayer was answered more speedily and fully than we thought.

A treasured letter to me from him says: "Thanks for that message about the worker being God in us; I have often thought of it, and found it helpful. It is a message we need to hear often—at least I do." But it was hardly necessary to remind him of a spiritual fact which was the constant inspiration of his life. His was no wearisome struggle to fulfil the demands of a Master infinitely beyond and above him, but of One who was "nearer than breathing." His life was hid with Christ in God; and therefore God's life, which is stored in Christ Jesus, was hidden deep in him, as a spring of living water.

Love endeavours to enshrine and perpetuate, however inadequately, by portrait and memoir, its impression of its friend who is with God, that others may know his worth and forgive its tears. Such, however, is not the main reason for the issue of this biography; but the hope that, as in the Old Testament story, many a young life, touching the grave of the prophet, may live, may be baptized for the dead, and may dedicate all to the cause for which Dr. Roberts counted not his life dear.

He sleeps in the English burying-ground at Tientsin, in a strip of land stolen from the featureless, desolate, and malaria-stricken plain, beside Gilmour of Mongolia and Mackenzie of Tientsin. Three kindred souls, whose graves hold the land for Christ, as that lorn cave of Machpelah held Palestine for the Exodus! And surely the spot where they lie, redeemed from the desert around, with its trees and flowering shrubs, is an emblem of what that moral wilderness is destined to become, when Jesus sees of the travail of His soul and is satisfied.

F. B. MEYER.

AUTHOR'S PREFACE

In the following pages an attempt has been made to show how, amid the holy influences of an English home, a lad of godly ancestry was trained for noble work in the Foreign Mission field.

The vast opportunities for service offered to the medical missionary in a populous Chinese city and its surrounding country districts are also portrayed.

It is shown how many a Chinaman who has heretofore looked upon the "Foreign Barbarian" with scorn and hatred, has had his heart softened by this benevolent work; and eventually, having his life transformed by the Spirit of Jesus, has become a missionary to his own countrymen. These things the writer, who had the high privilege of Dr. Roberts' friendship during his life in China,—being a fellow-worker in the same mission,—has endeavoured to relate.

But, in addition to this, the book is, as far as may be, the record (from his own letters and diaries) of a saintly soul, to whom the risen Saviour was, in a marked degree, a living, ever-present Friend.

Dr. Roberts proved experimentally that, in the strength which comes from the Heavenly Manna, the Christian can walk happily and victoriously amid any environment, and that it is possible to live a very busy life, and at the same time a life of closest communion with our Lord and Master.

Very many in this and distant lands, who received blessing from fellowship with Dr. Roberts, desired that others should share the privilege which they, for a season, had enjoyed.

It was with this desire that the writer, among many other engagements, while on furlough in England, has attempted, though very inadequately, to tell this story of a consecrated life.

She desires to thank the relatives and numerous friends who have so kindly placed the whole of Dr. Roberts' correspondence with them, and his diaries, at her disposal; and also the Directors of the London Missionary Society, for the same courtesy.

She sends the book forth with the prayer that a double portion of Dr. Roberts' spirit may rest upon many a reader. "God buries His workmen, but carries on His work." To Him be all the glory for the lives which prove to-day that we have not

"Lost the type of love,
Nor quenched the martyr line."

May many a Christian heart learn to look at the world through the compassionate eyes of Jesus, and give themselves and all that they possess to hasten the coming of His kingdom in lands which lie in darkness and the shadow of death.

MARY I. BRYSON,
Of the London Mission, Tientsin.

CONTENTS

CHAPTER I
A GODLY ANCESTRY

The Grandparents' Home—Religious Life in Wales early in the Century—Trevecca College—A Puritan Doctor—A Terror to Evil-Doers—The Hunting Squire—Early Family Worship—Bible Lessons—John Foulkes Roberts—University College of Wales—Maternal Grandparents—A Grandmother's Prayers—The Faithful Promiser   11

CHAPTER II
CHILDHOOD AND SCHOOL DAYS

The Manchester Home—A Child's Prayers—Bible Lessons—Influence of Elder Sisters—A Child's Blessing—Working for Jesus—Holiday Thoughts—The Coast of Wales—Serious Illness—A Child's Faith—Manchester Grammar School 21

CHAPTER III
ABERYSTWITH AND COLLEGE DAYS

The Boy-Student—Depth of Christian Life—Thoughts about Future—Influence over Others—Bible Studies Examinations—China's Need—Students' Prayer-Meeting—Answered Prayers—Work among Outcasts—The Joy of Service—Letter to Mother—Seventeenth Birthday—Separations—Principal Edwards—Success in Work—Confessing Christ—His Tutor on his Student Life . . . 27

CHAPTER IV
MEDICAL STUDIES

Student Home—Christian Friends—Infirmary—Drill Hall Free Breakfasts—An Edinburgh Sunday—An Ideal Friendship—Moody's Meetings—Dr. Schofield—Passing Exams.—Ward Services—At the Eleventh Hour—The Cambridge Party—A Never-to-be-forgotten Time—Dispensary Work—Jewels in Dark Places—Sister's

CONTENTS

Visit—A Leper Won for Christ—Success—Time of Testing—Home and Foreign Service—Murray's *Abide in Christ*—Spiritual Needs—Chinese Language—Hudson Taylor's Message . . . 45

CHAPTER V

ALPINE GLENS AND LAST FAREWELLS

Pastor's Recollections—Sunday-School Work—A Friend in Need—Italian Pictures—The Alpine Guide—Mountain Echoes—Avalanches—Thoughts on Qualifications for Missionary Service—Appointed to Mongolia—Consciousness of Weakness—Keswick—Many Prayers—Farewell 62

CHAPTER VI

OUTWARD BOUND, AND THE CITY OF THE HEAVENLY FORD

Voyage to China—Daily Occupations—Work among Sailors—Learning Chinese — An Ocean Grave—Shanghai—Gilmour's Welcome—Through the Yellow Sea—Up the Pei-ho—Tientsin Settlement—Result of Answered Prayer—Hospital Wards—A Crowded Dispensary—Medical School—Dr. Mackenzie—A Chinese Feast—Busy Days—Gilmour's Arrival—A Chinese Sermon—A Tablet—Frozen to Death—Chinese Soup Kitchens—Buddhist Temples—Spiritual Experiences 70

CHAPTER VII

MONGOLIAN SOLITUDES

The Feast of Lanterns—An Unknown Friend—Off to Mongolia—Roadside Inns—Chinese Industry—A Gate in the Great Wall—The First Mongol—Gilmour's Inn—A Comfortless Home—Progress in Chinese—Chinese Food—A Lama Letter-Carrier—Gilmour's Blue Tent—From Ta-ssu-kow to Ta-cheng-tsz—Pawnshops — Opium Smokers — Whisky Distilleries — Temples and Theatres—Dying Beggars—Journey to Chao-yang—Through the Robber-infested District — Crowded Inns — Mongol Priests — A Hopeful Sect—The Reformers of China—Joy in Work . . 83

CHAPTER VIII

APPOINTED TO TIENTSIN

The Messenger from Tientsin—A Heavy Blow—Dr. Mackenzie's Death—Dr. Roberts Recalled—A Momentous Conversation—Separations—The Lonely Colleague—Travelling through Mongolia—Crowded Inns—Hopeful Coreans—The Gate of Heaven—A Message from *Daily Light* — Newchwang — The Grave of William Burns — Chinese Doctors—On Board Ship—Christ my Pilot—Arrival at Tientsin—Mission Prayer-Meeting—A Man sent from God—Daily Life—First Chinese Address 93

CONTENTS

CHAPTER IX

GLIMPSES OF CHINESE HOSPITAL WORK

Chinese Medical Work—Lack of Sick Nursing—Winning his Way—Chinese Patients—Hydrophobia—Cholera—A Distracted Mother—Sight Restored—Gratitude of Patients—A Scholar Healed—Amputation Case—Baptisms—Increased Confidence—Overflowing Wards—The "Mackenzie" Ward—A Christian Drill-Sergeant—Soldier Patients — Liu Wei-hsien — Eight Inquirers — Before Rulers and Governors—A Noble Confession—A Christian Worker—A Chinaman's Gratitude—Dr. Smith appointed as Colleague—Wealthy Patients—Mandarin's Son—Mr. Massey's Visit . . 111

CHAPTER X

FAMINE, FLOOD, AND REBELLION

Famine Relief-Work—A Comfortless Journey—Ruined Temples—Dying of Starvation—Gratitude of Sufferers—China's Undeveloped Resources—Futile Attempts to Mend the Yellow River Breaches—Incapable Rulers—Mandarin "Squeezes"—China's Chronic State of Famine—A Winter Journey—The Husks of the Prodigal—Wars and Rumours of Wars—The Rebels occupy Chao-yang—In Hiding—A Colleague in Danger—A Happy Ending to Anxious Deliberations 127

CHAPTER XI

WORK IN THE COUNTRY DISTRICTS

Interest in Country Work—Lonely Chinese Christians—First Visit to Yen Shan—The Boat Journey—The Old Watchman—A Curious Crowd—A Deserted City—A Robber-infested District—Winning the People's Favour—A Sacred Tree—Thanksgiving Theatricals—A North China Sect—A Chinese Nun—The Golden Rule of Confucius—Village Chapels—Backsliders—Helpful Talks—Making Peace—Night Work—No Retirement—Singing Hymns all Night—Feast Day at Yen Shan—How the Gospel Spreads—A Christian Bricklayer—Rice Collections—Many Open Doors—An Appeal for Labourers 137

CHAPTER XII

DR. ROBERTS AS A FRIEND

Love for Children—Letters to Child-Friends—Interest in Chinese Children—Winter Games and Summer Rambles—Letters to Child-Patient — His Thoughts on Christian Friendships — Letters of Christian Cheer—Breadth of his Sympathies—Varied Testimonies—Ready for Unexpected Calls 150

CHAPTER XIII

PERSONAL CHARACTERISTICS AND GLIMPSES OF INNER LIFE

A Busy Life—Nothing Morose or Sad—Delight in Beauties of Nature—Secret of Happiness—Christ's Representatives—Spiritual and Temporal Blessings—"Weights" which Hinder—Witnessing for Christ—A Parable from Nature—Freewill Offerings—Spiritual Thirst—"Rivers of Living Water"—The Mount of Blessing—Light on the Daily Path—Obedience the Condition of Blessing—Temptations — Unconscious Sins—Devotional Reading — Peace Ruling in the Heart—Faith-Healing—The Needs of the Spiritual Life — *Bowen's Meditations* — A Year's Retrospect — Thoughts about being Cleansed from Indwelling Sin—Comfort in Trouble—Shallowness of Belief—Training Children for Christ—Dangers of Success—Progress—Joy in the Lord—Keswick—The Hospital Funds — Faith Tested and Rewarded — Self-denying Service — Saved to Save—Chinese Coolies—Sailors—The Last Christmas Eve—Teaching Chinese Boatmen—Holiday Service—The Forward Movement 165

CHAPTER XIV

THE LAST MONTHS

Chinese Revival Services—Special Blessing—Crowded Wards—Preparing for M.D. — Trip to Shan-hai-kwan — An Iron Bridge — Awakening among Solitary Christians—The Great Wall — A Frozen Sea—Country Labours—Need of Doctors—An Interesting Convert—Anticipations of Home-Coming—Thoughts on Deputation Work—The Unseen World—Service, not Rest . . . 193

CHAPTER XV

THE BRINK OF THE RIVER

Anxious Cases—Last Labours—Brotherly Sympathy—A Last Good-bye—A Happy Evening—"Kept for Jesus Christ"—The Evening Hymn—Grateful Praise—A Morning Thought—A Last Message—Asleep in Jesus—A Complete Life—A Chinese Mourner—The Graveyard at Tientsin—Loving Tributes—"Like Jesus"—Tribute of Hospital Workers—Letter from Country District—A Chinese Doctor's Letter—After-Results of Hospital Labours—The Barrowman—The Robber's Gratitude—An Opium Smoker Restored—Widespread Results of Dr. Roberts' Labours 208

ROBERTS OF TIENTSIN

CHAPTER I

A GODLY ANCESTRY

"Because He loved thy fathers, therefore He chose their seed after them."—
DEUT. iv. 37.

AWAY to the west of the grand sweep of the Cambrian range with the bold peak of Snowdon, stretches the "wind-swept, sun-bleached island of Anglesea." Here one sees little of the rugged mountainous scenery which we associate with the very name of Wales. The surface of the country is slightly undulating, the villages scattered, with farm-houses and white wind-mills here and there, while glimpses of the sea are visible from many sides.

In this peaceful and not uninteresting district, about six miles from an iron-bound coast, upon which, on wild winter nights, many a bark has been dashed to pieces, stood the old farmstead of Mynydd-y-gof. It was situated upon a slight eminence, not far from the village of Bodedeyrn, surrounded by shrubberies and smiling pasture-lands. In process of time, by repeated improvements and enlargements, it had assumed the proportions and appearance of an ancient manor-house. The old-fashioned porch was thickly over-grown with great bushes of scarlet japonica and pink monthly roses, while near at hand stood a huge hydrangea, which seemed to bloom almost the whole year round. Immediately in front of the house, two fine bay trees stood, like sentinels, keeping guard over the two long carriage-drives which led to the highway. What beautiful drives they were: the hedges grew at their own sweet will, and honeysuckle, hawthorn, and wild roses scented the summer air with their sweet perfume.

Mynydd-y-gof, as I have said, was one of those large rambling country houses which are the delight of all dwellers in towns. It had its parlour mawr (great) and parlour bach (little) on one side of the hall; and on the other, beside the front kitchen, another small room, in addition to the surgery. The front kitchen led into a still larger room, where the men-servants employed on the farm took their meals, and the white and black bread was baked. The ceiling was hung with abundant provision for the family wants, in the shape of hams, bacon, and salted beef.

The ancient chimney of this apartment was a wonder to all child-visitors, since several of them could stand together on the hearth-stone, and, looking up, see the blue sky at the top. Such was the residence—plain, substantial, and commodious—of David Roberts, Esq., surgeon, whose name was known all over the country-side for many a mile some sixty years ago.

He was the only medical man in the district, even though he superintended with interest the work of his farm. In addition to this, he was a leading man with the Calvinistic Methodists, a religious denomination at that time struggling into existence, but probably at present by far the strongest religious power in North Wales.

Mynydd-y-gof became famous as a stronghold of Methodism; and the leading preachers, such as the famous John Elias of Llangefni, and William Roberts of Amlwch, were intimate friends with its master, both in social and religious matters. The itinerant system of preaching was then in vogue, and the old homestead was known as an open house for all preachers, a special prophet's chamber being kept for their use.

It was through this itinerant system that Dr. Roberts was introduced to his wife, whose parents also kept an open house at Machynlleth in Montgomeryshire. She was descended from Mr. Simon Bowen of Tyddyn. He was the first gentleman to open his house for the preaching of the gospel in the time of Wesley and Whitefield, who used to preach to the crowds which assembled there. His daughter, Sarah Bowen, was one of those earnest Christians who at that time were desirous of going back to the apostolic practice of having all things in common, and made their home at Trevecca College. There, however, she met her future husband; with the result that there now exists a document, in the handwriting of the Rev. Howell Harris, returning the dowry which the young lady had brought in with her to Trevecca; one of the witnesses being Rev. Thomas Charles, the well-known founder of the Bible Society.

Mrs. Roberts of Mynydd-y-gof was a woman of intelligence and culture, calm and equable in temper, and free from oddities of manner. She was noted for the skill and wisdom with which she guided a pretty extensive household, and cared for the spiritual and temporal training of her family of eight sons.

As for Dr. David Roberts himself, his character is thus described by one of his sons, now Sir William Roberts:—
"My father was a Puritan, and displayed to the full both the excellences and defects of that type of character. He was a strict Sabbatarian, and would not even shave on Sunday. He would reproach his sons if he found that any of them had shaved on Sunday morning. He was a great Bible reader, and read the book honestly through, many times, from Genesis to Revelation; and believed not only every word but every comma in it. He taught his children the same knowledge with scrupulous conscientiousness, and would allow no criticism on the smallest detail. The Bible was to him the *ipsissima verba* of the Most High. In matters of doctrine he was, considering his information, decidedly liberal; and one of his most striking characteristics was that he never spoke ill of others, and never attributed unworthy motives to those who differed from him. My father very seldom petted us, and never played with us; he rarely laughed, and when he did, he would pull himself up suddenly, with a groan. To him life was too sombre for joking, and laughter and amusements of all kinds were forbidden indulgences."

Another son (Mr. Robert Roberts, Menai Straits), writes of him:—" Perhaps it was my father's strong individuality, both in private as well as in his public capacity, that made the greatest impression upon those who came in contact with him. Many are the stories told of him, and remembered to this day over the country-side. The following reminiscences may serve to throw some light upon the main lines of his character.

"Not long ago, a leading preacher remarked to me that, when he was a student, he remembered my father would exert more influence by the sheer force of his character and his known honesty—in a public assembly—than others who possessed much greater ability. He had the courage of his convictions at all times, and was the terror of evil-doers in his own neighbourhood. Sometimes this would show itself in an amusing way. Early one morning, on his way to the village to attend some case of sickness, Dr. Roberts met a drunken farmer, who sometimes spent his nights at the public-house. When he saw who was coming, the culprit straightened himself and tried to compose his features. Finding this a task beyond his power to accomplish, he turned aside, and, scrambling over a high hedge, tumbled down on the other side, to find his way home as best he could, rather than face the mentor of whom he stood in such awe.

"Another incident of a similar kind had a more tragic ending. On his way to service one Sunday evening, Dr. Roberts saw five or six young men loitering at a corner of the street. He walked into their midst, and remonstrated with them for not attending some place of worship. The wildest among them replied to his remarks in a somewhat rude manner. Some weeks after, this same young man was attacked with fever, and became seriously ill. He sent for my father, saying he could not die in peace till he had expressed his deep regret for his conduct towards him, and obtained forgiveness. I well remember the occasion, and the deep impression it made upon the young men of the village.

"On another occasion, while taking some of his boys to school, it was necessary to spend a night at an hotel on the way. Before retiring to rest, my father rang the bell, and ordered four or five Bibles, one for each of the party. The servant-girl was frightened, and called her mistress.

The mistress was also amazed at such an unusual order, but at length was made to understand; and, after much delay, brought one small Testament, the only one that could be found in the house. With this the party fell to work to read verse about, passing the book from one to another, till it was time to go to bed.

"We started early one Sunday morning for a chapel some two or three miles distant, to hear my father's friend, William Roberts of Amlwch, preach. We arrived a little too early, and, taking our seats in the vestry, found sufficient Bibles to read, verse by verse, according to our usual custom. A long chapter in Kings was chosen, and before we had reached the middle of it the congregation began to arrive. Quite regardless of this circumstance, we went on, verse by verse, till we could see the preacher himself at the back of the crowd; but my father would not stop till the last verse was reached. The preacher, knowing him well, was much amused, and took it in the best of tempers.

"Although my father took a leading part in the work of the Connexion, it was in spiritual matters that he carried most weight. At an important meeting he was nominated to a post requiring much skill and tact. William Roberts of Amlwch became alarmed, and, rising in his place, suggested that a more suitable selection should be made, for, he added, 'Dr. Roberts of Mynydd-y-gof takes everything so seriously.'

"At this time Anglesea boasted of a celebrated huntsman, Mr. Barton Panton of Holyhead, who kept a pack of hounds, and hunted all over the country. Dr. Roberts, hearing he was out of health, decided to call upon him, and speak to him upon religion, if possible. It is worth remarking that at this time, some sixty years ago, the Church of England in North Wales stood very low in public estimation; and although a man might be a member of it, yet, in prospect of sickness and death, his membership appeared of little value to him. Dr. Roberts carried out his purpose of visiting the invalid, and managed to introduce a few serious words. His character was so well known, and his earnest purpose so transparent, that the old squire took not the least offence, but thanked him for his visit, and offered him refreshments before leaving. Whether this visit deepened the religious convictions of the sick man is not recorded; but I am glad to say he recovered, and hunted over the green fields of Mynydd-y-gof for many years afterwards.

"My father was not an intolerant man: he allowed those who could afford it to hunt and shoot, but forbade his boys following the hounds, or taking part in games. One Christmas Day, when we were all at home, and most of us grown up, we played a game called 'cattio'—something like golf. Coming up, my father saw us, and became much excited. He seized one of the sticks and broke it across his knee, saying, 'How can you revive an old game that your forefathers spent their lives in banishing from the land? I forbid you to play on my fields!'"

Early rising at Mynydd-y-gof was one of the cardinal virtues that all were expected to practise.

"One of the most picturesque features of our Mynydd-y-gof life was family worship in the early morning," writes Sir William Roberts. "We were all up at six o'clock, and the farm-servants and maids, with the rest of the family, assembled in the roomy front kitchen. I well remember the scene. A chapter was read, a hymn was sung (not always in tune), and prayer was offered, either by my father or by Robin Lewis, who was an old and trusted servant of the family. During the singing, Robin's tall, spare figure would sway to and fro to the cadence of the music, and his sonorous, Oh, Ah, and Amen would accompany the petitions. Throughout the winter season, there were still some hours before daybreak when prayers and breakfast were over, and during these hours my father and we boys would read the Bible, verse by verse, chapter after chapter, right through."

"Most vividly do I remember those Bible-readings, in the winter mornings especially," writes another son. "In the dim light of a tallow candle, my father would have us read through, verse by verse, the histories and prophecies of the Old Testament. His taste and his reading at that time, and indeed all through life, was Puritan in all its associations. I can see him now. At the time of which I write he was about forty years of age—a dark, spare man, with stern and striking features; conscious of the dignity and sacredness of the work on hand, and that he was the high priest of the family.

"The labour and industry shown by the boys was a proof of good discipline; no register was kept, nor marks given for the innumerable verses and the long chapters that were repeated by old and young alike, with the greatest order and solemnity, and on the whole with wonderful accuracy. We used to follow, morning after morning, the accounts of the kings and prophets of Israel, and our father would point out their different characteristics, their successes and failures; and show us when they were guided by principles bearing upon religion and the fear of God, enforcing them as being applicable to ourselves and to our time. I have been surprised, in after life, at the pains he took with us; and have often found that I am more familiar with the events, and the lessons to be drawn from them, of these times, than with the history of my own country. The service would often last two hours, and, in the winter, the full light of day would creep in, while the candle burnt down in its socket, before we rose up.

"Later on in the day, our mother also had Bible-readings with us. These I remember, specially, because they interfered with our play. The portions that she usually chose for our studies were the Psalms and the life of our Lord. She used to vary English with Welsh, while she taught us; but our father's knowledge of English was not so good, and he always kept to his native tongue."

It was thus on religious teaching that this couple, so alike in earnestness and devotion to life's great end, concentrated their efforts, acting in perfect harmony, in the training of their family of eight children, all boys. They were also ambitious that their sons should be prepared for the battle of life, and secured for them the best available education—sending them to English boarding-schools, when they had reached the limit of the educational advantages to be obtained near home.

These parents of a time gone by thoroughly believed in what they professed, were simple in their ways and frugal in their habits. They passed a long life together in a quiet and out-of-the-way place, without parade or ostentation. It goes without saying, that such lives remain an abiding inheritance of priceless value to those that come after them, even to the third and fourth generation. The sons of this family, who had from their earliest days been the object of such earnest solicitude, and whose religious training had been a matter of such surpassing interest to their parents, became, like other families, scattered in the course of years.

The second son, Mr. John Foulkes Roberts, settled eventually in Manchester. There, through a long life, he has been held in high esteem, not only for his active interest in all religious and philanthropic objects, but for his care for the social needs of the community. In 1881 he became a magistrate, and in 1885 was elected an alderman of that city; and many a scheme for the enlightenment and prosperity of his fellow-townspeople is associated with his name.

But, like a true Welshman, the country of his birth has ever lain near his heart, and for upwards of twenty years he has taken an active part in the establishment at Aberystwith of the University College of Wales. He inherited from his father all those sterling Puritan characteristics which made him such a power in Anglesea in days gone by, but combined with these are the geniality and sweetness of disposition which characterised his mother.

He was particularly happy in his marriage, since he chose as a helpmate a Welsh lady, whose family had done much for the progress of Nonconformity in the Principality, and whose earnest interest in religion resembled his own. An old resident of Llanidloes, the home of Mr. Jones, the maternal grandfather of the subject of this memoir, writes out some recollections of him, which show that the ancestors on both sides were true children of the Evangelical Revival of the last century. Brought up as a strict member of the Church of England, at the age of eighteen Mr. Jones began to attend some revival meetings of the Calvinistic Methodists. Young Jones was much impressed, and anxious to connect himself with the Dissenters; but his father was strongly opposed to such a step, and had even been known to send and call him home from the meetings. After waiting for two years, the young man's "patience and Christian wisdom" won his father's consent. He became an earnest Christian worker, took up Sunday-school work, and was accustomed to seek out the poorest and most hopeless in the lowest districts of the town, many of them being saved through his efforts for lives of usefulness. In after years, he was three times elected Mayor of Llanidloes, and, until his death, was Chairman of the Bible Society for that district.

He married a lady of like mind to himself. After their marriage they kept an open house for all preachers. In those times many of them were very poor; and it is related that, on not a few occasions, they left that hospitable roof clothed anew from head to foot.

Dr. and Mrs. Roberts of Mynydd-y-gof were spared to a great age. One of their Manchester granddaughters has supplied some recollections of her later days. Her favourite seat was a large arm-chair; when too infirm for any work, she loved to sit there, lovingly ministered to by one or other of the younger generation. She liked them to read to her from the Book she had always loved the best. Not unfrequently she would become quite oblivious of their presence, and spend long intervals in pleading for her children at the Throne of Grace. "She spoke in the Welsh language, which I did not understand," writes her grandchild; "but I could always make out a few words, such as 'O Lord, bless,' repeated over and over again. It used to touch me very much, and especially the fact that her eyes were always wet with tears when her communion with the Unseen was over."

Not long before the death of this aged saint, her granddaughter, Mrs. Walker of Glenn, tells of a visit she, with her husband, paid to the old home of the family at Mynydd-y-gof. They took with them their little daughter, the first great-grandchild. Solemn indeed must have been the scene, when the aged saint, at this time about ninety years of age, blessed the little child, and, turning to the young mother with strong emotion, addressed her thus: "Annie, I lay upon you the sacred charge of carrying on the prayer for the Covenant-blessing for our family." She then quoted with deep feeling Isa. lix. 21: "As for Me, this is my covenant with them, saith the Lord; My Spirit that is upon thee, and my words which I have put in thy mouth, shall not depart out of thy mouth, nor out of the mouth of thy seed, nor out of the mouth of thy seed's seed, saith the Lord, from henceforth and for ever." "I have pleaded this promise for my children," she continued, "and for my grandchildren; I have heard my mother and my grandmother plead it; and I have heard my grandmother say she had heard her mother plead it: thus carrying out, in an unbroken line for six generations, the prayer for a godly seed."

Is the Lord faithful to His Covenant-promise now, as in days of old? Yes, assuredly; "He is the same yesterday, to-day, and for ever." I have taken the somewhat unusual course of dwelling at length upon the life and religious character of the line of godly ancestors from whom the young medical missionary—the story of whose consecrated life I wish to tell—was descended, for a special reason. I have thought that it cannot but be an encouragement to Christian parents and workers, to see how richly God does answer the believing prayers of His people, pouring forth on a single family, through successive generations, in a special manner, such a blessed insight into divine things, and such an abiding realisation of His presence, as to make them not only lights in dark places, but the rivers of water to which our Saviour likened the believer's life, blessing and reviving those who come within the sphere of their influence.

CHAPTER II

CHILDHOOD AND SCHOOLDAYS

"Upon our childhood rests the glistening cloud
Of His sweet benison—the unseen Hand
Holds up our steppings in that way of years
Which leads through life to the Eternal land."

MR. J. F. ROBERTS, the second son of the noble-hearted Puritan doctor of Mynydd-y-gof, having settled down in the great city of Manchester, made his home in an old-fashioned white house in the district known as Plymouth Grove. A merry band of boys and girls came to brighten the old house as the years passed by; and it was to an ideal English home that, on the 9th September 1862, the youngest child was received with joyous welcomes by his numerous brothers and sisters. He was the twelfth child of the family, but there were already several vacant places in the parents' hearts; and when the happy band gathered on winter evenings about the bright fireside, their thoughts would wander, in the midst of the merriment, to some little mounds in the graveyard; for three of the children had already gone to play in the streets of gold.

The baby boy received the name of Frederick Charles; and the prayers of his godly ancestors, down through so many generations, received a rich fulfilment in him, since from his youngest days he seems to have been a child of faith and prayer. All the early influences of his life were hallowed, and he learned to pray at his mother's knee. She still cherishes the sweet memory of quiet Sunday evenings, when all the rest of the family had gone to service, and she was left alone with the children. It was their custom to hold a little prayer-meeting together, before bedtime came; and when the turn of the youngest came round, he would take his part with the sweet, trustful earnestness of a child familiar with heavenly things.

His father's influence over the young life was also very strong. "I remember well," writes one of his sisters, "the Sunday afternoon Bible lessons which we all received as children. We used to learn the Catechism, and also an explanation of the portion of Scripture we read together. We were always encouraged to learn by heart a few verses of Scripture, to repeat at Sunday morning prayers. Father would urge it, saying 'it was such an important thing to store the mind with the Word of God while young.'"

His sisters were also a strong influence for good in the life of their little brother. One of them, Mrs. Walker of Enderby, writes: "When Fred was only about eight years of age, I remember distinctly, he would come to my dressing-room before going to school, to pray and read the Bible with me; and when he came home, he would look out for me, and we would often have prayer together again, when he would confess anything he had said or done wrong at school—I certainly never remember his doing a really wrong thing. We would sometimes remark among ourselves: 'Oh, Freddie is born good—he could not be naughty if he tried.' He was always a most religiously-inclined child, but yet always so simple and childlike, ever keeping himself in the background."

The marriage of his eldest sister, the dearly-loved "Annie" of whom he always spoke with so much reverence and affection, took place when Fred was about nine years of age. About two years afterwards, while on a visit to her old home, in delicate health, Mrs. Walker felt drawn to speak very earnestly to her young brother upon the necessity of definite decision for Christ. The seed fell into the prepared soil of the child's young heart, and it resulted in his acceptance of Christ as his personal Saviour. "I well remember the joy that came into his bright young life," writes this sister; "more especially as the necessity of daily abiding in our Lord was explained to him as the secret of the Christian's happy and victorious life."

Many years after, in answering the questions put to candidates for missionary service by the London Missionary Society, he wrote: "My conversion at the age of ten, at the sickbed of a Christian sister, presents nothing very striking. I had from my infancy been blessed with earnest Christian parents, who sought to bring me up in the fear and knowledge of God and of His Son; but I shall never forget the joy I had when, with a child's thoughts and understanding, I accepted Jesus Christ. I can say truly, 'all things became new.' From that hour He has continued to reveal Himself to me, so that, as I write, I can say, 'That which I have seen and heard declare I unto you.'"

I have heard him tell the same story in a mission bungalow in North China, to a merry group of English children, who would readily turn from their play when their grown-up playfellow was too weary with constant labour to join in their romps. Climbing upon his knee, sitting on a stool at his feet, or hanging about his chair, they would listen with rapt attention to the stories of the days when he was a child like themselves. He had a wonderful gift for interesting young people the secret of it being doubtless his intense love for them. Now and then the merry laughter would be hushed, and a shade of sweet seriousness fall over the childish faces, as their friend told of how God had spoken to him as a little child. He remembered it quite well, he said. Before that time, when playing with the other children with their waggon and other toys in the garden, he had always wanted to be the one to ride, and have his brother pull him; afterwards, the Lord helped him, and it was easy to give up things to his playfellows.

The early years of Frederick Roberts' life were spent, up to the age of fourteen, in Ashfield, the old Manchester home which was so full of brightness, where the will of the Saviour was recognised as the law of life. Till the age of eleven, he attended a school conducted by some estimable Christian ladies; the name of one of them, Miss Cave, being associated in after years with deeds of practical piety and philanthropic labours among the poor. Fred is described at this time as a sturdy little lad, gentle and affectionate.

He had the brightest recollections of his childish days—no cloud of austerity or unchildlike formality in religious matters hung over them. The desire to do the will of Jesus, and love for the Divine Master, like a golden cord, was woven into the whole fabric of his life. From the first, the child's religion was of that practical kind which desires above all things to find expression in the life. "He was always a most unselfish boy, delighting to do any errand or to be helpful in any way," writes his sister. "When only a child of four, I was out walking with him one day, just after some Fenian outrages had been perpetrated in Manchester. 'Let me walk on the outside of the path, Sister Annie,' he said; 'then, if I can have your umbrella, I will fight any Fenians who try to come and hurt you.'" While quite a child, he was touched with the deepest pity for the children in distant lands who had never heard of Jesus. When he saw his elder sisters distributing tracts, he would ask to be allowed to help them, and do something for Jesus.

The bright, happy holidays of these boyish days were spent either on the Welsh coast or at Mynydd-y-gof, the old home of the grandparents, which has already been described. On one occasion, while still very young, little Fred was staying with his parents at Llandudno. Taking a walk one afternoon, they sat down to rest; but the child ran along the road, gathering flowers, happy in the brightness of the summer day. A gentleman coming along the path in the opposite direction, was attracted by the bright-faced, happy-looking boy, and, sitting down on the grassy slopes, began to talk to him. After the conversation had gone on for a little while, the child looked up at his questioner with a grave expression in his gentle eyes, and asked, "Please sir, do you love Jesus?" The question opened the floodgates of memory: the child spoke with such evident simplicity of One who was a very real Person to him. After a little more talk, the gentleman said good-bye to his little companion. Meeting a lady and gentleman a short distance farther on, resting as they watched the waters dashing against the picturesque sides of the Great Orme, he asked, apologising for intrusion, if that was their little boy he had just seen. "I never met with a child like him before," he said; "it is very wonderful—he talks as if Christ and heaven were as real to him as the things of this world"; and then he repeated his conversation with the boy.

The summer of 1874 little Fred spent, with his brother

Hugh, among the green fields of Mynydd-y-gof. Writing on his twelfth birthday to his sister Annie, he says: "On Monday last, Hugh and I had a very nice bathe at a place near the cottage. We can both swim a little. I think the sea at Holyhead is very buoyant. After we had bathed, we gathered shells. Yesterday I asked the Lord to put the whole armour on me, and I believe He has given it me. We go back to school on Tuesday; and I want you to pray that we may get on, and get promoted, and get prizes next Midsummer; but will you also pray that I may become very fond of reading? I do hope I shall be a better boy this year: I have given myself up entirely to the Lord. I am glad to say I went this morning and did as you told me, and I hope I shall be a more earnest Christian. I have prayed that Jesus will keep me on the right road, and that my sword may never get blunt; and also that I may never try to do anything in my own strength."

In the spring of 1876, the child, who up to this time had hardly known what it was to be laid aside by illness, was attacked by measles, complicated with inflammation of the lungs. For some days his life was despaired of, the fever ran high, and he was frequently delirious. His mother, with the assistance of a trained nurse, hardly left his bedside. Her letters of that time, written to the sister in Leicester, who so anxiously waited for news of her dearly-loved little brother, tell of days of weary watching, brightened by the little patient's simple faith and trust. "When in the night little Fred had a lucid interval," writes his mother, "he used to pray aloud in the most affecting manner, clasping his hands and apparently not seeing anyone around him. 'Oh, dear Jesus,' he prayed, 'wash me in that blood which cleanseth from all sin! Oh, take me, dear Jesus, to heaven! Make me more like dear A.—she will have a crown of pearls.' To see his lovely face, and his eyes staring, as if he saw Jesus Himself, and to hear his weak voice—I never shall forget it." Writing from the sickroom, some days afterwards, the mother says: "The doctor came last night, and for the first time pronounced darling Fred better. My song this morning is, 'What shall I render to the Lord for all His benefits?' Oh, I do dread this visitation passing without a blessing for each of us."

Fred's first letter after his recovery from this severe illness, written to his sister Annie, runs thus:—"I do hope my dear, kind Saviour will help me to live more closely to Him, after all the great mercies He has shown me. Everybody has been so kind to me. George Gray has sent me a small aquarium, with seven tadpoles, which in time will lose their tails and turn into frogs or toads, as the case may be. I have two snails, one water-beetle, one minnow, and a few very young fresh-water cockles. At the top of the water is a spreading plant, which keeps it clean, and some shingle at the bottom."

At this time Fred was in his thirteenth year, and he had been attending the Manchester Grammar School since the age of eleven. In his fourteenth year, together with his brother, two years older, who had been the inseparable companion of his boyhood, he commenced his studies at Aberystwith, the University College of Wales.

CHAPTER III

ABERYSTWITH AND COLLEGE DAYS

"O God, who wert my childhood's love,
My boyhood's dear delight,
A presence felt the lifelong day,
A welcome fear by night.

"At school Thou wert a Kindly Face,
Which I could almost see;
But home and holy-day appeared
Somehow more full of Thee."

FABER.

It is a great change from the crowded streets and dull skies of busy Manchester to the fair, breezy shores of Cardigan Bay. The country is rich not only in scenery of the quiet sylvan type, with sleepy glens and wooded hills, but on its rocky shores there beats the ever-changing sea. It was here, as a student at Aberystwith, the University College of Wales, that Frederick Roberts spent the greater part of his boyhood.

He was admitted into the college at the early age of fourteen, on account of his father's interest in the institution, and because of his desire that his two younger sons should continue their education together.

His mother's letters, coming at regular intervals, kept the love of home fresh in his heart; while his elder sister, in the midst of a busy circle of her own little ones,—engaged, also, in not a little active public work for the Master,—never failed to send her young brothers a weekly letter of cheery counsel.

From Fred's replies to these letters, most of which have been preserved with loving care, we are able to gain a pretty clear idea of the young student's life at Aberystwith.

His early letters not unfrequently contain glimpses of the boy's delight in the great expanse of waters. "This morning," he says, "I saw the lifeboat being launched for practice. I enjoyed watching it battling with the waves—now hidden from sight, and now on the top of them. It is the custom among the crew, before they land, to jump into the water and swim to shore, which of course causes great amusement to the spectators, more so than to the men themselves—especially on a cold day like to-day," adds the lad, who was always so thoughtful for everyone.

Other letters tell of country rambles, and long walks round the bay, of grand sea-bathing, and how he became coxswain of the University boat, and went in for football, because, as he quaintly tells his sister, "it refreshes my mind"—for he was always a hard student.

The students were accustomed to hold debates upon various subjects; and in these, as time went on, Fred usually took part. "I think it may be useful for me to learn how to speak in public," he remarks. "Last night we had a very good debate on a question very dear to father—Ought Wales to have a University? The question was very fairly discussed. I, of course, supported the affirmative side, and spoke for it. The chairman and twenty more were in favour of it; but our opponents were equally numerous, so that the debate was a little inclined to be warm." With regard to another discussion, upon the Advantages and Disadvantages of Novel-Reading, his sister Mary had written asking him to send her a report of it. He replied: "It is by no means easy to give you the arguments *pro* and *con*, for I have not a good memory; and besides, there were few good arguments floating about. This was, I think, because each side was speaking in extremes. Those in favour of novel-reading spoke of the 'infinite' (and many other long adjectives) good to be gained by reading the best class of novels, such as *Uncle Tom's Cabin*, which they said brought about the emancipation of the slaves; while those going to the other extreme, brought into prominence the Penny Dreadfuls, etc. So you see, dear, out of such speakers it was very hard to get sound arguments."

The letters, even at this early period, are singularly full of a boy's thoughts about the Christian life and longing desire to follow Christ more closely. Fred Roberts had been trained in a home where religion was not—as is so frequently the case even in professedly Christian homes—the one subject which is never mentioned in ordinary conversation. The children were accustomed to hear the Saviour spoken of as a living, bright reality, and to feel His presence in their midst. It was natural, therefore, for the young student to write freely to the dear members of his home circle of the joys and difficulties of his inner life. There was never the slightest trace of unreality or self-consciousness in his conversation; but, to the end of his life, it was to him a very natural thing to speak freely of the Master he so joyfully served.

The letters of this period show very clearly what some have doubted—that a boy may indeed live a free, happy, manly life in the midst of his companions, and at the same time enjoy the closest communion with his Divine Elder Brother. "We find it hard to be earnest Christians here," he remarks. "So often, when I have a great amount of work to do, I entertain the thought of not reading my precious Bible; but then I just think of what our Lord said, 'Seek ye first the kingdom of God and His righteousness, and all these things shall be added unto you,' and, 'What shall it profit a man if he gain the whole world' (in my case all the scholarships) 'and lose his own soul?'—these, and many other verses, comfort me. What a sweet thing prayer is! Is it not kind of our Saviour to allow us to talk to Him, and to tell Him our every need? I feel, since I came here, the great need of watching and praying."

When about fifteen, he writes: "I am not at all sure what profession I am going in for: I have quite lost my liking for being a lawyer. I think I am too young to decide; but I have a great longing to do more for my dear Saviour. Oh that I may be a minister! We are going to be received as members of the Church to-morrow night. I hope we shall be able to comprehend this solemn step we have taken, and do a great amount of good in our chapel." Before long, Fred Roberts had induced a few other students to unite with him in starting a prayer-meeting, which seems to have been continued throughout his college course. He was also an ardent total abstainer. With a boyish straightforwardness, which won its way into many hearts, he tried to influence others to follow his Master.

"I was talking to another student, the other day, about trusting God for every little thing. I am sorry to say he did not think that God managed our small affairs, and he did not agree with me in praying that I might pass my examinations. He said that God had given us talents, and that it is for us to employ them, and that God will do no more for us. I told him that I should not feel safe if I could not trust God for everything. I was telling H. this morning, that if I did not look to God every minute, I should fall. I find, by taking the Lord's Supper, my soul gets strengthened. I feel so happy to-day, to think that I can tell everything to my Heavenly Father." Some months after, Fred was able to write home the good news that he had been successful in the examination. "I do feel," he adds, "that God has lent a listening ear to the voice of my supplication."

He was always an earnest Bible student. "I find it so good for my soul to have one hour, in the calm of the morning, alone with Jesus. I am now reading Ruth in the Old Testament, which I enjoy very much. I am going through the Psalms once more, and find new lessons in them every day. I have got to Luke ix. in the New Testament. This spring the sea has been like a lake; it reminds me of the calm in the Christian's life, when there ought to be fighting going on if people around are dead to Christ."

Soon after, he is busy again preparing for another examination. "I have to learn a good deal of Milton. Isn't the description of the Dawn beautiful? It is a great relief to me to be able to bring this matter of the exam. to the Lord, knowing that He will answer my prayer, if it is for my good."

He worked late and early; and sometimes his eager anxiety for success, for a time, dimmed the simple faith which usually distinguished him. "I find time for communion with God through it all; but not so dear and close as I have been enjoying, for the exam. is worrying me, and does not give me quietness. Next Sunday (*D.V.*) it will be all over, and I shall be at ease. I hope you will join me in fervent prayer to God, that I may get on well and succeed.

If I do not pass my examinations, I am thinking of going into business, or a bank. May the Lord direct my steps aright, and teach me what to do." It was a great relief when, some time after, news of Fred's success reached the college. Indeed, throughout his student course he never failed in a single examination, and on some occasions passed with honours. Yet he always distrusted himself, was never elated, and worked with steady conscientiousness.

After the delightful family reunion, which came with the summer vacation, among the Scottish glens or on the wild shores of Arran, Fred Roberts returned once more with fresh vigour to his studies. About this time we find his thoughts settling with some definiteness upon his future course. His youngest sister, Mary, who was privileged, in after years, to be the dear companion of his missionary life in China, had become deeply impressed with the thought of our responsibility as Christians, in view of the crying need of the heathen world. She wrote to her young brother, expressing a strong desire to offer herself for this service; adding her hope that, if it were the Lord's will, they might some day work together in distant China.

"Mary told me in a letter which I received a few days ago," he says, writing to his elder sister, "that she should very much like to go to China; and if she went, I think I should join her, as there is such a great demand for missionaries in that part of the world; but, of course, this is only an expression of my thoughts—I do not know if anything will come out of it. But I trust that it will please God to send me there, and that I may be the means of doing a great work, for there is room for a great work in China, and the labourers are few."

A few weeks later, he writes: "I feel that there is such abundant room for more of God to dwell in me,—to make me a living temple to Himself, to abide in me, to shine brightly through me,—that I hardly know whether I am worthy to be called one of His servants. There is such lukewarmness among the students, that I am quite anxious for my own spiritual welfare. At the same time, I am standing up for Jesus. H. and I have been talking about the Second Coming of Christ to a few of the students, and trying to arrange for a Bible class. We intend carrying it on in the same manner as you do. Will you pray for its success; also for the students who attend it, that they might like coming to it, and may stand up for Jesus? I never looked at the 22nd Psalm as referring to Christ before, and find it very beautiful. Surely if God hid His face from Christ, how much more from us, who are altogether born in sin; but my prayer is, that I may not find ease for my soul when God has hidden His face from me, but may pray, like Jesus, ' Why hast Thou forsaken me?' "

As the Christmas vacation drew near, he wrote to his sister Annie: "I always like to write to you and Ala, to tell you of my difficulties in living near to Jesus. I am delighted at the thought of your coming to Manchester in December; and also of praying the New Year in, and committing ourselves afresh to God, body, soul, and spirit. You will be glad to hear one of the new students is going out as a missionary. He is much older than I am; still, I am glad to have someone to talk to about God's work in foreign lands."

At about this time, some evangelistic services were being held in Leicester, which were very richly blessed, many souls being born again. Fred had been in the habit of praying regularly for this town, in which two of his sisters lived and engaged in Christian work. His heart was full of rejoicing when he heard the good news of blessing being poured forth. "God is indeed the hearer of prayer," he wrote. "I feel sometimes that you are really praying for me —that is to say, I feel in my actions some supernatural strength given me in answer to other prayers than my own. A friend was telling me, the other day, that I ought to commence preaching: at present I do no more than take part in our week-evening services, which prepares me, I hope, for the great work which is, I trust, before me."

On a Sunday evening, he writes: "My dearest Annie, I feel glad to have a chat with you once more, although not by word of mouth, yet through the medium of pen and ink. I have just returned from chapel, where I heard a beautiful sermon from our Principal on 1 Cor. iii. 9. I enjoyed the sermon immensely, and I feel greatly refreshed by it. I have enjoyed much *Helps to Progress in the Divine Life*. I do feel that I must look every moment to Jesus: unless I do this, I shall fall. Oh for a closer walk with God, to know more of His perfect will, and of His love, which passeth all understanding! Father and mother are much opposed to my going to China. . . . I trust God will reveal His perfect will to me. I was very glad to hear the joyful news about Leicester. I wish I were there; but I am, in spirit and thought.—Hoping and praying that you may have a very joyful winter, I remain, with best love, in which H. joins, ever your affectionate brother,   FRED. C. ROBERTS."

December 3rd, he writes to the same sister:—" I received your letter and its good advice this morning. I am sure, if I lived up to the things you said, that I should be much brighter than I am; for I must confess that self and a desire for the praise of men greatly mar my close communion with God. It is very hard for me to live every moment to God's glory; and yet that is my daily prayer and ambition. Oh that God would speedily grant my request! I feel that vain, and especially foolish words, keep me from enjoying this holy joy. I long to have a talk with you next Christmas, if we are spared, on many things in my personal experience. We had a glorious time at our missionary meeting. I was filled with a stronger desire to go to China. I trust that the desire for winning souls for Jesus will ever burn in me; and yet I am far from fit for doing this glorious work now—my Christian life is on far too low a level to undertake it. The Principal says that a man ought to be filled with the Spirit before he speaks to others about their souls, so that the words may force themselves out of his mouth, and he cannot help speaking. I do pray that the Lord may grant that to me. I had a class in the Sunday school last Sunday. There were about eight little boys; they were very attentive, and, I hope, derived strength from what I said to them. I prayed to Jesus to give me strength to speak for Him, and He did give it me. I have had the little tract you gave me, *Hints for Young Christians*, fixed upon cardboard, and I often read them. I wish I could realise the first point more: when I pray, my thoughts are very prone to wander; but the Christian life is one of progress, and I trust that my life will be so."

After the pleasant and refreshing break in his studies,

formed by the winter vacation, which was spent in the dear Manchester home, Fred resumes once more his letters to his sister. "I am glad to say," he writes, "that the last few days I have had much more joy in believing, but my difficulty is in keeping it. I must ask Ala and your prayers for a student who—it looks as if God had done it—sits next to me at meals, and who is one of the worst sort of infidels: he believes in nothing, cares not where he will go. I shrink from speaking to him on religious subjects, and yet I have done so two or three times. He doesn't believe in faith; without which, I told him, no man can see God. He does not want to see God, he says. Could you—and I know you can—give me some advice? If so, I should be much obliged. I am longing to enter on my ministry—at least such has been my feeling the last few days."

With reference to his sister's minister in Leicester, he writes: "What a treat to sit under such a highly spiritual man as Mr. F. B. Meyer. Truly you have in him a gem, which I hope will send its light deep into the darkness of unbelief, and be the means of bringing many souls from darkness to light. Could you get to know anything about that missionary college for young men going out to China? I should very much like to know more about it. I intend going to Edinburgh, a year next October, or thereabouts, to study for four years; at the end of which time I hope to take my degree. It will require very hard work, as at present I know no Science; but what other men, through God, have done, I hope I can do. After my examination in June next, I shall work for the Preliminary Medical Exam. in Edinburgh. I trust I shall, with God's blessing, succeed."

A week after, he wrote thanking his sister for a book she had sent him, entitled *The Inner Life*: "I sometimes find my case clearly represented in its pages; and think I also find out how to conquer my many shortcomings. On Sunday evening, I went to the mission-room in an obscure part of the town (the room is part of a lodging-house where tramps and outcasts and unemployed poor spend their Sundays). We had a glorious meeting. Mr. M. preached the simple gospel; and I said a few words, on the verse, 'I am the Resurrection and the Life,' to a very attentive audience. We also sang hymns; and I assure you, dear

Annie, the joy of being privileged as I was, I felt to be greater than all the joys of this poor earth."

"I thank God," he writes again, "that of late I have come to realise His presence more on my knees. I was much refreshed this morning in my prayers for God's people. Oh, what a boundless privilege to open one's heart to a great, yet compassionate God! I feel sometimes the selfishness of my soul. I am drinking of the fountain of living waters, and looking forward to the time when we shall all be with the Lord, if we faint not. Yet, while seeing so many walking in darkness, and ignorant of the love of Jesus, and the blessing of believing on Him, I can hold my peace!"

At about this time, mainly through the efforts of Fred Roberts, a prayer-meeting was started for the benefit of the young men attending the place of worship with which they were connected. He had many difficulties to overcome, and wrote: "I fear sometimes it is a characteristic of the Welsh people to be very zealous for any new thing they undertake; but, by degrees, they cool down into a more stagnant state. I hope, however, it will not be so in this case." Passing on to his own personal affairs, he says: "I am in doubt whether to spend four whole years in Medicine, or merely to get a knowledge of practical work, and spend the remainder in some good college for missionaries in London —What is your advice?"

"I was much pleased," he writes, in April 1879, "to get the information about Mr. Grattan Guinness' missionary college. To me it would be a great pleasure to go there, even next October; for of late my interest and desire to go out to the inner parts of China has been greatly increased. I read of the great need of young men who have given their hearts and lives to God, and who are desirous of obeying our Lord's last command to His disciples, 'Go ye into all the world, and preach the gospel to every creature'; and then I say, 'Send me, send me.' I feel, dear Annie, sometimes that time is very earnest, and is flying fast. The time for us to appear before our Lord, and tell Him of our feeble efforts to obey His commandment, is drawing nigh. Oh, how little have I, so far, done for my Lord, who has done so much for me! I feel I am worse than an unprofitable servant. The Lord grant I may be, some day, a great and spiritually-minded missionary, and that I, even I, may be the means of bringing many a poor Chinese to the feet of Jesus. I know and feel that you are praying for your brother; and I trust that the prayers which are offered up to God may be abundantly answered. Oh for a closer walk with God! I am reading a very nice book, by Rev. Samuel Pearson, M.A., of Liverpool, *Home to God; or, A Guide on the Way*, which I enjoy very much.

At the same date, he writes to his mother of the great refreshment the visit home had been to him: "We felt your kindness and love so much; for when in college, there is little but books and communion with God, which we never forget, and which, I am glad to say, is becoming a great source of comfort to me. Often have I been encouraged to look up, and not be cast down. It is no difficult thing for a student to acquire a gloomy and morose attitude in dealing with his fellow-students; and it is also very easy to become hateful to man. I feel the truth of that verse which says, 'Ye cannot serve God and mammon'; and, 'Woe unto you when all men speak well of you.' I feel that the temptations of college make me throw myself more entirely on God in prayer; and, dear mother, it is to you and to our dear father that I owe my present happiness. It is through your influence that I have been brought to love the Lord; and I trust that the good example of my parents will, with God's blessing, bring forth abundant fruit in future usefulness."

On the 12th May, he writes to his sister Annie: "I always get more or less good from your advice, and from reading the verse and poetry at the commencement of your letters. It is a very good idea, and I think much good may be done in that manner. They say that the great Richard Baxter was converted by a tract; and no knowing but the verses you put on your letters will be abundantly blessed in quickening some dead and lukewarm Christian. I am now reading Baxter's *Saints' Rest*, and Dr. Doddridge's *Sermons*. It is astonishing to think what an amount of reading can be got through in spare moments. I find it is true in my own case; and I have read of a great naturalist who, although surrounded by outward duties, found time to write many volumes of books. I am glad to say, dear sister, that I do not neglect my private devotions, but endeavour to read my Bible regularly three times every day; and also to pray to my God for more light on my way. I trust God will find a great work for his poor and, at present, timid servant to do, both at home and abroad."

During the next week, in reply to a letter from his mother, he writes thus:—

"MY DEAR MOTHER,—I was very glad to receive your beautiful letter, which was indeed a model for all mothers' letters, and one which made me feel how wicked it was to give way to gloomy spirits. It shows, as you, I think, intimated, lack of trust in God; for, having committed our way unto the Lord, it is our duty also to trust in Him to do for us all that which is for our good. But, beautiful as your letter was, I could not agree with the hope you cherished, that, as I grew older, I should see differently from what I see now. I feel that if, when I grow older, my longing to go and preach the gospel to the perishing millions of China is less, then truly my love to God must have grown less warm. If the disciples had only been willing to stand up for Christ in their own country, what would have become of the future Church? No, dear mother; if God calls us to work for Him in foreign parts, it is only our duty, as children of the Heavenly King, to say, 'Here am I; send me.' If we love father or mother, or brother or sister, more than God, we are not worthy of Him; and by considering home comfort (which may last but for a moment) before God's will, we do Him great dishonour, and are not worthy to be called His servants. I hope you will agree with me in all I say, and especially when I say that, if in future years my desire to go to foreign lands has ceased, it is only because my love has grown cold."

On the same date, he writes to his sister Annie: "I am getting more decided for foreign work the more I think of all Jesus has done for me, and of His will towards those unconverted. May the time soon come when I shall be working hard in His vineyard, and reaping souls for His glory! I feel it is the grandest of all occupations. The Lord of the harvest prepare me for it, and pour out upon my thirsty soul His Holy Spirit, that He may teach me all things, and prepare me for a mighty work. I go forth into an unknown future, but trusting to God and knowing that all things are mine, whether Paul, or Apollos, or the world, or life, or death. Knowing this, I go forth to the conquest, and feel sure that the victory is mine, through Christ.

"I am now enjoying the *Life of Bishop Patteson*, a very good missionary in the Pacific Islands. I wish I were now engaged in the work; but I think, as the Principal does, that it is very essential that every missionary should have a good education, and be thoroughly grounded in all things, that the gospel of Jesus Christ may not be put to shame."

Writing again to his sister, on September 10, after her recovery from sickness, he says: "May we renew our vows to the Lord now, in the presence of all His people,—may we be drawn closer and closer to Him,—is the fervent prayer of your youngest brother, who has now entered upon the seventeenth year of his life, and in that year has once more consecrated that life to the service of Him who is the Guide and Counsellor of his youth, and will be, I trust, the support of his old age, if it is granted to him. May your dear prayers find acceptance before God, so that I may have a life not only full of usefulness, but also full of fruit, which is a sign of God's blessing attending any work in His name."

Up to this period, Fred and his older brother had been inseparable companions at school and college; but at the commencement of this term they were parted for a time. The lad loved his brother with that strong and intense affection which was one of his characteristics all through life; and when he returned to the old rooms and the old familiar haunts, he missed his former companion every hour of the day. A letter he wrote to his brother at this time gives us some idea of how keenly he felt this trial of separation: "I cannot go anywhere but it brings to my mind some bright recollection of the very pleasant time you spent with me in Aberystwith—a time never to come back in our lives, and never to be forgotten. As for our old rooms, they are quite different from last term, when you were in them. Then all was so lively and comfortable; now all is so desolate." The letter continues in a most melancholy strain; but was interrupted by "a boy,—you will know if I call him 'Canary,'—who, I am sorry to say, came to kick up a row in the corridor. May he fail in his endeavours!"

Writing soon after to his sister Annie, to whom he always confided his difficulties and sorrows, and who answered her young brother's letters with the wise, tender counsel of an elder sister, he says: "I am very thankful for the advice you gave me in to-day's letter; it has helped me to calm down my sorrow, which, I am glad to say, was only a surface wave, and has not disturbed that deep peace which, I trust, I have in my soul, which proceeds from the Father, and is promised to His children. I feel sure that my separation was for my good. I think it has brought me closer to God; for, being more alone, I can think more of Jesus, who is the same always, and, as you say, 'the Friend that sticketh closer than a brother,' whose heart is always open to receive His beloved. I am truly blessed in my family ties, that, through one dear sister, and others indirectly, together with a parent's advice and instruction, I have been brought to know Jesus, to enlist in the roll of His servants, to take up my cross daily, and follow Him. But oh how feebly do I carry that cross, as if it were a burden that would sink me down, and cause me to lag behind in the race of life! May I draw strength from the Word of Life, and so, reading of Jesus and His precious example, try and follow it more perfectly, and live a more devoted life in His service!

"I have a class of eight scholars in the Sunday school; may I be greatly blessed to them. I felt the Holy Spirit helping me this afternoon to speak for Jesus. I fully agree with you in your admiration of Paul's prayer for the Colossian saints. I heard a beautiful sermon upon it from the Principal. He thought it ought to be the prayer of every true Christian, not only for himself, but for all Christians. As regards being faithful in every good work, that will take a lifetime to obey fully."

A month later, he writes: "As I look back upon the work of the term and its results, I feel they are very few; and the influence of my life upon those around me, I fear greatly, has not marked, as it ought to have done, the contrast between Jesus' life in me and the careless, thoughtless life of those we associate with. Still, I trust that what feeble attempts I have made in His name, and for His glory, will not be without their fruit. May we, one and all, through bitter failures and many shortcomings, seek to trust more entirely in His strength, and look more fully to Him, for 'there is strength in a look at the Crucified One.' Though feeble-hearted and ready to fall, yet if we have our gaze concentrated upon the King in Zion, He will be with us and help us; and, knowing this, I take courage, and hope, some day not far hence, to be declaring with power the glad tidings of the gospel, following Jesus in His work of going through all the country healing the souls of men. May I have a true missionary spirit, one of entire reliance on Him; and oh, may He never have to say to me, 'Depart, I never knew you.'" In a postscript to the same letter, he adds: ",I have just received your welcome letter, and the card of membership for the Prayer Union. I will endeavour to carry out your advice about the prayer, and trust I may have the Holy Spirit given to me. I agree with you, in one way, about coming out from the world, and not being corrupted by its sin; but do you not think, dear Annie, that there must be care taken lest we walk in our own shadow, and keep our religion for ourselves? I am this evening going to a meeting very dear to me—a missionary meeting. Oh that I may be refreshed in my desires to serve my Master! I sometimes think little E. will be a missionary. Would it not be nice if we could work together?"

The next letter contains an account of a chat the young student had enjoyed with Principal Edwards regarding his future: "He recommended me to go to a university, Oxford or Edinburgh, and get a good education, as he thought it especially desirable for a missionary to have a good education. He said he thought I had better take a classical degree, but study Medicine as well; and he thought I ought to get my B.A. in three years next October (*D.V.*). Then, being twenty years of age, I could devote two or three years to the study of Divinity and Medicine, and, all being well, start on my work at the age of twenty-three. But my way is dark; and I can only leave it with a greater than myself to decide. I told the Principal about China, and gave him some facts, with which he seemed greatly interested. He asked me to bring him Hudson Taylor's periodical upon China, that he might read it. He has been very kind to me this term; he is such a fine character, and does his best always for the students."

After the Christmas vacation, in January 1880, Fred resumes his letters: "I am now working for two entrance examinations at Edinburgh; so you see, dear sister, I am still fixed on the missionary life and work. May I be trained for it in a higher school than that of earth! I am always thankful to receive news of China, and trust that God has allotted me a place in the mission field of that dark land. I had a very pleasant day of Sabbath work yesterday. Oh the power of prayer! I feel sure that there is One who is ever by the side of His people, from the very fact that my prayers are often answered, if I pray aright. Although I am not so active as you are in Leicester, still I had yesterday the pleasure of speaking in a mission hall in this town. The number of hungry souls was large: they were, I fear, most of them, unsaved, living prayerless lives; and oh! dearest sister, may I say that I think God has been pleased to accept me for a minister of light—oh, glorious title, but unworthy supporter! I had power to speak, although of myself unprepared; and who knows but the seed may, after much delay, bring forth abundant fruit! Do you think I am wrong in supporting this movement, through inexperience? But I am sure you do not; for I know not when Christ will come; and if He comes now, I fear I have not added a jewel to His glorious crown. I pray, yet not enough, for you, dear sister, that you may be a still more powerful instrument in God's hands; and may I ask you for prayers on my behalf, that I may not hide my light under a bushel, but speak of all the glorious things I have received from the hand of the Lord? Having tasted and seen that the Lord is good, may I tell others of the treasure I have found! Oh, how I thank God that I was not persuaded to go in for the Bar; but of His favour, and, I trust, through the influence of the Holy Ghost, led to consecrate my life to His service!"

In a later letter, he says: "Is not the process of coming to God often slow, and to the human eye, unobservable? The disciples had not a clear vision of Jesus all at once. May we, too, draw nearer and nearer to Him, till at last we are laid at the throne of God in heaven—spotless, complete, and entire, wanting nothing; then we shall be not only near, but in Him; standing not in our own strength, but in His. I was so delighted to hear what mother said with reference to me,—that she is perfectly willing to give me into the Lord's hands for China, as the mother of Samuel gave him to God's service. I trust I now see my way clear for a work which is the most glorious attainable."

Fred still continued his work at the mission rooms in Aberystwith, and as in after life, so now, when only a lad, he sought in many ways to find opportunities of loving service. There are letters extant which he wrote to the sick and the dying, full of Christian consolation and tender sympathy. Among the students there were some who caused the Principal much anxiety, and whose conduct received the severe censure of the other students. These, young Roberts not only prayed for constantly, but tried, by acts of kindness and friendly letters, to allure to better things.

Though he saw little of the great success which blessed the work in which his sister was so much interested in Leicester, yet signs of future harvest were granted to him. After one of the Sunday-evening meetings, a young man stayed behind, deeply affected by the young student's words. After some conversation, in which the power of Christ to save the worst of sinners was clearly shown to him, he left, with clearer light upon the heavenly path.

The work at this lodging-house was interrupted for a time, since many of the inmates, who preferred to spend the day in drinking and swearing, objected to the presence of the young workers. "God has found us another place," he writes, "where we may tell the old, old story of Jesus' love. We have some true followers here, but they all seem to be of the class Christ loved when on earth—not the rich, the great, the scribes or the Pharisees, but the poor and the outcast. Yesterday we had a splendid meeting—a large room fairly filled with grown-up people, ragged and torn. I remembered that it was for them the gospel was specially fitted. Our subject was, the judgment to come on all men. Much of God's Spirit was present. I walked home with a poor woman and her daughter. She said she had lost her husband one and a half years ago, and she had drawn comfort from our services, and the hope of meeting him once again. We talked of Him that sticketh closer than a brother, to our great joy."

Thanking his sister Annie for her helpful letters, he adds: "What a glorious thing is the communion of the saints—the comforting of one another—helping those who are in darkness—and praying for one another! I think we may tell a true Christian from his praying for others, especially for his brothers and sisters in the Lord. I wish sometimes I had more time for the contemplation of heavenly things; and yet, as I read in the *Inner Life*, if we are working for Him, and feel our need of His presence, He will come at once to our side. I quite agree with you, that happiness is not to be found in the things of this world; but it is the secret joy of the believer, who realises that God is near, that Christ reigns, and is about to return to us once more.

"How strange it is that we do not feel more grateful to Jesus for His atoning sacrifice, and for His life of sacrifice for us! It seems a mystery that we, like the centurion of old, can sit and watch Jesus suffering for us on the cross: sit comfortable and with indifference, while He who came from the Father's side to save sinners is suffering before us. Oh that the power of Calvary might stir us up to greater works of love and self-sacrifice! Alas! I confess to you, my dear sister, that the spirit is willing, but the flesh is weak—that when I would do good, evil is present with me. This morning, I awoke feeling that God was near and working out all things for the best; but my conversation while with the students was not what it ought to have been. Then a student came to my room to ask me for *The Days of Bruce*, a book not for Sunday. I felt I might speak to him about the advisability of reading better books on this day; but then he was an old student, and I had expressed my views to him before upon Sunday novel-reading, though to no purpose, and I thought it would not become me to preach to him. What ought I to have done, that I may in the future do it? I have to read a paper on 'Warren Hastings' at the Debating Society: this takes up a good deal of my time."

This is the last of the series of letters, written so regularly throughout a period of several years, to the sister to whom

Frederick Roberts owed so much of strength and counsel in the spiritual life. Her daily prayers, and the love which watched so tenderly the development of the Christian life in her young brother's heart, have surely had a rich and abundant reward.

With reference to the period spent by young Roberts at Aberystwith College, the Principal, to whom he became so deeply attached, now well known as the Rev. T. C. Edwards D.D., Principal of the Theological College of Bala, thus writes to his sister Mary :—" He was, in comparison with the other students, very young when he came to Aberystwith, but from the first he inspired me with a deep conviction of his unusual piety. More especially in the Society, as we in Wales call our weekly meetings for religious instruction, his addresses and prayers impressed us frequently with their reality, freshness, faith, and humility. He could weave Scripture into his petitions with the greatest naturalness, so that his prayers always gleamed with rich thought. They were not studied compositions: the expressions were beautifully simple and fit, and full of ripe experience, the result of delightful fellowship, as of a child with his father. His influence in the college was even then very considerable. There were other influences which grieved my heart, because they endangered the moral tone of the students. But your brother's quiet, unobtrusive, holy life prevailed over every sinister tendency. I know that at this early age he was full of the missionary spirit. He accustomed himself to arrange and pursue sedulously a plan of house-to-house visitation among the poor and neglected inhabitants of the town. He was our first missionary student; others followed, belonging to different sections of the Christian Church. The college has its representatives to this day in the mission field, and by this time its pioneer missionary has finished his course and reaped his reward."

CHAPTER IV

MEDICAL STUDIES

"True-hearted, whole-hearted, faithful, and loyal,
   King of our lives by Thy grace we will be ;
Under Thy standard, exalted and loyal,
   Strong in Thy strength we will battle for Thee.

"Half-hearted, Master, shall any who know Thee
   Grudge Thee their lives who hast laid down Thine own?
Nay, we would offer the hearts that we owe Thee,
   Live for Thy love and Thy glory alone."

F. R. HAVERGAL.

THE environment of the next few years of Frederick Roberts' life is to be found, far away from the breezy shores of the quiet Welsh coast, in the busy streets and romantic surroundings of the "grey metropolis of the North." It was at Edinburgh, in the autumn of 1880, when he was just eighteen years of age, that he commenced the medical studies which were to fit him in future days for that loving service among the sick and the dying, which made his name a household word in many a home over the bare plains of Northern China.

The brother in whose company Fred's early years were spent, pictures him at this time as "a sturdy youth of constantly cheerful temperament and deep religious feeling."

He soon settled down to the ordinary life of a medical student; and from his regularly-written home-letters we glean the main facts of these Edinburgh days. It was a new experience for the lads to have to cater for themselves in the great city, after the sheltered life at Aberystwith. The deep earnestness with which they both entered upon their University course comes out in an amusing pen-and-ink picture, drawn by the younger, of how they sat over the fire in the evening, discussing the serious question of orders to be given to the landlady for the next day's dinner. Fish was eventually decided upon, because it was considered "nutritious, and medical men praise its value for students." They were very ambitious to do well in their examinations; and in one of his letters Fred remarks, that he " hopes to get a scholarship next March, while H. has his eye upon another honour."

Many prayers were being offered by Christian friends that the young students might be guided into safe paths, and kept faithful to their Lord during the time of testing, which new experiences of life always bring with them. They felt that these petitions received an abundant answer when they were introduced to a most devoted Christian lady and gentleman, Mr. and Mrs. Melrose by name, who for many a year served the Master by inviting young students to share in the hospitality of their home. "After the daily routine of work was finished," writes the elder brother, "we were wont to meet there for social intercourse and reading of the Bible. Fred loved to join in a game of draughts or chess. He could be serious even in games; but never a ripple disturbed the sweetness of his temper should his opponent win. He could laugh the loudest of us all; and would fall in with every suggestion that did not fall out with his conscience, and was the merriest of the party. He was often called upon to lead in prayer: it was his seriousness here which impressed me. His religious exercises were always the outflow of an overfull heart. This heartiness, indeed, manifested itself in the very shake of his hand, in the ring of his voice, and the expression of his eye. Sympathy was deeply woven into his nature, and took men captive."

These friends secured the help of the young students in the Sabbath Free Breakfasts for the Poor—"it will not interfere with our studies, and will go far to keep up the life within," Fred remarks. He also connected himself with the Medical Students' Christian Association, and was one of the most active members of the University Temperance Association.

"This morning," he writes, "I went, with the son of Mr. Macfarlane of New Guinea, who is also going to be a medical missionary, to pay my first visit to the Edinburgh

Infirmary. It is a splendid building; only opened last year, thus having all the recent improvements." They went through the women's ward, and were able to speak a few words to the patients, and distribute tracts. The simple faith of a child of eleven, touched the young student's heart, and also that of an aged woman suffering from a lingering disease, but happy in Jesus.

The New Year, 1881, found young Roberts rejoicing in the blessing which had so evidently attended the Week of Prayer. Dr. Bonar and Major Whittle conducted the meetings; and at a consecration service at the close, three hundred persons gave themselves to the Lord. Fred was deeply interested in these meetings; and yet felt that it was impossible to attend them night after night, without neglecting his studies. "I am so busy preparing for my March examination, that I feel I cannot spare the time; but someone has said that the student can make his studies an act of consecration to God," which illustrates his brother's remark, that "one of his chief characteristics was fidelity to duty."

In a letter to his sister Ala, he thus describes one of his Edinburgh Sundays: "I am now a settled worker at the Free Breakfast, and shall never repent having taken it in hand. There are over 2000 fed—first with earthly bread, and afterwards with the Bread of Life. The people are the lowest of the low; many of them with scarcely any raiment upon them. After this, I hurried on to the service for workers; subject, 'Being filled with the Spirit.' Major Whittle showed us that it was the heart emptied of all earthly ambitions that received this blessing, and that there is no Christian but may obtain it, if he is only willing to receive it. Truly it was good to be there, for it was the gate of heaven to our souls. Then we went to chapel, and heard a splendid sermon from the text, 'Every eye shall see Him.' Then came the Students' Meeting, when fifteen stood up, seeking peace. Afterwards came the gentle dew from heaven upon our souls, as we went, in the evening, to a gospel service in the lowest part of Edinburgh; and we came home, having tasted of the spirit of prayer, and felt what a blessed thing it is to win souls for Christ. Such was last Sunday. Dearest sister, do you not rejoice with me in answered prayer? I feel sure I shall leave Edinburgh strengthened in my soul with holy aspirations, and, above all, with increased missionary zeal for the extension of God's kingdom. I am determined to know no other God but the God of heaven and earth. He has been near me in the past of my life, has led me hitherto, and revealed Himself time after time to my view; and I feel something within me which tells me that there is a work allotted for me in China; but oh for greater zeal to live every moment to Him and for Him!"

There is an old and beautiful story told in that Book whose simple human histories are more pathetic than any other, of a strong yet tender friendship which grew up suddenly between two men in days of yore, and continued even to life's latest hour. It was during his first year in Edinburgh that Frederick Roberts met with such a friend, whom he loved ever after with the full strength of a singularly affectionate nature, and who was destined to share his labours during the last years of his life in China. The story of their meeting is best told in Dr. G. P. Smith's own words:—

"It is more than thirteen years ago since, at a chemistry tutorial class in the old University in Edinburgh, I sat next to a student whose face attracted me, and to whom I ventured to address a remark—this was Frederick Roberts. During the winter session we were constantly meeting in the lecture-theatres and dissecting room, and I soon saw the beauty and remarkable consistency of his character. There are few like him; and now, after thirteen years' friendship, which, as time went on, only seemed to grow deeper, I can only say he was the most consistent man I ever knew—a God-given friend. Students and professors alike respected him, and those who knew him more intimately, loved him. One only needed to see his face in order to be able to read his character. Whether in the lecture-theatre, dissecting room, or hospital, he went about his work in an earnest, conscientious way. As far as I know, he never missed a lecture. He took careful notes, and worked on steadily, always endeavouring—and successfully too—to understand his work. Each subject received equal attention: he was a good student all round, and his name was always high upon the lists."

"Gifted with a fair memory and the power of perseverance," writes his brother, "it is no wonder that he was successful in his examinations. I do not think he had any intellectual bias, for I do not remember him to have shown preference for one subject over another. He could turn from one subject to another, as regularly as the hands of a clock from one hour to another. There was in him a wonderful inward harmony, which seemed to spring out of silent communion with his Creator. There was nothing erratic or fantastic in anything that he did, for his judgment was sound. I do not think he was ever troubled with doubts or questionings—his nature was too trusting and confiding for that. His life seemed to flow serenely to its goal, like a deep river between its banks. When Mr. Moody was in Edinburgh, he took an active but unostentatious part in his meetings; but nothing was allowed to hinder his regular studies. I never knew him to neglect one duty in the over-zealous performance of another. His gentleness was strikingly shown when he was called upon to nurse the writer through a serious illness. He was never ruffled by the fretfulness which accompanied my complaint. Modesty was a natural trait in his character: I never knew him to be self-elated. He was nothing in his own estimation but an instrument for good works. There was no posing even in this modesty,—it also was the outcome of a beautiful inward spirit. He was ever leading men to look at the great Pattern and Example."

As the months went by, Fred Roberts' thoughts were often filled with the deep need of those who had never heard of Christ; and everything connected with China missions had a special interest for him.

"Have you heard of Schofield, that London Gold Medalist who has given up all, and joined Hudson Taylor's work as a medical missionary?" he asks his sister. "Seven or eight of the Drill Hall workers at the Free Breakfast with which I am connected, are going out next autumn as missionaries to foreign lands. We are going to have a missionary prayer-meeting next Monday evening, and are trusting to have a great blessing that night."

At about this time, Dr. Griffith John, while in England on furlough, paid a visit to Fred Roberts' home in Manchester; with the result that the desire that his sister had long cherished, to engage in foreign mission work, became greatly strengthened; and the correspondence of this period contains many references to it. "May the fact that I heard yesterday, that there are in the world 700,000,000 living without Christ, fill us with greater earnestness than ever before. We are having our missionary meetings next week. Please pray that many may be encouraged to give themselves to Him who bought them; and that fresh love for that work may be rekindled, if indeed it ever has been kindled, in my heart."

Writing to his mother, he says: "I am so glad you are willing for me to go wherever the Lord may call me. Of course, at present, I can only wait upon Him and learn His will concerning me, and what is the work He has allotted to me. When I look to myself, I feel and I know I am not sufficient for the work of upholding the Cross of Jesus Christ before the gaze of perishing millions abroad; but with the Lord is the power I need, and also the grace; and perhaps it may be my happy experience to say, from the bottom of my heart, 'I can do all through Christ, who strengtheneth me!' May His life be more fully manifested in ours before the world and all we come in contact with. Is it not a solemn thought, that we are Christ's representatives to the world? They don't read His Word or pray to Him, much less have fellowship with Him; and the only conception they can form of Him is in and by His disciples. May we become brighter mirrors of His beauty and grace, and, walking in His ways, find them indeed, in our happy experience, ways of pleasantness, leading to that City whose foundation and light is the Lord."

To his sister Mary he writes: "The straight and level roads on which I have been far too content to walk hitherto are now becoming monotonous, and there is present a desire —not indeed earnest and abiding—to soar up nearer to Jesus. I can entirely sympathise with all you say about experiencing the power of self. I do not think anyone has been more tempted in this respect in our family than I have been, and certainly none have less cause to think one good thought of self than I. Yet I can say, that of late the clouds have been breaking up, and the Sun of Righteousness shining through them on my cold and barren soul. Oh, life divine!

flow on, flow in, breaking down every barrier that Satan and self have raised, making my life to redound ever more to Thy praise alone."

The letters which Fred wrote so regularly during his student life to his sisters, as well as his parents, show how faithfully he worked, while at the same time he prayed and trusted in the Lord to grant him success in his examinations.

In reply to his sister Ala's invitation for them to spend part of the summer vacation in her country home, he writes: "We should enjoy it much, but it is out of the question; for directly after our trip, we shall have to sit down to books, books, books. For the true medical student there are very few holidays: I fear they are a thing of the past. From what students say, our holidays will have to be spent in the dissecting room. We shall also have to reserve some time for revising lecture notes and preparing for new classes."

In 1883, Fred was able to write home the good news that he had passed with honours the examination for which he had been so diligently preparing. "Please don't mention the fact," he adds; "I merely tell you to show that we are working. The peace I enjoyed in my 'orals' was something wonderful, and I had the very questions that suited me in chemistry. We both felt sure of success, and success has been granted us by our ever faithful Friend. Truly, as I look back upon the past period of study in Edinburgh, I can say the Lord has been with me to help me, and has kept me amid the many temptations of a student's life."

Early in this year, young Roberts met with a heavy loss, in the sudden death of his kind friend Mr. Melrose. After writing of his earnest Christian character, Fred continues: "One thing in his life made a very deep impression upon me; and that was, his anxiety for the salvation of all he came in contact with. May the Lord grant that a double portion of his spirit may fall on us, that we may be made valiant soldiers of the Cross of Christ, and burning and shining lights, shining more and more unto the perfect day."

From the letters of numerous fellow-students, written since Fred Roberts' call to higher service, we find that not only was he regarded as a most diligent and successful student, but that he found time for a large amount of Christian work. His friend, Dr. G. P. Smith, writes that, in consequence of his early Sunday morning's work at the Free Breakfasts in the Drill Hall, he had not been accustomed to take part in the religious services the students were allowed to hold, two by two, in the wards of the Infirmary; but he always appeared at the prayer-meeting which succeeded it, in the chapel, and many seem to have been struck by the earnestness and eloquence of his prayers. "One Sunday morning he left his Bible behind him in the Infirmary chapel, and, returning to look for it, he found me asking some men for assistance at a service in one of the large medical wards that afternoon. Several men offered; but, turning to Fred, I said, 'Will you come and help us?' To my delight he said, 'Yes.' He met me at the appointed hour. Just before beginning our service, the staff-nurse sent a message asking us to go and speak to a dying man in the side ward. The service over, I left Fred to speak to the patients individually, while I went to see the man; it was only too evident that he was dying. I tried to point him to the Cross, but he only groaned out, 'No, no!' I tried to pray for him, but it seemed as if the heavens were shut against me. Then the thought struck me—Get Roberts. Just as I reached the corridor, he was hurrying off to a Sunday-school class which he taught. He said he could not remain—he was already behind time. I said, 'Never mind, you must come in and speak to this man; he is dying.' Entering the man's room, he went up to the bedside, and in a clear voice said, 'The thief upon the cross was saved; all he said to Jesus was, "Lord, remember me when Thou comest into Thy kingdom." The Lord at once replied, "This day shalt thou be with Me in Paradise." I believe that God has sent Mr. Smith and me here to give you this message. Will you believe it?' The dying man looked up at the pitying face of the young student bent over him, and gasped out, 'Yes, yes; I will.' Roberts then repeated the same thing over to him in different ways, and he always replied as before. Later in the evening, thinking the man might still be alive, Fred went round, to read and pray with him. I was sitting alone, in my house, when he rushed upstairs to my room. 'George,' he said, 'that man is in glory.' He added that, as he was walking across the Meadows to the Infirmary, he passed a small crowd gathered round a godly cabman, who was known as 'Preaching John.'

They were just singing the hymn, ' Rescue the Perishing,' and
the chorus rang out clearly, ' He will forgive if they only
believe.' Thinking of the man to whom he had spoken in
the afternoon, he felt ' that man has believed, and is now forgiven.' When he reached the Infirmary, the man was dead.
The nurse told him that he had passed away quite peace-
fully, though before Fred spoke to him he had been writhing
in agony and distress of mind. We could not find out who
the man was. He was only an unknown stranger; but Fred
felt that some day we should, without doubt, meet him
beyond the river. He then resolved, in addition to his other
work, to join us in conducting the ward services."

It was towards the end of 1884 that Edinburgh received
a visit from the band of young volunteers for missionary
service, known as the Cambridge Party, who were shortly
sailing for China in connection with the Inland Mission.
The self-sacrifice and devotion to their Divine Master which
induced Charles Studd, captain of the University Eleven,
and Stanley Smith, stroke of the Cambridge Eight, to accept
Christ's last command as a call of lifelong service in the
foreign field, attracted the attention of many students who
had little interest in spiritual things. "As soon as Studd
and Stanley Smith entered the building," writes Dr. G. P.
Smith, "the students met them with quite a round of
applause. Again and again, as they told their simple story,
they were applauded. At the close of the meeting, Professor
Charteris asked those who wished to bid the missionaries
God-speed to come forward; and quite a crowd eagerly
accepted the invitation. They were to leave that night by
the Great Northern express, and a large number of students
gathered on the platform at the Waverley Station to see
them off. They begged Mr. Studd to address them again,
and, standing upon one of the seats, he did so, while the men
crowded round. 'Who are these fellows?' inquired a
commercial gentleman of a railway porter. 'They are
medical students,' replied the man; 'but I think they are
all off their heads!'"

At this first meeting, which was held in the Free Church
Assembly Hall, some of the best men in the classes were
present, and all were deeply impressed. It was decided to
invite the two young missionaries to pay another visit to

Edinburgh before they left the shores of England; and this they consented to do. Meetings were arranged for students only, and one for schoolboys; those who attended being checked-in by their class or matriculation tickets. They were crowded gatherings; and at the close, the hall, till a late hour of the evening, was filled with groups of men speaking earnestly with Stanley Smith, Studd, or their fellow-students, regarding the way of salvation. When the last meeting came, many were rejoicing in the peace for which they had sought. Others were still in darkness and doubt. Roberts might have been seen passing from one group to another, trying to point men to the Saviour he so truly loved.

"When Studd and Stanley Smith left us," continues Dr. Smith, "we found ourselves face to face with a great religious movement, which no one dared to take the responsibility of stopping. The Oddfellows' Hall was taken, and it was decided to ask Professor Drummond to continue the services every Sunday evening during the session. These meetings were crowded to the doors with students, and were always followed by large after-meetings."

With reference to these gatherings, Fred Roberts writes to his mother: "There seems to have been very much permanent good done; and very many have, we fully believe, begun to live the new life. I do not remember ever having been at such a meeting as last Sunday evening's. Professor Drummond was the preacher, and Professor Greenfield was in the chair, and many other professors and ministers were present. Quite a large number of students have decided to serve the Lord, and many beside are very deeply moved. One professor said there had never been such a time of spiritual blessing among the students for certainly twenty years." In a later letter he continues: "Last Sunday was a day never to be forgotten. We had a splendid meeting of students in the evening. It was turned into a testimony-meeting, during which many fellows got up and testified to the power of the gospel, and to the change which, by the grace of God, had taken place in their lives during the last few weeks. Over one hundred and sixty, who had received blessing during the meetings, went into a special room, and were addressed by Principal Cairns and Dr. Wilson.

"One young fellow I was speaking to was quite in the dark about the truths of the gospel. He did not believe in a God or a Saviour. He said I could have no idea what it cost him to hold such views. When his dearest friends are speaking about these things, he is obliged to leave the room, for fear of hurting their feelings by his remarks. From 2 Cor. iv. 4, he understood how it is he cannot see the truth, 'because a veil is over his mind.' We told him to go in prayer to Him who alone can give light and joy and peace in believing. We have great hopes that he will yet come out into the light. He would be a great power for good if he did so."

Towards the end of the winter session, Professor Simpson suggested that Edinburgh should send deputations to the other Scotch Universities—Aberdeen, Glasgow, and St. Andrews. Roberts formed one of the Glasgow deputation, which was headed by Professor Sir Thomas Grainger Stewart; and more than seven hundred students gathered in the lesser St. Andrew's Hall to hear them speak. Professor Drummond afterwards suggested that men should be asked to give their April holiday, spending it in doing evangelistic work in various Scottish towns. Roberts was among the one hundred men who volunteered. The recollection of this never-to-be-forgotten session was one of the most precious memories of Fred's University life; and often in after days, in far other surroundings, he loved to talk over the experiences of those days, in the company of the friend who had with him shared the joy of harvest.

Not only did Fred Roberts thus engage in the more public forms of Christian work, but in the quiet byepaths of daily service he ever sought to do the Master's will.

Writing during the course of 1885 to his father, he mentions his dispensary work, and remarks: "One of my last cases had a strange and sad interest about it. It was that of a poor lad, aged fifteen. I was called in to see him the day before yesterday. When I arrived at the house where he was, I found a starving, almost naked, person lying on what answered for a bed. He was very thin and weak—in a most critical condition. His little brother, about seven years of age, lay on the opposite end of the bed, asleep, suffering from a severe skin disease. I almost shrank back with horror at the loathsome sight: there was no one else in the room. Their mother was dead, and the father out of work; the poorhouse refused to give him a bed in their hospital, because his father was in good health; the town Infirmary refused to admit him, because his case was too far gone. The sight was truly heartrending."

He tended his patient with loving care, supplying him not only with medicines, but with necessary food. His delight was great to find in this poor sufferer a fellow-believer. "He spoke in a firm, unhesitating manner of his trust in the Saviour and his hope of heaven." Roberts was called in to the next room of this same house, to see a sick woman, and, on his return, found the poor lad breathing his last. "In a moment," he writes, "his soul had left that scene of unspeakable misery, and, I doubt not, gone to be for ever with the Lord—can we not truly add, especially in this case, 'which is far better.' I feel it to be a great privilege to have been called into the medical field of work, and hope I may have more and more of the self-denial and love of Jesus Christ, and give my life—it is all that one can do—for the work of a medical missionary."

In July 1886, the young student successfully passed his final examination. Writing to thank his sister for her letter of congratulation, he remarks: "I am indeed happy, and feel like a bird that has been let loose from a cage. Medical work has all at once become doubly interesting to me, because I am for ever free from the slavery of exams. I feel I shall make far more progress in my work now than ever before; and this is just what Uncle William said in his kind letter I got this morning. I have much to thank the Lord for: to Him be all the honour."

At about this time, his youngest sister paid a visit to Edinburgh, and Fred anticipated with great delight the walks and talks they would have together, amid the lovely surroundings of the Scottish capital. "I hope we shall have a pleasant time, in the truest sense of the word," he writes; "doing all things for the gospel's sake (1 Cor. ix. 23), even our pleasures, because, through the recreation, we may be strengthened and enabled to further the gospel of Jesus. Much prayer is needed for the evangelistic work among the students, that now, when so many are on the eve of entering upon life, and are soon to attend the sickbeds of the suffering, they may commence by consecrating themselves to the Lord's service, and openly becoming His humble but faithful followers.

"Last Saturday I saw a leper, such as our Lord cured when on earth. It was a very sad sight. He is beyond the power of any earthly physician, and suffers much pain: he can only sleep a little at night; and in many parts his skin is as white as snow, and quite dead. A week yesterday he accepted the Lord Jesus as his Saviour, and seems now rejoicing in the blessed hope of eternal life in heaven. What matters it now if his outer man is daily perishing, seeing he has been healed in soul by the Great Physician.

"There is more illness just now among the medical students than I can remember. This afternoon I am going to the funeral of a student with whom I was well acquainted, who three weeks ago was studying in the same classes. He was seized with typhoid fever, and died in a few days. His father is in India, and he had only one relative in Edinburgh; but I rejoice to be able to say he was a true Christian, and had recently received a great blessing, and was hoping to become a medical missionary. I shall ever look back to my acquaintance with him with joy; and trust I may follow in his footsteps, even as he did in Christ's."

For many a year, as is clear from his letters and the testimony of all who knew him, Fred Roberts' heart and hopes had been set upon foreign mission work. But it is not to be supposed that the young and brilliant student never felt any temptation to turn aside from the prizes which he knew the world could offer him, and seek to follow his Master in the path of lowly self-denying love.

When the final struggle for his University degree was over, and kind congratulations poured in on every hand, though he never for a moment wavered in his allegiance to the Master whom he loved, he did feel the power of temptation alluring him to a life of service other than that which he had for years looked forward to. This was not strange, surely, when we know that the same temptation, to carry out the work of the world's salvation by some easier way than the thorny path of self-denial, beset the Saviour

Himself, when in the desert of Judea He suffered, being tempted by the great enemy of souls.

"What next?" he writes, "is the cry on all hands; and I suppose, sister, it is the cry of mankind the world over. No sooner is one duty accomplished than another care is manufactured, or eagerly sought for. Against this restlessness of mind I desire to strive and pray. All I can do, while resting for a few short hours, as it were, upon my oars, is to look up and watch the eye of the Lord, and the message which I trust He will soon send me as His will concerning my immediate future. I feel strongly, at present, that my work is in Edinburgh—to more practically equip myself for the life of a medical missionary, if God's will is to send me out. More I cannot say at present; more I cannot see. Why seek to see the distant scene? one step's enough for me. I feel as free as a lark, in every sense, now my exams. are over. My way is beginning to open up, but I am still undecided what to do."

"I have little news to communicate," he writes to another relative, "except of a personal character; and, after all, one is safer when he is writing on other topics than self. My last term with H. Yes; the time when we shall have to separate, and go each in his own path, is coming near; and I have to brace myself when I think of it, because I find excessive brooding over such facts is, to say the least, injurious. One thing I may say about myself—that God is, I believe, bringing me to see myself in the pure and searching light of the Cross of Christ. This last month has been one, to me, of literally wrestling against principalities and powers. Very humbling to the flesh, is it not? but I fully believe that God is by it preparing me for my life's work, which is close at hand. Let us both wrestle on and conquer, and take all these experiences of life as occasions for becoming increasingly useful to others."

Writing to his father, he says: "I would have written sooner, but thought things would clear up somewhat if I delayed my answer. I believe, upon thinking over the matter, and your advice that, after all, I had better not be too hasty in coming to a conclusion, and in presenting myself to the L.M.S. So I will wait till I can see my way clearer, and God's hand leading me in this matter. My way is indeed dark, and my consciousness of inability for this work has of late come over me with very painful reality. I think I am not deceiving myself when I say I am anxious to do God's will, and that I am willing to go where He would have me, and when He would have me. I pray that, in His mercy, He would keep me from entering on anything to which He has not called me, and that He would lead me on in the right way."

His sister Ala had sent him, as a birthday gift, a copy of Andrew Murray's *Abide in Christ*. In his letter of thanks he says: " I trust the future will show that the book you have so kindly given me has been blessed to my soul, in creating within me more love to God and to Jesus Christ, in return for the perfect example He has given me in His life on earth. I am indeed greatly blessed in having your prayers on my behalf. I felt the Lord was answering them yesterday; for He drew near, and enabled me to consecrate my life and few powers to His service anew, and He gave me good counsel through the author of *Abide in Christ*—that if self was not dead, yet I was to be dead to it. Many a time does self fight hard for the mastery over me; and often, I must confess, have I been led captive away and put under bondage. But thanks be to God for the way of escape He has shown me. I have been reading of late the travels of Dr. Moffat in Africa, and have enjoyed it very much, and received strength and more love for the missionary work from reading all he went through for the gospel's sake. May a double portion of his spirit rest on me, that I may glorify our loving Father in all my walk here below."

One matter that at this time caused him some anxious thought, was the suggestion that had been made to him by some relatives, who knew his high professional qualifications, that, since he desired to give himself to the Lord's service in China, he might very well go out there as a medical practitioner to one of the Treaty Ports, and at the same time do much good among the Chinese in the adjoining native town. He replies to some of their arguments as follows:—" If I go out to China and set up at once as a practitioner, which I should have to do, I could never find time for the work of acquiring the language; and the great object of my going abroad, *i.e.* to try, God helping me, to follow in the footsteps of Christ, the greatest physician and missionary, would be lost. Your reference to Paul seems to be erroneous. True, he supported himself; but it has been well said he had no new language to learn, and a tentmaker may take on as much or as little work as possible without giving any cause of offence. . . . But I fully believe in being connected with a society, and receiving at first, if not later on, a definite salary, that, free from the extra care of making a livelihood, I may give up the whole of my time to the work to which I believe God is calling me. In the meantime, all I can say is, if the new idea is of God, He will make it clear to me what course to adopt: in the meanwhile I can only wait on Him, to be guided and prepared for a work the grandeur of which is only just beginning to dawn on me, and for which I know and feel I am utterly unworthy."

Later on he writes to his mother: "I cannot close without asking you to remember me in your prayers. I realise in a way I have never done as yet, the fact that I am soon to start on my life-work. I long for the baptism of power from God for the work. I know I need it, and that apart from it all work done must be of no avail. How I can enter into the feelings of those disciples when they were tarrying in Jerusalem for the baptism for service! What a sense of weakness and absolute dependence must have been present! Somehow in these days we hear little of this baptism, and yet I feel, as I have never felt before, that I need more than the eleven disciples did to tarry for this great blessing. The gospel is still the same; and oh, how grand the thought—whatever sceptics and doubters may say—that blessing which those helpless disciples got upon the day of Pentecost may be mine too! Their pure and steadfast love for the service of Jesus Christ may be mine; and their zeal, which no selfish consideration of worldly interest could touch, may also be my own. May He who alone can give it, in His own time give it me, that His cause may be furthered and souls won."

Another occasion for some anxiety was that which has been a rock of stumbling to so many when first thinking of the China mission field—the great difficulty of the language. "I know," he writes to his sister Mary, "God is able to help me; and if He sends me out, He will not leave me to defeat on the score of the language. What I am now doing is like Gideon—seeking clearer guidance in the great step I am contemplating taking. I feel my work is not in England—I don't wish it to be. The teeming multitudes of sick in soul and body call for help louder than any Macedonian messenger. Mine is the upward look for the pointing of God's hand to China and its millions. Oh, when will the message come, and with it the needed power and grace?"

And the sign for which he waited in faith and prayer came, as it ever comes, now as in olden days, to those whose vision is made clear by the purifying influence of the Holy Spirit. "I had such a happy time last Sunday in Dr. Whyte's church," he writes. "Mr. Hudson Taylor spoke with great power, and the Lord, I believe, spoke through him to me, assuring me of His will to send me to the heathen abroad. I got comforting assurance also that He would help me to learn the Chinese language from Matt. xi. 11; 1 Cor. i. 30; and 2 Cor. ix. 8. This has been a question of some difficulty to me; for I have no gift for languages that I know of, and a pitiable memory. But I am glad to say it is a difficulty no longer. The Lord will guide me in every step, and prepare me to become a workman that needeth not to be ashamed."

Later he writes to the same sister: "I am glad to have these quiet months before going out. They are for my good. I am trying to study two lives fully before leaving England—the life of Jesus Christ and St. Paul's life. I am making but slow progress. I am in the middle of the first, and studying Geikie's *Life of Christ* for a short time daily. But I am painfully conscious of my need of a greater Teacher than Geikie—of the Holy Spirit to so reveal Christ in me, that one day, God willing, it may be my work to preach Him among the heathen, and heal the sick. I was struck by a remark in Geikie to-day—that when the Holy Spirit was poured forth upon the disciples, He quickened their intellect and heart. Mary, how encouraging is that thought, or rather fact. Oh to have the same transformation ourselves!"

CHAPTER V

ALPINE GLENS AND LAST FAREWELLS

"To start thee on thy outrunning race,
Christ shows the splendour of His Face :
What will that Face of splendour be
When at the goal He welcomes thee ?"
C. ROSSETTI.

WITH regard to the outer life of the young student whose inner experiences we have been depicting from his letters, Dr. G. P. Smith writes : " Fred was capped in August 1886, receiving the well-earned degree of M.B., C.M. He came up to Edinburgh again for the following winter, and acted as one of the demonstrators at the Minto House Anatomy Classes. Here he was highly appreciated by Dr. Symington and the students. Whenever a man was in a difficulty about his dissection, he generally tried to secure Roberts' help for a short time. Thus, in teaching others, his own knowledge of anatomy was increased, and that made him a good and fearless surgeon. During the winter he also studied the eye, the throat, and other special subjects, with the one aim of fitting himself for his life-work as a medical missionary."

Referring to the years young Roberts spent in Edinburgh, the Rev. James Gregory of Augustine Church, of which he was a member from 1881 to 1887, thus writes : " He was a most interested and assiduous Church worker. Students are not always very satisfactory Church members. The studies and interests which grow out of their student life are apt to absorb their energies, and leave them little or no time to cultivate fellowship with those outside their own circle. It was not so with Frederick Roberts. His place in the church at the Sunday services (my eye travels now to the well-known spot in the gallery where he used to sit) was seldom empty. He was still more seldom absent from his post in our Mission School at Gilmour Street, where, year after year, he taught a class of rough, unkempt lads, and undaunted by their trying and often riotous behaviour, threw his whole soul into the task of seeking to win them for Christ.

"Only yesterday I had a letter from one of his fellow-workers, a personal friend of his and my own, from which I venture to extract a sentence or two : 'I am deeply grieved to hear of the death of Dr. Roberts. The last time I met him was in Manchester, quite unexpectedly, and very shortly before he sailed for China. I have never forgotten his affectionate farewell, nor the glowing hope with which he then, as always, spoke of his future work. I was a teacher at the mission for only a few Sundays while Roberts was there. . . . One fact, and a noteworthy one, I do remember— that his prayer in closing the school, by its earnest eloquence, seemed to reach the hearts of many, for the roughest lads seemed quieter then than at any other time.

"'Privately, I saw a good deal of Roberts. It is now a good many years ago ; but never before nor since have I known anyone so filled with the spirit of love to men, springing from a devoted love to Christ. His entire lack of self-consciousness, of self-love in any form, and the absence —so it seemed to me—of any desire to criticise others, left him at liberty to win his way into many hearts. I owe much to him. He did not enter into my difficulties at the time when I knew him ; but he drew me upwards and away from them. In his presence the coldness of the modern spirit thawed, and the hearts of those who talked with him burned within them. Very many must have loved him.'"

The spring of 1887 found Frederick Roberts bidding farewell to the scenes of his student days. Just at this time a heavy bereavement fell upon his friend, Dr. G. P. Smith, who in the course of three short weeks was called upon to suffer the loss of his beloved wife and two children. Dr. Smith was at that time in practice in Edinburgh; and although he had long felt attracted to the work of foreign missions, and had taken an active part in maintaining the interest aroused among the students by the departure of the "Cambridge Band," his own way to the foreign field seemed closed.

The shock of this sudden and severe bereavement was so overwhelming, that it seemed necessary his friend should have complete change of scene, and Dr. Roberts immediately arranged to accompany him on a long continental tour. They visited the Italian Lakes, and then crossed the Simplon Pass into Switzerland. After travelling through the magnificent scenery on the banks of the Rhine, they followed the line of march of the German Army in the war of 1870, visited the battlefields of Spichern and Gravelotte, and made their way, through Paris, home to England. "During this time of anxiety and sorrow," writes Dr. Smith, "Fred was more than a friend to me. For the first time I was able to devote my life unreservedly to foreign mission work. I shall never forget the day when I announced to him my intention. 'George,' he said, 'you know I am going to China. I want a companion, and there is no one I would rather have than you.' 'In that case,' I said, 'we will here and now devote our lives to China, and to work together there, if it be God's will.'"

With reference to this heavy sorrow, Dr. Roberts writes: "How true that we must through much tribulation enter into our rest. Sometimes I am alarmed at the freedom from sorrow in my own life; and yet I trust God is preparing me for all He is preparing for me."

Before he had determined to accompany his friend to Switzerland, Dr. Roberts had made no formal offer of his services to the London Missionary Society; but, some months previously, Dr. Lowe of the Edinburgh Medical Missionary Society had written to the Rev. Wardlaw Thompson: "You will be getting an application from Dr. Roberts soon. He is not one of our regular students, but has worked with us in all departments as if he were. He graduated last year, but has been assisting since in the Medical School. He has been up having a long talk with me as to what he should now do. He thought of spending another year at home, as resident physician or surgeon in the hospital here or in London. I strongly urged him to offer to go out this autumn and stay for a time where there is a good hospital, learn the language, and at the same time acquire experience in Chinese hospital work. He is one of the most talented of last year's graduates. As a Christian, an evangelist, and a

medical man, I cannot speak too highly of Dr. Roberts. He
is one of the best men I have known—highly accomplished
professionally, and greatly appreciated by the students as a
teacher of anatomy." " His high character, great kindness,
and marked capacity for his work, are guarantees of success,"
wrote Professor Greenfield. "I have had abundant means
of forming an opinion as to his character and attainments,"
writes Dr. Symington of the Edinburgh School of Medicine.
" Students have repeatedly expressed to me their appreciation
of his abilities as a teacher. By his kind and obliging
manner, no less than by his powers of exposition, he has
gained the respect and esteem of his students and colleagues.
I can only say that the London Missionary Society is to be
congratulated in the prospect of adding to its staff such an
accomplished, able, and energetic man."

The series of letters which Frederick Roberts wrote so
faithfully to his home circle, when absent from them, are
continued from the shores of Lake Como. He sketches a
vivid picture of the terraces of vines, the acacias, and olive
trees; among them the pink, white, and yellow houses, with
their chocolate-coloured tiles, looking down upon the blue
waters of the lake, encircled by snow-capped mountain
peaks.

On the 13th June he wrote to his mother, from the top
of the diligence, half-way to Geneva: " The road runs
along pine-clad defiles, with the Arve flowing by our side,
while the snow-clad Alps form a matchless background.
We have seen the grand sights of Chamouny under the
most favourable circumstances." He then describes how he
made the ascent of Mount Anvert, crossed the Mer de Glace,
and the next day ascended Mount Brevent, 8300 feet high.
" During the climb I had some novel experiences of walking
up snow slopes—the guide, going before me, made steps in
the frozen snow, and I literally followed in his footsteps.
After a while he began to ascend an almost perpendicular
snow precipice. Planting his alpenstock deep in the snow,
he made good steps for me, and the road became as easy as
going upstairs in a house. Reaching the summit, we got
a superb view of the Alpine range under a cloudless sky.

"On the way up to the hotel we heard the most
exquisite echoes of the Swiss horn. The original sound was

nothing extraordinary, but the music that came echoing back from the precipices opposite still rings in my ears." Some days after, he writes, while still among the mountains: "We were awoke this morning by the horn blown to tell us it was time to get up and see the sun rise. People were on the scene in no time—some in blankets, some looking sleepy, and all only half-dressed. We stood looking eastward, where a bright light heralded the approach of dawn. A universal silence fell upon us all as the sun came forth, rejoicing as a young man to run a race. Peak beyond peak caught the morning rays; not a cloud obscured our view of the one hundred and twenty mile range of Alps."

Describing a glorious sunset on the Jung-frau, he adds: "Far better than all, the Master is near, and is blessing us unspeakably, giving us happy times of Christian fellowship: a foretaste of future blessing in His service. I am hoping to see the Directors of the L.M.S. before the Long Vacation; so I earnestly hope, before I see you again, I shall be a step nearer my life-work." To his father he writes: "I feel truly grateful for the guidance I have received in so many ways from our Heavenly Father, and I feel sure He will still guide me through each path along which He calls me to walk; and if, as I fully believe, He is calling me to China as a medical missionary, to China I shall go, though all the directors of all the missionary societies in London unanimously reject my services."

Leaving Grindelwald, Dr. Roberts and his friend crossed a sea of ice in the heart of the Bernese Alps. "Our guide was Johanne Josse, an excellent fellow, who knows his work A 1. When we reached the glacier, we were deeply impressed with our position—on a sea of ice 2500 feet deep. After a while we struck up the mountain-side: to our left was Schreckhorn, over 13,000 feet high, where more than one life has been lost by avalanches. Now and then, with a sound like loud claps of thunder, we heard them falling down the precipices in solemn style."

It was among these Alpine solitudes that Dr. Roberts answered the questions which are supplied to its candidates for missionary service by the London Missionary Society. His reply to the question, as to what, in his judgment, were the general qualifications for the work of a Christian missionary, and the trials and temptations to which he would be exposed, was characteristic:

"The qualifications of a Christian missionary I take to be: (1) Complete distrust in himself, in his worthiness for such a work, in his faithfulness and zeal, etc. (2) Complete trust in the living God, in the indwelling Saviour and Holy Spirit, and in the power of the Spirit to convince the world of sin, righteousness, and judgment. (3) A thorough belief that Jesus has died for all, and therefore that there is hope for every living creature. (4) Patience. (5) Entire consecration to His service. (6) Sanctified common sense."

In a small diary, kept at rare intervals, the following note occurs, on his return to London:—"A never-to-be-forgotten day. I said good-bye to George, and then made for Blomfield Street, where I had an interview with Mr. Wardlaw Thompson, and learned that Mongolia was my probable field of labour, with Mr. Gilmour."

To his father he writes: "It will be a great honour to be fellow-labourer with a veteran missionary like Gilmour. The Lord knows what is the best thing for me; and I rest assured He will guide me in every step, and will open up the way as He sees best. Oh, it is a privilege so soon to enter on the list of medical missionaries to the heathen! My fitness and strength are not in myself, but in Christ Jesus, and the power of the Holy Ghost, which every child of God has received. Were it not for this,—believe me, I say it in all sincerity,—I would not entertain the thought of going out on such a mighty work, the extent and responsibility of which I am only beginning to realise."

To his sister he wrote: "I hope, Mary, you will remember me in your prayers, that I may be guided in this very solemn and important step by our Father in heaven. Only He knows fully all that is bound up in the issues of the next few weeks. Many loving ones are supporting me in prayer. I am on the eve of a great undertaking, which I can't face in my own strength. I am longing for a great blessing, God knows, and am expecting it. He will not disappoint, but exceed our request. Oh for the true, refreshing showers from the King's presence! —no other refreshment can be permanent."

"It was Fred's great wish," writes his sister, "to attend the Keswick Convention, before sailing for China; but the tender pleadings of our mother, not to leave her, overcame his desire. He thought, and rightly too, that God was able to make up to him at home the deeper blessing he sought for at Keswick, and determined to stay and comfort his mother." "Annie and Mary are now at Keswick," he writes to Mrs. Melrose. "You can easily understand why I am staying a week longer in the old nest; and perhaps it is as well not to accustom oneself to spiritual delicacies, when one cannot depend upon them in the future. Praise God! one has always a glorious conference in and with Him. The Lord bless my dear parents abundantly in all this trial; for it is a sore trial to them, as there is no great likelihood of our meeting again in the flesh."

A valedictory service was held at the Manchester church with which Dr. Roberts' parents were connected, and his earnest appeal for greater interest in the work of foreign missions touched many hearts.

A service of a similar kind was also held at Leicester, conducted by the Rev. F. B. Meyer, his sisters' pastor at that time. With reference to this, he writes: "Yesterday, the last Sunday in the old country, was a day never to be forgotten. My faith has been strengthened, my hope enlarged, my desire to labour for Christ abroad deepened. Oh for a greater zeal,—the zeal of God to eat us up,—for such a revelation of Christ and His kingdom, and the privilege of service which costs us self-denial, and is thus made doubly precious, that we may go forth to do His will! Have you heard of the consent of many in Mr. Meyer's congregation in Leicester, to pray every Sunday before breakfast for me and my work? Am I not rich with such fellow-workers to support me? The Lord is keeping us all very cheerful; and as our day, so is our strength. The evening meeting was rich in comfort to us all."

The date of the steamer's sailing was several times postponed; but on September 29, he wrote: "I am to be on board the s.s. *Glenshiel*, in the S.W. India Docks, not later than 10 A.M. on Thursday. Happy day, when I shall start on the work towards which my thoughts and studies have been directed for so long in the past!" To such an affectionate nature the sad hour of parting was no common trial, but he kept outwardly brave and cheerful to the last. Many members of the dear home circle accompanied him to the steamer, from which he sent a letter of loving farewell to his parents: " May the Lord abundantly make up to you for the loan of your son for His service, is my prayer and belief. I wish I could tell you all I feel and would like to say; but you know what I would like to say."

The last sight the little company of his loved ones had of the young missionary, was his bright face smiling farewell, as he pointed upwards to that Home where partings never come.

CHAPTER VI

OUTWARD BOUND, AND THE CITY OF THE HEAVENLY FORD

"A wealth of love and prayer behind,
    Far-reaching hope before ;
The servants of the Lord go forth
    To seek a foreign shore.
And wheresoe'er their footsteps move,
    That hope makes sweet the air ;
And all the path is paved with love,
    And canopied with prayer."
                        S. G. STOCK.

THE little company of missionaries on board the s.s. *Glenshiel* were favoured in having for their senior, one whose long years of service have endeared him to many Chinese hearts—one, also, whose youthfulness of spirit and warm-hearted sympathy have through all these years cheered the hearts and brightened the lives of his colleagues. The Rev. Jonathan Lees and his devoted wife, whose names are widely known and loved through all the missions of North China, did all in their power to make the voyage a happy one for their young colleagues.

"I stood on the deck," writes Dr. Roberts, "till the white, waving handkerchiefs of our party were lost sight of. ' I would that my *pen* could utter the thoughts that arise in me.' I have gone back more than once in thought to that group of dear ones. How kind of them to come and make the parting hour cheery by their presence. In the evening, Mr. Lees and I paced the deck in the moonlight, which made the limestone cliffs of Dover look very grand. Mr. Lees interested me much by telling me some of the incidents of his first voyage of four months in a sailing vessel round the Cape. They had very rough weather and unkind treat-

THE CITY OF THE HEAVENLY FORD 71

ment, not being allowed even to sing hymns in their cabin. What a contrast to our trip!"

He thus describes their daily life on board: "After breakfast and dinner, we meet for prayer and reading of the Bible in Mr. Lees' cabin. These are times of quickening, I hope, for all. At 10 A.M. we meet on deck for Chinese lessons, which Mr. Lees kindly gives us. He is teaching us the numerals, a few simple sentences, and to read the Gospel of St. John in Chinese. It is slow but interesting work, and Mr. Lees is as patient as Job! Of course I find the language very difficult, as do the others, but perseverance conquers all things; and one has the consolation, that what others of moderate ability have, with God's blessing, achieved, we may hope to do also.

"The lessons last two hours. Afterwards comes lunch; then some play lawn tennis, others quoits, in which I take my share, and afterwards letters and diary-making. From four to five o'clock I devote to medical studies; and after that, Chinese again. More Chinese after dinner. This applies to every day; and, I assure you, time flies quickly, and I have little, if any, time for leisure moments of thought over past sunny memories. I know that you are glad that it is so; and that I could not please you better than by working hard."

Opportunities were also found for Christian work among the sailors in the forecastle. "Mr. Annand of the Scottish Bible Society and I had a service the first Sunday evening. We sung many of Sankey's hymns; and the way was, I believe, opened for future work. Some of the crew seem to be seeking to come into the light. We have had many earnest talks with some of the sailors. May the Lord guide us. We are being very closely watched by many on board, who stand aloof from Christ. Oh for the outpouring of the Spirit through us upon one and all!

"For myself, I have never before experienced such strength and comfort in Christ; and I know that this is in answer to your prayers."

There was little incident to mark the voyage, though the passage of the Red Sea and the glimpse of the Sinai range were naturally full of interest to the earnest Bible student.

Half-way across the Indian Ocean they passed a tract of ocean full of sorrowful memories for the seniors of the missionary band; for here, within sight of the low-lying coral island of Minokoi, four years before, their bright young daughter Laura, who was on her way to school in England,—her parents remaining at their post in Tientsin,—had died of fever, and been buried at sea.

We cannot linger over the bright descriptions of tropical scenery, the Chinese population of Singapore, the wedding in Hong Kong, and the evangelistic service among the soldiers stationed there, at which Dr. Roberts spoke; for we must hasten on to the scenes of his life-work in Northern China. "A verse was much in my mind as I neared Shanghai," he writes. "I take it as a voice from God: 'Be strong and of a good courage, and I will strengthen thy heart.' Taken in its fullest meaning, what grander keynote could I have, what better motto! ... As far as I have learnt to know myself, this was the message I needed; and I trust each returning year will find this communion more perfect. Oh for the faith and spiritual strength which overcomes all obstacles, and finds one better prepared for every battle and fiery trial that may befall us. Already I am beginning to see that there is a fuller meaning in the Christian life than I had dreamt of. May we be led to rejoice as Paul did, that we may know the fellowship of Christ's sufferings here, and (though, as I write it, the flesh shrinks from the experience) may we enter into deeper fellowship with Jesus in His sufferings now, that one day we may also have fellowship with Him in His joy and glory."

"I have had a good time in Shanghai," he writes to his mother. "It is in some respects a charming spot. The river is studded with Chinese junks and English ocean-bound ships; and along its banks are public gardens, well laid out. The foreign settlement is divided into English, American, and French quarters. As you walk through the English quarter, the shops, houses, streets, electric light, and a thousand and one other things, make you fancy you are still in the old country."

Dr. Roberts found a letter of welcome awaiting him from Dr. Griffith John, which greatly cheered him, for he had always a great admiration for the veteran missionary, and, had the way opened, would have been glad to work as his colleague.

"What is before me no one knows. Mongolia, so it seems, with its poor, lapsed masses, as sheep without a shepherd, vainly groping their way in the dark. What changes, what shifting scenes are before me! But we are all pilgrims here. This is not our resting-place. May we never make it such."

There was also a letter awaiting the young medical missionary from his future colleague, the Rev. J. Gilmour, which ran as follows:

"MY DEAR ROBERTS,—It was with much thankfulness that I heard, on September 30, that you were coming out to Mongolia. Come, brother, and may the blessing of God come with you. . . . I believe we have a splendid field of work here: a hard one, I know, but nothing is too hard for the Lord. I am coming to depend more on God in my work, and on prayer; and I want much your help in prayer. God has been very good to me, but two can pray better than one. Come along, brother, and help me. In this respect you can be an efficient help the day you enter the field. I am praying and longing for large blessings. I have one thousand and one things to say and ask, but I will wait till I see you. I pray that your life in China may both be more consecrated and more fruitful in conversions than mine has been. I have been here twenty days to-morrow. I'm off east, to be at a fair for eight days, then a month at Chao-yang, then eight or nine days at fairs, etc., then I hope to start for Pekin.—Expecting soon to see you, and praying that we may be a blessing to each other, believe me, yours very truly, JAMES GILMOUR."

While in Shanghai, Dr. Roberts greatly enjoyed making the acquaintance of missionaries of his own and other Societies. "I took tea twice at the China Inland Mission," he writes. "I found them a happy, united band of consecrated workers. It was curious to see them in the Chinese dress." He was also much interested in the hospital, once under the care of Dr. Lockhart of the London Missionary Society, and saw there several cases of leprosy, and one of elephantiasis. After a visit to one of the large opium dens, capable of accommodating 600 persons, he writes: "There are six of these in the English concession, and six in the French, though Mr. Muirhead told us the Chinese officials had in the strongest terms requested their suppression."

"The nearer I am to Mongolia, the clearer does my way open up," he writes'; "but Tientsin is the first step, and I hope to spend some valuable months there, preparing for Mongolia."

Transhipping at Shanghai, the little party of missionaries appointed to Tientsin made their way up the eastern coast of China, through the Yellow Sea and Gulf of Pechihli, till they arrived within sight of the far-famed Taku forts, from whence, in 1859, Admiral Hope's squadron, on its way to Pekin with the newly-ratified treaty, was fired upon without warning, and repulsed with the loss of three English gunboats and 300 killed and wounded. "The other vessels lay anchored at the bar," writes the doctor, "which, during a season of low tides, often prevents steamers from ascending the river for days together." They were especially glad, therefore, to find they could cross with little delay.

They then passed up the winding, muddy Pei-ho, or North River,—every bend of which a Chinese official estimated as being worth a couple of ironclads to China, because it makes their capital more difficult of access to a hostile army,—and in six hours reached Tientsin, the port of the capital, a city of 500,000 inhabitants. It stands on a featureless plain, which at no very remote period must have been below the level of the sea, and is at present almost as destitute of any natural beauties as the alkali deserts of the Western plains of America. Yet energetic spirits from the West have, with unwearying energy, transformed this bit of mud-flat, conceded to the Foreign Powers by the Treaty of 1858, into a fine settlement, with well-built European residences, and broad, well-kept roads, shaded by trees, which have only attained to their present growth in this saline soil by constant watchfulness and care.

The destination of the missionaries was not, however, this foreign settlement, but a cluster of buildings at the extreme end of the Taku road, where it touches the native quarter known as the compound of the London Mission. Its surroundings would be considered most unsanitary in any Western land, consisting, as they do, of crowded native huts, built on land innocent of anything but the most primitive attempts at drainage. In front, we have the prospect of a treeless plain, dotted with innumerable graves, interspersed with stagnant malarial pools, bounded by the low mud-wall which bears the name of San-Ko-lin-Sin's Folly.

The London Mission commenced work in Tientsin in the year 1861. Nine years after, the city obtained an unenviable notoriety by the terrible massacre of Tientsin, during which twenty-two European lives were sacrificed to the fury of the mob, urged on by the systematic circulation, by those in high places, of rumours crediting the "foreign barbarians" with unmentionable atrocities. This massacre was, for a time, a serious hindrance to work in North China—not that the missionaries left their posts, but the people stood aloof, and were inclined to look upon them with greater suspicion than before. It is given only to the workers themselves to know how long it takes to lay the foundation of a Christian Church in China. The years of slow and painful teaching of those, willing to learn, emerging out of heathen darkness into glorious light, yet, at first, only "seeing men as trees walking,"—the bitter pain which rends many a missionary's heart as he sees converts struggling upward, yet fettered by the bands of the heathenism of countless generations,—these are the trials of mission life. It is these and similar anxieties that call earnestly for the constant upholding of the Christians in England, and not so much those seasons of storm and bloodshed, which loom so largely in the minds of those at home.

Just emerged from this baptism of fire, Tientsin did not seem a very hopeful field of Christian effort. But in the space of ten years the aspect of things had entirely changed, in answer—so the founders of the mission believe—to constant, united prayer.

In the first place, a new Viceroy held sway, who was so far in advance of his age as to believe that it was possible for China to learn a few things from the despised nations of the West.

When his home was invaded by sickness, and his wife lying at the point of death, he dared to violate all Chinese rules of etiquette, and call to her aid Western physicians.

The story of how the skill and constant care of Dr. Mackenzie, with the blessing of God, brought about her recovery, has been told elsewhere. Upon Dr. Roberts' arrival in Tientsin, he found a large Chinese building, known as the Viceroy's Hospital, under the charge of Dr. Mackenzie—His Excellency himself forwarding to the doctor a monthly cheque for its support. The dispensary was daily thronged with patients, and between five and six hundred persons were treated yearly as in-patients in the wards. In addition to this, there was a flourishing medical school, in which young English-speaking Chinamen went through the curriculum required of medical students in England—the whole of this work being actively superintended by Dr. Mackenzie.

The Directors of the London Missionary Society had expressed a wish that Dr. Roberts, although appointed to Mongolia, should remain in Tientsin for some months, for the study of the language, and to assist in the hospital, thus gaining experience of Chinese medical mission work.

It had been settled that, during Dr. Roberts' stay in Tientsin, the two medical men should reside together. This arrangement was a source of much satisfaction to them both. In a letter of this date, written by Dr. Mackenzie to a friend, he speaks of the entire consecration and Christlike character of his young friend. "Roberts is only twenty-five," he writes, "and I am thirty-six; and yet he seems to have such a wonderful grasp of spiritual realities, and such a knowledge of Christ, as I have never yet attained to."

In his letters home, Dr. Roberts constantly referred to the help and strength he received from Mackenzie's companionship. "I am living with Dr. Mackenzie—rejoice with me, for he is truly an excellent fellow, and a deeply spiritual man. He has a very large work here, and it is ideal medical missionary work. He has great ability, and success also. We have many talks daily upon spiritual things. He is much used of the Lord in His work, and always has some seeking Christ in the wards. It is a great privilege to be with him." Dr. Roberts' first letter tells of the great Chinese feast prepared by the native Christians to welcome the new arrivals, and to show their joy at the return of their old friends, Mr. and Mrs. Lees. "The chop-sticks were a new experience to me; but I broke the ice, and my appetite too, with them. Certainly, to use the same sticks for every course was comical and objectionable to our notions, though in keeping with our surroundings. But to refuse food would have been to hurt their feelings.

"I have a bedroom to myself, and am going to make it into a study for my teacher and self. My teacher is an elderly man of sixty-four. I am to have four hours a day with him to begin with, beside private work and hospital work, and other things; so my time is well filled up.

"This is our daily programme: Rise between 6.30 and 7— breakfast at 7.45. Then, over to the hospital with Dr. Mackenzie for prayers with the patients and assistants. We are reading the Gospel of St. John. At present, of course, I am only a listener. Anyone can ask questions about the verses read. How the Chinese enjoy the Parables!—they are admirably suited to the Chinese mind, Dr. Mackenzie says. At nine o'clock we return home, and my teacher is waiting. We then set to work, reading John's Gospel. My aim is to master every character. Afterwards, I go over Wade's Exercises, and generally finish up with learning one of the translations of Sankey's hymns. Last Sunday I enjoyed a Bible class with the medical students who speak English— our subject was Paul's conversion."

On 12th December he writes: "The chief news is, that Mr. Gilmour has arrived. I had been out with Dr. Mackenzie, and, on our return, heard he had come. Entering the doctor's study, we found Mr. Gilmour, dressed in Chinese clothes—no hair on his face and very little on his head, as he had only a short time since been shaved. He is of average height. Great determination and force of character are clearly seen on his face. When he speaks, one is reminded that he is in the presence of a man of power. There is in him a most pleasing combination of great earnestness and cheerfulness. He can enjoy a joke, as well as make one. I never saw a man who was more absorbed with the spirit of the gospel, and who had greater zeal for Christ and the salvation of souls. Mr. Gilmour was in good health, notwithstanding that he has been living in Chinese and Mongol inns on a vegetable diet for nearly a year.

Last Sunday he spoke to the native Christians in our Ma-chia-kow chapel. You should have seen how thoroughly they enjoyed it, leaning forward to catch every word he said. He has a happy knack of illustrating everything by the Mongol habits, and their way of dealing with him. In the evening he received news of his youngest child's serious illness, and left at 2 A.M. in a Pekin cart. The other day, two mandarins and their suite of servants called, in very handsome sedan-chairs, to present Dr. Mackenzie with a tablet, in recognition of his kindness to them when ill. I went over with the doctor to the dispensary."

The front of this building is painted a brilliant scarlet, and it possesses the queer curled eaves which are so characteristic of Chinese architecture. The pillars which support the roof, where it extends over the narrow verandah, are black; and upon them, and the elaborately carved doorways, hang what appear to the uninitiated a series of Chinese signboards. These are the tablets which, according to Chinese custom, are presented by wealthy patients to the physician whose skill has restored them to health again. It was one of these tablets which the mandarins had called to formally present.

"Upon our arrival at the dispensary," writes Dr. Roberts, "there were great salutations and a display of fireworks. We went into a room, where tea was being served,—in Chinese fashion, minus milk and sugar,—and the Chinese officials had a smoke. . . . Meanwhile, the band was performing outside. I believe it would have driven Hallé mad—everyone played with a total disregard of tune. This is the Chinese ideal of harmony, and they can find nothing attractive in our music. The tablets were nailed up amidst a deafening chorus of fire-crackers. Lunch was then announced. It was the signal for an amusing struggle, as to who should lead the way or go down the steps first. The officials had a relative present who was not in uniform. Eventually they literally dragged him down the steps, and made him go first."

Dr. Roberts' first home-letter, in 1888, tells of the Christmas celebration, when he heard two hundred Chinese Christians singing, in their own tongue, "Hark! the herald angels sing." On New Year's Day, large numbers of Chinese friends called, in groups of twelve or fifteen at a time, to offer the best wishes of the season. The Week of Prayer, when the Christians of China united their petitions with fellow-believers the wide world over, was also a season of great joy to him. "I am glad to say that I am making some progress in the language," he writes; "and I believe your earnest united prayers, that I may be helped, are being answered. I pray God none will grow weary of praying because they hear so little of the answers, or because I am so far away. I feel my success in my future work will largely depend on your united prayers. God can make even me anything that you ask Him to make me. Is anything too hard for Him? In the middle of January, the extreme cold of the Tientsin winter caused great distress among the people. Twenty bodies were found frozen this morning outside the West Gate. Well-to-do Chinamen wear robes lined with fur and sheepskins. I am glad I am a total abstainer—there is nothing like it for enabling one to resist the cold.

"If father were on the Watch Committee of Tientsin, there is one improvement he would be inclined to make in the night-service. The policeman goes his rounds every hour; but the comical thing is, that he beats a wooden drum as he walks, as much as to say, 'I am coming—look out!' which gives thieves a chance of escape. The air being very clear, you can hear his drum at a great distance. This performance over, the watchman enters his little box on the roadside, and, I regret to say, is soon fast asleep. 'How do you like the Chinese?' you ask. There are some very nice Chinese at work in the hospital, and all of them seem to understand the language of love. Some of them are very grateful, and, when leaving the hospital, carry a good report of the work far away into the country districts."

On one occasion, the two doctors made a tour of the native benevolent institutions of Tientsin. During the time of great distress, which the severe weather always brings to those who live ever on the brink of starvation, many thousands of people depend entirely upon the benevolence of wealthy men for their support. "Near the East Gate, 16,000 women are fed daily. The streets around the Benevolent Hall were crowded with beggars; for, though a large basin of millet gruel is given to the inmates morning and night, they are expected to make up the rest of their food by begging. Five hundred persons are cared for in this way in one place. I saw a room, 10 feet by 30, which had forty men and boys sleeping in it. The air, as you may imagine, was terribly foul, and the inmates were in rags. Besides these, 6000 more are provided with shelter, the Viceroy having rented a large number of small inns for their accommodation. They slept on the usual brick bedsteads of North China, with no other covering than their rags, and most of them looked unspeakably wretched." Leaving these sad sights, they made their way through crowded streets, past tea-houses thronged with customers, listening to conjurers and story-tellers, who were attracting larger crowds.

"We also visited a Home for Widows and Orphans, supported by the Viceroy and his wife. The grounds were nicely laid out with a few trees.

"We then went into a Taoist temple, filled with plaster images showing the terrors of the world to come, and also a grand Mohammedan temple with elaborate carving. We returned home very full of all the suffering and sorrow of this great city, and of its deep need of the gospel of Jesus. The task of bringing its people to know Him and believe in Him, seems almost too great to grapple with, and only makes one pray for the advent of that happy time when a nation shall be born in a day. Till then, how great the privilege of having any share, however humble, in preaching to those who have never heard of Him."

To Mrs. Melrose, his kind friend of Edinburgh days, he wrote: "I seem, as yet, to have scarcely begun to know what Jesus is, or the power of His resurrection to lift me from things seen, and to fill me with an unspeakable yearning to do His will. But I am beginning to see a meaning in those words, 'Follow me': I was a stranger too before. I know there faces me (when, I can't say) experiences which will be like the gale which shakes the very foundations. These things must have one of two results—to bring me into clearer, stronger light; or, as in so many cases I have heard of, to drive me farther from Christ. My verse this morning came as a voice from God: 'My help cometh from the Lord, who made heaven and earth.' Our last great request at the Throne of Grace, that it might be our meat and our drink, every hour of our lives, to do His will, is often on my mind; but how far from being realised, God only knows.

"It is impossible to make headway out here unless you are fully surrendered to Christ. I have heard of men who have grown cold, or become wholly engrossed in the secular part of their work. Pray that I may never be one of these. I know almost nothing of that yearning to be used for the salvation of souls compared with what I should know, and trust, through many prayers, that I shall soon know."

To his brother-in-law, Mr Ralph Walker, he wrote : "I am only coming into the very twilight of the light of the knowledge of the glory of God. But the Lord is very near and very patient, and He will reveal Himself and the glory of His gospel in a fuller sense than He has done as yet, for the sake of these multitudes who seem so comfortable and contented in their present blindness, and whose consciences seem dead indeed. Terrible are the manifestations of the subtlety of Satan in this land and this city. He lets his darts off in every direction, and works as an angel of light on every hand.

"The other day, I gave an address to the sailors of the English gunboat wintering at Tientsin, on the Medical Aspects of Total Abstinence. The operation case I had last week is going on well. The patient is a poor man, who tries to make a living by picking up shells found on the plain which have failed to go off. He secured one of them; and, while attempting to take out the powder, it exploded, injuring his hand severely. He was a frequenter of the soup kitchens of which I spoke. No one leaves the hospital without having often heard the gospel, and had it explained to them; and many in a short time learn to read the Testament and Catechism. We have some deeply interested and truly hopeful; and how they love and respect Dr. Mackenzie!"

At the Chinese New Year season, Dr. Mackenzie went into the country for a few weeks, to make a round of visits to a number of the eye patients who had become Christians while under his care in the hospital. During his absence, Dr. Roberts took charge of the class of medical students, thirteen in number, giving them instruction in surgery. "This helps to keep up my book-work," he writes, "and I enjoy it very much." One of his last letters before starting for Mongolia, was written to his sister Mary. "I can't but believe," he says, "you will be here in China some day. You know William Burns had to wait years before his desire to go out to the heathen was realised. I strongly advise you to learn to paint, with a paint-brush, all the Chinese radicals. Then, if you like, take the radicals in the first chapter of St. John, and trace them out. This will be of great use if ever you come to China. I wish someone had told me to do it before I came."

CHAPTER VII

MONGOLIAN SOLITUDES

"As labourers in Thy vineyard,
Send us out, Christ, to be
Content to bear the burden
Of weary days for Thee.
We ask no other wages,
When Thou shalt call us home,
But to have shared the travail
That makes Thy kingdom come."

IT was on an evening early in March of the year 1888 (according to Chinese reckoning, the 15th of the 1st moon), the day kept universally throughout the Celestial Empire as the Feast of Lanterns. The Tientsin streets were gay with many-coloured designs of every conceivable shape. Vegetables, insects, fish, animals, and even boys and girls, had their paper representations. These strangely-shaped lanterns were either carried along the street in people's hands at the end of a stick, or, in the case of the larger ones, suspended above the houses at the end of a pole—the lights inside brightening the colours of these very effective decorations.

Inside the mission-house, also, the little folks were keeping high holiday, for some Chinese friends had sent them an assortment of wonderful designs.

They were busily engaged in admiring and comparing the merits of their respective treasures, when their old friend Dr. Mackenzie made his appearance, telling them, with a twinkle in his eye, that he had brought a Chinese gentleman to see them.

The older children looked a little shy at the idea of a stranger breaking in upon their festivities. Who is it? they asked. Is it Chang Sien-sang, or anybody we know? But the doctor only smiled in a mysterious manner. Meanwhile a little one had trotted off, to examine more closely the tall figure in the shadow of the doorway. The stranger wore the usual long blue wadded gown of a Chinaman, and over that a wadded black jacket. His cap was of black satin, finished off with the usual knot of scarlet cord; and his black cloth shoes had thick white soles.

In a few minutes there was a chorus of laughter, mingled with shouts of "Why, it's only Dr. Roberts!" The supposed stranger was quickly taken possession of by his young captors, and merrily ushered into the room where the lanterns were burning, and was soon busily at work fixing new candles into those which had burnt out, and rescuing others from the devouring flames. Soon Dr. Mackenzie suggested that it was quite time to say good-bye, to the great regret of the little party. Then Dr. Roberts told them he was starting at daybreak, to join Mr. Gilmour in distant K'ou-wai, or "beyond the Wall," as the Chinese commonly call Mongolia. He had changed his usual garments for Chinese clothes, because they were better for travelling in, and for work "beyond the Wall."

Life is full of changes; and perhaps there is no place like a foreign mission station for impressing this truism upon one's mind. Still, none of us dreamed, as we gave a loving God-speed to the young Mongol missionary,—Gilmour's long-waited-for, earnestly-prayed-for medical colleague,—that it was the last time we should see together in this world the two doctors, so alike in entire consecration and glad devotion to their common Lord.

Eight o'clock next morning found the Chinese Christians and some foreign friends gathered round a Pekin cart drawn by two strong mules; inside the cover of which— wedged in among the Chinese bedding, which serves in some degree to preserve European travellers on Chinese roads from concussion of the brain and fractured bones—sat Dr. Roberts. His box was secured on two small shafts protruding at the back of the cart—his "boy," or servant, sat on one of the front shafts, and the carter on the other. The Chinese friends shook their own hands, according to their custom, wishing him "peace on the road"; and he was soon on his way through the crowded Chinese streets

—crowded, even though at eight o'clock in the morning, for Chinese business is always transacted in the early hours of the day. That strange custom of "the barbarians of the West," of sitting up long after the sun has set, and spending the morning hours after dawn in bed, thus wasting oil in the most reckless manner, is only one thing among many which no Chinaman can ever understand.

"We crossed the Pei-ho by an iron bridge of French construction," writes Dr. Roberts. "Once in the country, we said 'good-bye' to the smooth macadamised roads of the settlement, and a simple mud construction took their place. These roads, as each day showed more and more clearly, were noted more than anything else for their ruts. In China, everyone seems to like to go in ruts in more things than roads, and our carter kept faithfully to them. On our right hand was the river. Along the bank walked a number of men, pulling large house-boats and other craft up the stream. They had ropes passing from their waists to the top of the ships' masts.

"We had plenty of company, as we were on the high-road to Pekin, and dozens of carts were journeying in the same direction.

"Passing through a village of mud-huts, the carter immediately in front of us got into a row, and gave me an opportunity of noticing at least one use for the pig-tail; for a man came up and seized the carter by it, and carried him off.

"A little farther on we saw a woman and two children grinding corn, with a pole fixed through two mill-stones. At 4 P.M. we made our first halt, stopping at a native inn. As soon as the mules were unharnessed, they rolled over and over for some time in the dust, which is their usual custom on halting. I secured a room for myself and boy: it contained a little table, an arm-chair, and a brick bed. This sounds bad; but if the bed is clean, as it happened to be on this occasion, and you have plenty of your own bedding, and are sleepy, as you are sure to be after travelling in the cart all day, then they are splendid. They warm these beds, if required in the winter season, by a flue running beneath them.

"Having got into our room, we settled down for our first meal that day. They brought us some beef, which was very good, some native flour-cakes, and some tea. I fell asleep early; but had no means of telling the time, for it is awkward to carry a watch when wearing Chinese dress. Yet we have two excellent clocks — the Chinese, in truly Eastern fashion, go, first, by the sun; second, by the cock-crowing. I never valued a cock half so much as I do now. Morning after morning these 'heralds of the dawn' would tell us it was time to be up and preparing for our journey.

"The Chinese rely implicitly upon the cocks, and speak of the first, second, or the third cock-crowing as the time they wish to start on their journey.

"One morning I found I had mistaken the light of the moon, always so brilliant in China, for the sun, and got up, I imagine, about midnight, and prepared for starting. This mistake never occurred again—my faithful friends the cocks kept me right. The industry of the Chinese struck me much. In the early dawn, while stars were still shining, shops were open, and men selling fish by the river-side.

"The country was low-lying and partly submerged, which accounted for the unpleasant experience of the cart occasionally sticking in the mud. We had to be ferried, cart and all, over one river.

"On the third day after Tientsin we sighted hills, and soon were near enough to find they were parched and barren, but still a welcome prospect after four months of the perfectly flat and barren plain of Northern China."

About four o'clock on Saturday afternoon the travellers arrived at Tsun-Hwa—a large city with an American mission station. "I made for the missionaries' houses," he writes, "and was soon very kindly welcomed by them all. What an oasis in the desert this was! A band of warm-hearted Christians united together in seeking to win this city and its many neighbouring villages for Christ. How refreshing it was to speak to someone in English once more, I leave you to imagine."

After giving an account of the services for the natives, including a Chinese Sunday school, the young missionary continues: "We had a very blessed time in the evening together, talking over God's covenant with Abraham, as contained in Gen. xvii. 1-8. How grand the thought that this covenant implies the conversion of all nations to God. Through

faith the heathen shall become the sons of Abraham. The
'I wills' there are full of comfort to one surrounded by a
heathen people, when he realises his utter helplessness, and
leans solely on the promises of God and His almighty power."

In good time next morning, Dr. Roberts was once more
on the road to Mongolia, his kind hostess having thought-
fully made some provision of English bread and cakes for the
way—a boon indeed to those who know how unpalatable
Chinese provisions, to be obtained at inns, are to new arrivals
in the country.

The sight of the Great Wall of China, which soon loomed
before them, was full of interest to one who thought, at that
time, his life-work lay beyond it.

"We halted within a short distance of the famous Wall
for lunch, and I had a fine opportunity of examining it.
It runs for many a mile over the mountains and down into
the valleys. I climbed up it, and found it was made of large
bricks, with a stone foundation. It is about 40 feet high
and 15 feet broad. It is solid, being filled with stones in
the interior. Mr. Willits told me it was built 200 B.C.,
and this part of it is said never to have been restored.

"A broken-down wooden gate formed the entrance into
Mongolia. Here my passport was demanded; but the men
in charge seem to examine it more as a curiosity than anything else—so few foreigners pass this way.

"I was now in Mongolia, but not yet 'among the
Mongols,' for they have withdrawn farther north, and left
the Chinese in exclusive possession of this part."

Passing near the rich copper mines of Pa-kow, worked
under the direction of an Englishman, Dr. Roberts remarks: "What would not the opening up of a few more
mines and railways do for China? Why, in England I
could have gone this distance, from Tientsin to Ta-ssu-
kow, in five hours instead of ten days!"

At an inn, in which they put up for the night, the
Mongol missionary met the first representative of the people
among whom he had been appointed to work. "He was a
miserable-looking lama (or priest): his head was shaven; he
wore a chain of beads, and a long light-brown robe, much
the worse for wear; he seemed to be on a lower stratum to
the poor Chinese peasants, and spoke only Mongol. My

room at the inn was crowded with visitors, but they gradually left; and though it was freezing outside, I was soon asleep on my heated brick bedstead, dreaming of Old England."

Early next morning he was on the road again. "Everywhere," he writes, "I found complete ignorance of the gospel and of Jesus Christ; yet everywhere they read gladly John iii. 16, and other verses—saying they seemed good words. Early on Saturday morning we crossed the summit of the pass, 2000 feet above sea-level, according to my aneroid bar. Such a glorious sunrise! We had a grand view of the valley we were soon to enter; and soon passed an ancient pagoda, built of carved stone and bricks. About 4 P.M. we sighted Ta-ssu-kow, a comparatively large town, and were soon at Gilmour's inn. He was out preaching and healing the sick, but soon appeared; and before long we were enjoying a chat upon many subjects in common."

Dr. Roberts did not send to his Manchester home, or any of his English friends, a description of the rooms in the squalid Chinese inn known as the "London Mission Premises." Another member of the mission, who stayed there some months later, has thus described them: "The place is known as the 'Inn of Benevolence and Harmony.' Entering the high gateway, we passed across the small outer court to a larger inner one, which contained rows of stone feeding-troughs for the use of the mules. The floor was unswept, covered with drying manure, and surrounded by poor-looking buildings out of repair. Gilmour's quarters consisted of a three-roomed house, with a low mud-wall in front separating it from the general court. The doors and sideposts were covered with the torn remains of the usual Chinese New Year's scrolls, wishing health, honour, and fame to the tenants. A few broken steps led into the middle room of the three, which contained a Chinese cooking-range and several native utensils. The rafters were smoke-begrimed, and the walls dingy. The next room, furnished with a table, a bamboo-chair, and two benches, belonged to the native helper.

"To the right of the kitchen, a screen, bearing the words, 'The Glad Tidings Hall of the Jesus Religion,' covered a door; lifting it, the visitor entered Gilmour's sanctum. A brick bedstead occupied one side of the room, and the furniture consisted of a table, old and rickety; one bamboo-chair, and two benches for the worshippers who came to prayers in the evening." Such was the home that awaited the young missionary at the end of his wearisome journey; but he never at any time alluded to its outward discomfort, for the Christian fellowship with his senior colleague made it often the very gate of heaven.

"Poor Gilmour," he writes; "he is a grand pioneer missionary—a very Livingstone,—but he has been sorely tried since he came to Mongolia. Lately the Roman Catholics have being doing their best to draw away one of his most promising converts, by the offer of large sums of money if he will join them. Some of the Christians are asking for Government protection, and what not; others are proving faithless deceivers, and worse; and here Gilmour has been labouring on for many years, out of sight. Oh, pray for him! Pray much for souls, for sustaining grace. The Lord lay it on all your hearts to plead much for him and for Mongolia."

It was a great joy to Gilmour to find what rapid progress his young medical colleague had made in the study of the language.

"You all know," he writes, "this is of the Lord; you know my bad memory. I can only ask you all to remember to give Him the praise, and Him only, for answering your prayers. There is not much prospect of your hearing again for a month or so. Do not be anxious, as we shall all be safe in our Father's keeping. I am gradually getting into the Chinese food. Ta-ssu-kow is a first-rate place to stay at. Splendid hills and good Chinese food."

About three weeks after this letter was written, a lama, or Mongol priest, known to Mr. Gilmour, walked into the inn one evening, and expressed his willingness to carry any letters or messages to Pekin for the missionaries. They gladly seized the opportunity of communicating with the outside world; and Dr. Roberts' letter gives some glimpses of their life in the lonely mission outpost:—

"I rise at daylight, drink a cup of tea, and have prayers in Chinese with my man, who shares my room. Meanwhile, Gilmour has sallied forth with his far-famed wooden medicine boxes and blue cloth tent, and, taking his stand in a sheltered corner of the broad Mongolian street, or in the open square, preaches and heals the sick all day long. After breakfast, I settle down to the study of Chinese. This was difficult at first, as visitors are very numerous; and to refuse them admittance would give great offence, being so contrary to Chinese custom.

"At noon, I join Gilmour on the street, and assist him in distributing medicines and selling tracts from his tent, which bears upon it the characters for the 'Gospel Hall,' 'The Saviour Jesus Christ,' and 'God, the Heavenly Father.' This work goes on till the time for the evening meal. After it, many people come in to ask questions, and talk about the new doctrine."

So loyally did the young doctor follow the lead of the senior colleague, who, though he had received no medical training, had for many years relieved much suffering throughout this large district, that the general impression of the people at first was that the young missionary had come to learn the art of healing from Gilmour by residence among them. This fact speaks volumes for the humble and brotherly spirit of the young doctor.

After ten days' stay in Ta-ssu-kow, the missionaries went on to the town of Ta-cheng-tsz, where the few Christians soon found their way to the inn at which they stayed. "The chief shop in the place is a pawn-shop. Opium smoking, gambling, and immorality abound, and native whisky-drinking is very prevalent. One of the largest buildings in Ta-cheng-tsz is a spirit distillery. Whisky is very cheap,—about four tablespoonsful for a farthing,—and both Mongols and Chinese in this district drink heavily. Another large building is a Buddhist temple, with, opposite to it, a theatre. Every large temple has a theatre attached to it, the acting being in honour of the gods.

"No women are to be seen on the streets, but there are large numbers of beggars. Oh, what specimens of humanity! wearing nothing but a ragged piece of sacking round their loins. Their hair has not been cut for many months. They are everywhere in China, and possess power of a certain kind. They will crouch down in front of a shop, and, with plaintive moans, cry for a "cash." They refuse to leave off till at least one is given to them.

"Should the shopkeeper persist in refusing, it sometimes

means a mob of a hundred beggars round his shop within half an hour, plundering or pulling it down. Should a beggar die in front of a shop, it means ruin to the tradesman, as no one will purchase anything from him. So a dying beggar receives a few 'cash,' and crawls away to some quiet spot, where he can die in peace."

After a few days at Ta-cheng-tsz, the missionaries proceeded to the third station, at the town of Chao-yang, where Gilmour usually made his longest stay, and which has since become the headquarters of the mission.

It is three days' journey from the the sea-coast of the Gulf of Pechihli. For the first twenty miles from Ta-cheng-tsz the travellers had to pass through a district frequented by robbers.

An attack from them had been provided against in the usual way, by placing some lumps of silver in a Chinese purse attached to a girdle tied round the waist beneath the outer robe. Had they been attacked, the travellers would have been compelled to make their way back to the nearest city. The robbers are usually mounted, and soon manage to escape with their booty.

"The people here, both Chinese and Mongols, are very kind. As Gilmour walks through the streets, they nod to him in a friendly manner. They thoroughly appreciate his labour of love and the medical work he has done among them. He tells me he considers the Mongols more inclined to heart-religion of some kind than the Chinese, whose idea is rather—try many religions, one of them is sure to save you at the last. The people here will come in and drink tea with you as long as you like; and, after you have spoken to them of our Saviour's death and God's love for them, will say, 'Yes, the words are very good, I believe them,' when in reality they care nothing about it.

"There is a sect in Northern China, having its centre in Tientsin, called the 'Tsai-li-ti' sect. There are over two hundred members here in Chao-yang, and in Tientsin they number many thousands. Three of their rules are : abstinence from opium, from alcohol, and from tobacco; if they break any of the rules (there are eight in all), they are dismissed."

The missionaries passed unmolested on this occasion through the mountainous, sparsely-populated district separating their stations, and arrived at the inn at which Gilmour usually lived, to find the rooms filled. In an apartment containing two brick bedsteads they found six traders already settled for the night, and had to share one of the beds with two strangers.

"There are two Christians here and several inquirers, and any amount of medical work daily. I am deriving much benefit from living so much among the Chinese, and believe some day I shall be able to speak with ease and comfort. Every morning I go over to the innkeeper's room, where there are usually a number of men assembled. One of them acts as my teacher, while the others look on and make remarks. In this way I get a number of words from them, by hearing them speak to one another.

"There are three fine pagodas near here, and a famous Buddhist temple, which swarms with filthy lamas, old and young. I often hear them chanting their anthems, and see them walking about with their strings of red beads.

"We hope to remain here till May. Gilmour is a grand man—his whole heart is in his work; it is very helpful being with him.

"I can't close this letter without asking you all to join in thanking our loving Heavenly Father for His blessing, and for the loving way in which He has already heard your prayers for me. I am very happy, and would not exchange my life and calling for any other. I feel more than ever the grandeur of the work, and my utter insufficiency apart from the Lord's presence; but our sufficiency is of Him, and all power is His."

CHAPTER VIII

APPOINTED TO TIENTSIN

"Use me, and let my weapon be
The clear brook's polished stone:
The weakness of the work be mine,
The glory all Thine own."

BRIGHT days seemed at last to have dawned for James Gilmour, the lonely worker on the bare Mongolian plain. All the North China missionaries who knew Dr. Roberts felt that the Lord had indeed answered the many prayers that had been offered, and sent to Gilmour a medical colleague after his own heart, and no whit behind him in burning zeal and entire consecration to the Master's service. What might we not hope for now, we began to ask, in that long-neglected field? But God's ways are not as our ways, or His thoughts as our thoughts; and those who seek most earnestly the coming of His kingdom, have not unfrequently to see their dearest plans broken and shattered, and to learn to trust with simple faith, that the things that seem most like hindrances are all a part of His omniscient plan, working together for the coming of His kingdom in the earth.

It was on a bright April day, while Gilmour and his young medical colleague were busy attending to the crowd of those afflicted with many diseases, who daily thronged their blue cloth tent in the market-place. Suddenly there was a stir among the people, as a dust-covered courier appeared, looking as if he had travelled fast and far. In his hand he carried a sword, encased merely in a cloth scabbard. This was somewhat alarming to those who remembered the terrible massacre of Tientsin, for the man announced himself as sent off in hot haste from that city. "What news do you bring?" asked the missionaries; but the man only shook his head, and groaned audibly. On the way to the poor Chinese inn which they called home, followed by a curious crowd of Chinese and Mongols, the question was repeated, but with the same result. Too anxious to wait longer, Gilmour drew the man aside into a quiet corner, and demanded the news at once. It came slowly and sadly —"Dr. Mackenzie is dead, after a few days' illness."

Entering the bare room of the inn, the man opened his broad blue girdle, and took out of it a little bundle of letters, wrapped in Chinese oil-paper.

They told the sad story of the illness and death of the man who had won the confidence of the great Chinese Viceroy, and whose name was a household word in Tientsin and all Northern China.

It seemed as if no more crushing blow could have fallen upon any mission. Gilmour was trying to realise what it meant—that he had lost the friend with whom he had so often spent happy hours of Christian fellowship. He never dreamed that a still heavier blow was yet to fall.

Suddenly his young colleague looked up from his letters, and said one of them enclosed a telegram from the Directors of the London Missionary Society, requesting him to leave for Tientsin immediately, and take charge of the hospital there.

To Gilmour, at first, this double blow seemed almost overwhelming, while to Dr. Roberts the situation was perplexing beyond measure. Yet to men accustomed, as these two were, to submit the minutest details of daily life to the decision of a living Saviour, there was light even behind this cloud. For forty-eight hours, Gilmour writes, he "felt like a ship suddenly struck in mid-ocean by a mountain sea breaking over it." From Dr. Roberts' letters we gather something of the impression produced on his mind. "The Directors have telegraphed to me to succeed Dr. Mackenzie in the work of the Tientsin Hospital," he writes to his mother. "I know not what to say. Perhaps I should say nothing, but wait only upon God for guidance. You cannot think how hard it is to leave Mr. Gilmour in his lonely work for Christ in Mongolia. For over eight years he has agitated for a medical colleague

—now, is he again to be left alone? You say, 'Not alone, for Christ is with him.' Ah! but true though that is, it is not good for man to be alone, either in mission work or any other work.

"Can it ever be that labourers are so few? ... We are in great perplexity. How to leave my dear brother alone I know not; yet to refuse to fill up the ranks, and in the strength of the Lord, as His humble instrument, carry on the work in Tientsin to which I am appointed, is also difficult. ...

"I have lost more in Dr. Mackenzie's death than I can possibly realise. I had learned already to lean on him, to be guided by him, and to love him deeply. He was a man full of the Holy Spirit, and with a burning love for perishing souls. He had great power in prayer, and many rare qualifications for his post. Oh! what a loss to the London Missionary Society, from our point of view; but not from God's, is it? He does all things well; and who knows but that, by his death, our dear brother may be a greater blessing to our Tientsin mission than during his life even?"

After much united prayer, Gilmour and his young colleague came to the conclusion that it was the duty of the latter to proceed at once to Tientsin. The sea route was decided upon, as Dr. Roberts' health had already suffered from the poor fare and lack of the ordinary comforts of life, which were such distinguishing features of Gilmour's life in Mongolia. The night before the doctor left Chao-yang,—as the colleagues sat talking together, after the crowds that thronged them through the day had dispersed,—a subject was broached which was to have far-reaching issues, not only in the brightening of Dr. Roberts' own life, but also to the great strengthening of Christian work among the women of Tientsin. As they sat there by the dim light of the Chinese candle, which, flickering over the walls, brought into relief the dingy surroundings of the desolate room, Gilmour's thoughts were busy. Not so much, however, with his own grief, in the coming parting with the young colleague, whom he loved till death with the deep affection of a strong nature; he was thinking most of all of his Father's business, and the progress of the work in the port of the capital. "We want to get a stronger hold of the family-life of the people there," he said. "We want more workers among the women." This remark at once suggested to Dr. Roberts the thought of his youngest sister, the only daughter now left in the old Manchester home, towards which his heart ever turned so fondly. "I have a sister," he said, "who has wished to come to China as a missionary ever since I was a boy at Aberystwith. If the way were only open, she would come at once."

To Gilmour, who had learned during his lonely years of communion with God, what the majority of Christians are slow to believe, that the call of the Lord of the harvest must have precedence over all other claims, this fact was sufficient. He based upon it an earnest plea that Dr. Roberts should write at once to his parents, stating all the facts of the case, and urging them to give up their sole remaining child under the old roof, for the Master's work in China—sending her out as an honorary missionary, supported by the family. "I believe with all my heart," the doctor wrote, "dear Mary has been called of God to China. When shall that call meet with an eager and glad response from all concerned? If she were to be married at home, and go to some remote part of England —would any hinder, would any one say it was wrong? The far higher call has come—can she do other than obey? The God whom we worship, and have learnt to love and trust in, will a hundredfold more than make up for the gift of a second child for His service among the heathen. Has your giving me up for China proved a grief or a joy to you? I mean, in the true sense of the word. Speaking for myself, I feel it has been a richer source of blessing to our family, and certainly to me, than ever we had dared to hope for. If you give up Mary, I feel sure you will find that, by taking her, God has been making way for greater gifts, for richer spiritual blessings, and you will know more of the unspeakable love of God, when He gave up His ALL, His ONLY Son."

The 23rd of April found Dr. Roberts once more in a springless Chinese mule-cart, jolting over the rough, narrow track which serves as highway between Chao-yang and the city of Chin-chow, in Manchuria. "It was a sad parting with Gilmour," he writes, "and, but for much prayer and meditation on the Word together, would have been sadder still; yet we both felt strongly, that though we would, for personal reasons, wish to raise objections to my being removed to Tientsin, and even refuse to comply with the Directors' request, we found our mouths stopped, and could only say, 'It is the Lord; let Him do what seemeth Him good.'"

The first night on the road was spent at an inn, containing only two bare rooms for the accommodation of travellers. The brick beds of the larger room, supposed to be sufficient for thirty or forty men, were already full; and several had already made themselves comfortable in a smaller chamber. "The crowded state of the inn was accounted for by the rain," writes the doctor. "Some were smoking tobacco, some opium, and all were talk, talk, talking about the 'foreigner.' I tried to speak to them about the gospel, but was much discouraged to find I spoke so far from accurately that I was not understood. I think, though, it was a blessing, as it is calculated to stir me up to greater efforts than ever before to learn the language."

Another day, he writes of meeting two Corean merchants, dressed in white silk clothing. He was able to talk with them a little, and found they had some knowledge of the gospel.

The first Sunday was spent in a small Chinese inn; a poor place, with its mud floor, paper windows, and brick bedstead; but to the young medical missionary, far away from all human companionship, it proved the very gate of heaven to his soul. In the little well-worn copy of *Daily Light* he always used, the text for the day, 29th April, is thickly underlined, and the name of the place noted where, in a special way, the Lord met him, and spoke words of cheer and comfort to his soul. "'Consider how great things the Lord hath done for thee,' was the text for the day," he writes. "I reviewed my whole past life that quiet Sunday, that lull in the recent rush of events; and many an illustration of the things God had done in the past came up before me, and I was able quietly to wait upon Him for His blessing." In his diary he wrote: "Heavenly Father, can it be that I am to succeed Dr. Mackenzie in Tientsin? Oh, why hast Thou sent me? Why chosen me, who am so dull and slow to learn of Thee; so lukewarm? Thou surely knowest the deceitfulness of my heart, to-day and every day; the unfathomable depth of my need. I don't shine in society; far from it. I have a slow ear for languages, and a very bad memory. O Lord, why hast Thou called me from the sheepfold to the high places in the vineyard? Lord, there can only be one answer: the labourers are so very, very few, and Thou dost condescend to use the weak and base things of this world. Thou dost say: 'Follow Me. Look to Me alone; find in Me your all in all. I can supply every need of yours *in Christ*. You will always continue in yourself to have the consciousness of weakness and insufficiency for My service. Your strength will come from union with Christ, from being a passive instrument in His hands to accomplish His purposes. Be strong and courageous, do great exploits (truly this is one, Lord!), be calm and restful in Christ.' Lord, help me always to watch and pray, to take heed to myself, to be clothed with humility, to be filled with the Holy Spirit, that through me He may testify to men of Christ, and convince them of sin, righteousness, and judgment.

"I feel how far I am from being filled with the Spirit of Jesus, whose heart was full of love, to speak and live for His Father's glory. Lord give me also this Spirit in power. I can ask for nothing short of being filled with the Holy Ghost—kept by Christ, and used by Him whose I am, and whom I desire to serve. Lord, prepare me for all Thou art preparing for me; and grant, whatever else comes, I may please Thee in everything, and bring forth much fruit to Thy glory."

Writing home, he says: "What awaits me in Tientsin, I do not know; but there is One who knows all—the work is His. His presence I find, as I write, a source of power, peace, and hope. In His strength I can meet the task which, without Him, would be too difficult for me to face. Yet what an interesting, happy work is before me! A hospital which will accommodate over sixty in-patients, a large dispensary and consulting-room, a strong staff of Christian assistants; while for colleagues in the spiritual work, I shall have a band of happy, united workers I have learned to love."

Next morning, the young missionary, strengthened in spirit by his day of rest, took passage, on a native boat, down a rapid river, to the port of Newchwang, where he was kindly received by the members of the Irish Presbyterian Mission.

"I had a very interesting chat with Mrs. Carson over breakfast," he writes, "about William Burns. One of their converts knew him, though at the time he was yet a heathen. He made his coffin, and with great difficulty was persuaded by the English constable to assist in preparing his body for burial. Though an unbeliever for years, he says, 'eventually the lives of the missionaries convinced him of the truth of Christianity.' He has been much blessed, since his conversion, in bringing others to Christ.

"I walked to the foreign cemetery, and there spent a profitable time at William Burns' grave. There is an iron railing round it, and a cypress-tree at the head, while a climbing plant creeps over the rail. What a glorious corner it will be on the resurrection morning! I called on Dr. Morrison, who is greatly interested in the medicinal botany of the neighbourhood. He tells me that the Chinese have a very extensive list of medicines, some of ours among them, but they are much in the dark about their use. Two Chinese doctors called this morning. They gave me some curious information as to their ideas about the numerous pulses of the human body."

Next day Dr. Roberts took passage for Chefoo. "It is a lovely morning," he writes in his diary. "I have a little cabin to myself on deck—nice and breezy. The Lord is good. He crowneth me with loving-kindness and tender mercy.

"I had a very solemn talk with one of the officers on spiritual things. He believes in God's love, but loses sight of His justice, and finds difficulties in the way of believing many parts of God's Word. I left him, feeling how utterly powerless I was; but he said, 'Well, you won't forget me?' —a quiet way, I think, of asking me to pray for him.

"In a talk with the pilot, I found he was resting in the fact that he 'does sometimes think of religion, and is not so bad as some others he knows.' I stayed some time on the bridge, watching him manage the ship—it was grand! I was full of joy to know that Christ is my Pilot, and in full command of my little bark—that the hospital is under His care, and I only a bond-servant to do His will."

Dr. Roberts stayed a few days in Chefoo, leaving upon the missionaries who met him there the impression of a man whose one desire was, in all things to do the will of God. Taking ship for Tientsin, he reached the Pei-ho early on Thursday morning; but the steamer stuck fast in one of the shallow reaches of the river, about six miles from the city. So he came ashore, and, making his way up the river-bank, arrived at the mission compound soon after noon.

Few of his fellow-workers in that great Chinese city can forget the day when the quiet figure, in travel-stained Chinese clothes, suddenly appeared in the midst of our midday prayer-meeting. Especially do they remember the same meeting, on the following day, when the young, newly-appointed doctor led our devotions. Upon each one of us he left the impression of a man who had heard God's call, and obeyed it, sure that the needed strength and wisdom would be granted by the Master, from whom it came.

It did not seem wise that Dr. Roberts should be allowed to take up, at once, his residence alone in the house where he had lived so happily with his well-loved friend Dr. Mackenzie. It was therefore arranged that, if willing, he should for some months make his home with us. To many an earnest and devoted worker the offer of a home in a house which was filled from morning to night with the sound of children's voices, and the patter of little feet, might not have been altogether acceptable. To the doctor, however, their presence was rather an inducement than a disadvantage. He always interested himself in their studies and play alike, and they helped to make up to him for the loss of the dearly-loved nephews and nieces in the home-land. "It reminds me of dear old Ashfield in days gone by," he wrote," to see all the children's faces round the table at meal-times."

It is said sometimes, that to know a person's real character you should live with them during the ordinary wear and tear of daily life, through the "strain of toil, the fret of care." Dr. Roberts certainly bore this ordeal well; for it was a common remark of ours, that it was helpful to the spiritual life to have him living in the house, so attractive and Christlike was his " walk and conversation." Dr. Roberts had been barely six months in the country; but the day on which he took up the charge of the hospital was memorable for an address delivered in Chinese, asking the prayers and help of the native Christians and his fellow-missionaries in the new and important work to which he had been called. Writing home on the subject of his acceptance of the post, he says: "I gave my final answer to the members of our North China Committee of the L.M.S. on Friday, feeling I was doing the Lord's will, and Mr. Gilmour's too. It was encouraging to find that all the brethren here wished me to accept it. So, as Dr. Macfarlane had already been appointed to an inland station requiring a married medical missionary, and no man here or at home seemed forthcoming, I felt I could only refuse on one ground—that of inability to carry on the work. This I could not confess to, or even believe, with God's Word by my side, telling me the source of all sufficiency. Unbelief would unfit me for any service: so here I am in the post."

To his sister Annie he writes: "I never valued your prayers more than I do at present: the Lord has called me to a responsible position, and I realise, dear, my need of Him. I am realising His help every hour of the day, both in the treatment of disease and in all the new duties of this new work. May I be made more conscious of my dependence upon Jesus for all! To take on such a work as Dr. Mackenzie was engaged in is no light task, but it is easy and happy service when One mightier than man is our Helper. Our sufficiency is of God. Oh, may the day never come when I may think my sufficiency is of self!

"I had an interesting interview the other day, in Mr. Lees' house, with one of the principal officials of this province, and one of the Viceroy's interpreters, who, of course, speaks English. In the course of conversation he asked 'if we had any philosophical defences of the Bible and our religion?' I left them to attend a prayer-meeting with a few ward-workers and patients, all of them comparatively poor people. Yet we felt in the presence of the King of kings and the Ruler of the kings of the earth. These poor Christians were not only His servants, but His sons. Pray that, though as yet I cannot speak much to the patients, I may magnify Christ by every word, look, and action. The Lord knows my thousand-and-one needs. He will teach you what to pray for, and fulfil all your requests in Christ Jesus."

But though the Christian workers and the suffering patients had given a hearty welcome to the young doctor, it was otherwise with the high Chinese officials.

For some time they had been feeling the incongruity of supporting a work so entirely Christian in character, and had been contemplating the possibility of withdrawing their support. The Viceroy, however, had a high regard for Dr. Mackenzie, to whom, in years past, he owed, under God, the restoration to health of his wife. But he had no sympathy with the religion of Jesus, and was accustomed to say of the doctor, and also of General Gordon, that he considered them "enthusiasts in matters of religion."

When, therefore, the death of Dr. Mackenzie was announced, it was considered a favourable opportunity for withdrawing from the hospital all pecuniary aid. Accordingly, they made a suggestion to which they could hardly have supposed that the London Missionary Society would agree. It was: that in future the Chinese authorities, while supporting the medical work, must have entire control in their own hands, selecting their own medical officer, and allowing only one missionary on the board of management. There was also in existence a large sum of money, known as the Hospital Trust Fund, consisting mainly of the balance not expended of the monthly sum allowed by the Viceroy for the carrying on of the work. Dr. Mackenzie had spoken to the Viceroy about this balance, which was such an anomaly, according to Chinese ideas, that His Excellency felt quite perplexed about it. He readily agreed to the doctor's proposal that it should be allowed to accumulate, and be put out to interest, forming a fund to be used for the extension of medical work throughout the province; but, unfortunately, the agreement was only verbal, and no document existed to prove it.

At the time of his death the doctor had begun to cherish the bright hope that this scheme might be carried out.

But "Put not your trust in princes" is as wise a maxim to-day as in days of yore. The Chinese officials soon laid claim to everything, even the buildings erected on mission property, in which, for nine years, Dr. Mackenzie had carried on his benevolent work.

Within a few short months the Viceroy erected a large Government hospital in the immediate vicinity of the mission, and staffed it with the most distinguished of the medical missionary's students.

At the same time, overtures were made to the dispensers and ward-attendants of the mission hospital, to come over and accept posts in the Government institution at greatly increased salaries. The love of money being perhaps one of the most distinguishing features of the Chinese character, the missionaries felt it a cause for special gratitude to God that, without exception, the men refused these tempting offers, and rallied round the young doctor who had come to fill the place of the lamented " Ma Tai-fu."

When the news reached England that Dr. Roberts had been appointed to the charge of the large hospital which had so long enjoyed the patronage of the Viceroy Li, it was not unnatural that many letters of congratulation should be written to him by members of his large home-circle.

His replies to these letters, taken from several sources, are very characteristic.

"I received by the last mail many hints that I should accept this position because of its importance; and it was not difficult to see, underlying all the suggestions, a secret pride in such a post having fallen to me. Now, dear ——, may we all be forgiven if there has been any such thought, like a secret, unknown enemy in our hearts. . . . Anyhow, the wish is not going to be gratified; for at this very moment the high officials, headed by Li Hung-chang, are at daggers-drawn with the London Mission and its Tientsin representatives. They claim that all the buildings, drugs, and instruments belong to them. . . . As for me, I am sure that God is with us; and though we shall seemingly have to start again in the medical work, yet He will not fail us. 'The cattle upon a thousand hills are His,' and the money in a thousand banks.

"I am convinced the loss of official patronage is a blessing, and the best thing for me individually, and for the work which has brought me to China. Of late I have often found that practically I attach more importance to the outward prosperity of the work than to the real success.

"By the outward prosperity, I mean such points as—a large number of patients every day at the dispensary, numerous indoor patients, official patronage and pecuniary support, and a grand list of successful surgical operations. By the spiritual success, I mean patients being moved by the constraining influence of the Holy Ghost, souls born again and rejoicing in a newly-found Saviour. May we be led earnestly to desire these last things, and then our lives will be successful and victorious, even though those to whom these spiritual realities are but an empty dream will be sure to regard them as fanatical and worse than wasted."

At this time Dr. Roberts' days were spent in the following fashion: he rose early, and took breakfast with us at 7.30. At 8 o'clock the great gong was sounded for prayers, which took the form of a Bible class for the hospital assistants and all the patients able to attend. It was conducted by Rev. A. King, but Dr. Roberts always accompanied him. After this he visited the more serious cases in the wards. At 9 o'clock he came home, and had one-and-a half-hour's study with his Chinese teacher. By 10.30 the time had arrived to return to the dispensary, and prescribe for the crowd of sick people who thronged the room and the steps of the hospital. Dr. Mackenzie was always assisted in this work by a band of qualified English-speaking medical students. On account of the rupture with the Viceroy, Dr. Roberts had to take it up single-handed, as the dispensers and other assistants left him were not accustomed to the diagnosis of disease. He therefore gave to each case his conscientious personal attention. During the hot season and the autumn there were often as many as from one hundred to one hundred and thirty patients to be attended to in the morning. During the healthier seasons the numbers fell to seventy or eighty.

It was sometimes necessary for Dr. Roberts to remain in the dispensary till long past the hour for the midday meal, and he would come in looking pale and exhausted. The afternoon was occupied with attending to the numerous serious surgical cases in the wards, and was often devoted to operations.

For some time he changed every dressing and bandage himself. Remonstrated with about the heavy additional work this gave him, he explained that, in a climate so malarious, and a hospital with such unsanitary surroundings, he felt the absolute necessity of thorough antiseptic precautions in order to ensure success in operative surgery, and at present he did not feel able to trust the ward attendants, now for the first time free from the supervision of Dr. Mackenzie's trained native staff.

Thus, through the heat of several Tientsin summers, Dr. Roberts, while struggling manfully to obtain a firm grasp of the difficult Chinese language, was weighed down with the medical and surgical work, which had been all too heavy for his predecessor. During the months he had spent in Tientsin before leaving for Mongolia, Dr. Roberts had seen all the various meetings for evangelistic work which, during the course of years, had grown up in connection with the hospital, in full operation; and, upon his appointment, he determined, with God's help, that they should all be continued. All day long the spiritual part of the work was ever in his thoughts, and no patient passed through his hands without some loving appeal to pray for healing, or give thanks to the Great Physician. The most careless and indifferent were touched by the earnestness with which he spoke of the Master he loved, and entreated them to accept Him as their Saviour. One friend who accompanied him to the hospital, some weeks after he had commenced the charge of it, writes: "I was greatly surprised at the influence he had already obtained over the Chinese. It was amazing how quickly he had learned their peculiarities, and how soon he had succeeded in winning their confidence and affection."

Yet although from the first he undertook the tasks of several men, he often grieved that he could not find more time for evangelistic work. He longed to be able to sit by each bedside and speak quietly to each patient, every day, of the love of Jesus for each one of them. Often in that first year, as well as afterwards, when he came in wearied with another hour's work with his teacher, he would speak regretfully of this unfulfilled longing. When I replied, as I usually did, that the Lord Himself portioned out our work for us, and did not expect from us more than we had time and strength to perform. "Ah, yes," he said; "but the sight of these poor Chinese, in their darkness, does make one long so to make heavenly things clear to them."

Once, seeing he was working visibly beyond his strength, I suggested that it sometimes occurred to me that, when our great Enemy found he could not otherwise hinder the usefulness of the Lord's servants, he tried the plan of tempting them to shorten lives of usefulness by too great asceticism, or else by over-work—we had illustrations of both in our North China Mission. About this time he received a letter from Dr. Griffith John, for whom he always had a high admiration, which was helpful to him. It was written with reference to Gilmour's failure of health, and ran thus:—

"Is it not to be ascribed, in part at least, to the new method of living which he has adopted? I am sure it would have broken me down long ago. I feel as strong, and am able to do as much work now, as I felt and could do fifteen years ago. I can walk twenty miles without fatigue, and preach half a dozen times into the bargain. I walked the other day nearly thirty miles. It is a common thing with me to preach three times in a day, and work hard in my study for two hours beside. Now, I ascribe this to the fact that I have been living in a good house, and eating plenty of wholesome food. I mention this now, because of the absurd things that are being written and spoken these days about missions and missionaries. People seem to be coming to the conclusion that a missionary, because he is a missionary, ought to live at starvation-point. Were missions to adopt the principles laid down for them by some people, they would soon become far more expensive than they are—sickness and death would soon rob us of our best men, and women too."

With regard to this matter of asceticism, Dr. Roberts was always willing to allow there were two sides, but he never felt it was quite right, at anyrate for him, to slacken his efforts, when the need was so great and the labourers so few. He always tried to shape his life after the pattern of our Saviour's life. "Just see," he would say, referring to the record of Christ's labours, "what a crowded life He lived—no leisure so much as to eat, no quiet room such as I have now, but people thronging His room as they do Chinese inns, whenever He had a place to lay His head. Yet, to gain time for communion with His Father, He rose a great while before day. He was never deterred by over-fatigue, but went on quietly day after day, filling each hour with deeds of love and mercy."

I remember, one day, he showed me a text which he thought had a bearing upon the subject of conversation. It was, "His end had not yet come." The reference being to the useless efforts of our Lord's enemies to take His life before His work was accomplished. He thought it applied also to the daily strain of over-work undertaken by His followers, if clearly laid upon them.

Arguments of this kind usually ended by a feeling, on my part, that it was more than likely he was right, combined with a dread that I might be seeking to deter him, as Peter did our Lord, from the path he felt to be clearly marked out for him by divine love.

But, while settled down happily in the work at Tientsin, Dr. Roberts' thoughts were often with Gilmour and his lonely work in Mongolia, and his name was constantly in his prayers.

In his letters to the Mission House, he repeatedly pled for another colleague for his friend. "Should you find a medical man for Tientsin," he writes, "I should rejoice at the prospect of rejoining Mr. Gilmour, if that was the wish of the Directors." Later on he writes: "I trust a suitable man will be forthcoming for Mongolia. He can surely never be other than thankful for such an opening, and such a colleague as Gilmour."

On the 19th November of this year, a great joy came into Dr. Roberts' life, in the arrival in Tientsin of his sister Mary, whose loving companionship and sympathy brightened all the years until his call to higher service came.

Very earnestly he had written home about the need of workers among the women of Tientsin; and how, in his view, the call that had come to his sister must not be disregarded.

But when his beloved parents, in answer to his appeal,

sent forth a second child to the Lord's service in China, many also were the words of tender sympathy and love which he wrote to comfort them.

He sent also the following letter of affectionate welcome, to greet his sister as she landed upon Chinese soil:—

"MY VERY DEAR MARY,—The time has come to write you a letter of welcome to China. I am truly rejoiced at the thought of seeing you so soon, dear, and having you as a fellow-worker in the same city. It is very wonderful how it has all come about, and how one obstacle after another has been removed, and you are, after years of waiting, about to realise your constant desire to be a missionary. This firm conviction, that it is God alone who has called you to the work, will help you more than you can now realise.

"I can never forget one thought Mr. Haslam gave us at the church at Northenden—'When God calls us to any work, He fits us for it, and gives us the necessary wisdom to fill that post.' How comforting that the qualification has not to come before the call. . . . You will soon realise, if you have not done so already, that you are coming to a very difficult uphill work. There will be much labour, in the way of pulling down, ploughing, sowing, and watering, before you can see the golden grain. You will soon learn the truth of the words, 'Who is sufficient for these things?' and then there will also certainly come the experience— our sufficiency is of God, who also will make us both able ministers of the New Testament. Whatever strange experiences you may be called to pass through in Tientsin, dear, will only manifest the 'all power' of your risen Saviour. My prayer and heart's desire, as I write, would not be, what we are so apt to wish, the absence of all crosses and trials, but rather that you may learn, more than in the past, to count it all joy when you fall into divers trials (or temptations). A life free from these things must necessarily be ignorant of the peace in the midst of storms which God desires to give us. And yet, if ever there was a life which promised to be one of cloudless sunshine, yours is the life."

After describing the work among the women, and her future companions in it, he continues: "I hope, dear, your coming will be a blessing to me. God keep us from running

APPOINTED TO TIENTSIN

in grooves, from becoming satisfied with low aims, poor results, and a low standard of Christian life and work."

Accompanying Miss Roberts came also, to the great joy of her brother, Dr. Smith, his old friend of Edinburgh days. He had desired that they might work together, but was more than satisfied when he found he had been appointed by the Directors to strengthen Gilmour's hands in Mongolia. Dr. Roberts' first home-letters, after hearing that his strong hope that his sister might join him in China was to be realised, were full of joyful anticipations of the happiness it would give him to have her sharing his home in Tientsin. Before her arrival, however, he began to feel that probably it would be rather to the advancement of the work among the Chinese women that the two unmarried lady workers should at first live together, in the beautiful Home erected in memory of Mrs. Lance. It was characteristic of Dr. Roberts, that he did not hesitate at once to sacrifice his personal feelings in the matter. Greatly to the perplexity of friends at home, who could not understand the necessity for such an arrangement, they lived for about a year in different homes. They saw as much of each other as their busy lives would allow, and his sister's presence near him was a constant source of strength and comfort. At the end of the second year of his life in China, it became clear to both that this sacrifice was not required of them; and from that time till his call to higher service, the brother and sister shared the same home.

Writing at the end of his first year in Tientsin, Dr. Roberts was able to report nearly eleven thousand attendances at the dispensary, while 459 patients had been treated for longer or shorter periods in the wards. This was an increase upon the previous year, as far as the outdoor attendance was concerned; and this in spite of the withdrawal of official patronage, and the establishment of the Viceroy's hospital in the immediate vicinity of our own.

There was, however, a slight decrease in the number of in-patients. "The reason for this decrease," writes the doctor, "is, I think, to be found in the death of Dr. Mackenzie. The Chinese are slow to trust themselves to a foreign doctor, though they may venture to the dispensary. It required the magnetic attraction of the late Dr.

Mackenzie's fame, which nine years of work had justly secured him, to induce so many to enter the wards last year."

He writes with joy, also, of twenty-nine patients, who, upon their recovery, had been baptized upon confession of faith in Jesus; and of a large number of others who had left with an intelligent knowledge of Christian truth.

"We are poorer, as regards funds and the favour of the great; but richer, in having been brought to feel our dependence upon the Lord to supply our every need."

CHAPTER IX

GLIMPSES OF CHINESE HOSPITAL WORK.

> "And ever with the same unwearied pace,
> From one to another, down the weary walls
> He walked, unconscious seeming of himself,
> Beholding but the sad, sick faces turned
> To him for succour; or that other Face
> To which he turned himself, (that you might see
> Was shining on him full and clear to him),
> When the rapt eyes grew glorious in their gaze,
> That comforted and helped him and upheld
> Him happy, though the tears were in his eyes
> For pity."
>
> H. E. HAMILTON KING.

THE dawn of 1889 found the Tientsin hospital, after a year of storm and conflict, giving perhaps clearer evidence than ever before that it was a work which the Lord of the harvest graciously deigned to bless. During the previous year, as we have seen, its founder had been called to his rest; and the official support it had so long enjoyed had been summarily taken away.

It was no easy task to succeed so able and successful a worker as Dr. Mackenzie; and especially when the patronage of the Viceroy was withdrawn, and a rival Government institution was commenced on the opposite side of the road. But the equal ability of the new doctor, his Christlike spirit, and unwearying attention to every patient, even the poorest and most loathsome, could not fail to be immediately acknowledged by the observant Chinese.

To those who are familiar only with English hospitals, the sight of Chinese wards is not inviting. The brick or wooden bedsteads possess only a sheet of straw matting, and are destitute of mattresses or bedding, except such as is supplied by a Chinese wadded coverlet. At first sight they seem comfortless and bare, and the patients themselves anything but attractive.

Attempts to introduce Western sleeping arrangements into the hospitals of the *Middle Kingdom* have ended, in some cases, in all the patients able to move, depositing themselves upon the floors, rather than endure the discomfort of a night upon the extraordinary barbarian invention known as a "spring mattress." Sick cookery is a meaningless term in China, for people who are ill are never supposed to eat anything. If a person is sick, it follows, as a matter of course, that "he cannot take his rice."

Serious objections are made by patients when beef-tea is offered to them, because it is supposed, in some mysterious way, to increase the heat principle in the system which causes disease; while a great aversion is always felt to milk.

The surroundings of a Chinese hospital are usually anything but sanitary, and native prejudice generally prevents any improvement being made. The environment of the Tientsin hospital consists of numerous graves, and a plain frequently inundated—a fruitful source of ague. A large majority of the patients who present themselves for treatment suffer from chronic diseases of many years' standing, and only come to the foreign doctor after lengthened periods of maltreatment by native physicians.

It will be seen, therefore, that a medical missionary in China has to contend against many disadvantages; and yet, surely there is no land under the sun where Western medical science, once known, is more highly appreciated by the suffering millions, to whom the cures wrought by Western doctors seem little less than miraculous.

In each of his patients Dr. Roberts saw one whom Christ loved enough to give His life for; and his home-letters constantly contained requests that Christian friends might pray for an increase in him of the spirit of love for them, and earnest desire for the salvation of their souls.

How these prayers were answered may be gathered from an extract contained in the recollections of a friend who saw much of Dr. Roberts in his daily work in the hospital. "In the dispensary," he writes, "he was most courteous and gentle in his behaviour to the poorest coolie. How his merry laugh and cheery remarks caused the shadows to flee away from many a sad face. He was tender and almost womanly in the sympathetic way in which he listened to, and entered into, the sufferings of the patients. How gently he touched limbs covered with the most repulsive sores! His manner towards children was most winsome. His kindly remarks, as he placed his hand on a little one's head, won the affection of the child and the confidence of the father. Even through the rush of the dispensary work, the message of Truth was winged home to many hearts by his apt and pointed sentences and attractive bearing."

The sympathetic interest Dr. Roberts felt in every patient comes out constantly in his home-letters, where he often gave graphic sketches of special patients, pleading that prayer might be offered for them.

"One day this week," he writes, "a man was carried on a mattress into the consulting-room, where I was seeing the patients, suffering from hydrophobia. It was truly a sad case. Nothing could be done for the man—he was quite mad, could swallow nothing, and was very much worse when water was sprinkled over him. They took him away to die—a heathen, ignorant of the gospel of our Saviour. Many are the sad sights one sees daily here: some come to the foreign doctor, as the last resource, when dying, and nothing can be done for them. But there is the bright side of the work, and it is as bright as the other is gloomy. Many come with faces all lit up with feelings of gratitude for disease cured, and relief from pain.

"Many have died in Tientsin this autumn of cholera; it is of a very deadly type. Two days ago I was asked to see a case in the heart of the city. The man was dying. It was most sad to see his mother on her knees, imploring me to heal her son, as he had been given up by all the native doctors. His legs were blue with the marks of the sticks used by them in the treatment of cholera. They beat the limbs severely, and also introduce needles. One poor man, a small shopkeeper, who comes many miles once a fortnight to be tapped for dropsy, brought a gift of 2000 cash, equal to about three shillings, to help on the work. This is the largest subscription, in proportion, we have received this year.

"Last week I had the joy of restoring sight to two men

who had been blind, in both cases for over a year. Their gratitude was very touching; and one of them seems to have learned many things about the gospel since his admission. It is a great joy to receive the numerous cases of cataract, as very frequently they can be quite cured by an operation."

At another time he writes: "I operated upon a case of cataract of ten years' standing about eight days ago. It has been quite successful: the man now sees distinctly. I feel very happy about it. We are very full of work every day, and have as much as time and strength will allow of. The poor are friendly to us, and appreciate our motives, as a rule. Poor things, it would touch your heart to see the gratitude of some after treatment; and many of them are friendly to the Christian faith.

"This morning some of them asked very kindly about an abscess I have had on my hand. They were very pleased when I told them it was better, and said they had been praying to God to make it well. When one remembers that they were not baptized Christians, I see in it an instance of the goodwill of many of the Chinese.

"Another patient, a simple countryman, is very happy in the hospital. The other day he said to me: 'How can I fret or worry about my complaint here?—this place is heaven.' 'Oh no, my friend,' I replied. 'Heaven is much better than this: there are no sick or suffering ones there.'

"Another case is interesting in its way. A scholar came to us from Port Arthur, on the other side of the Gulf of Pechihli, with a surgical malady. On admission, he assumed the usual antagonism to Christianity; but the kindness and attention he received, and the reading of Christian books, touched his heart, and he told us he should never again worship idols, as he saw they were powerless. He then confessed that, as yet, he had not prayed for the gift of the Holy Spirit, to teach him about Jesus, and show him his own sinfulness. I am not without hope regarding him. He has been suffering from stone since five years of age—he is now twenty-nine. It weighed two and a half ounces when removed. He is now well, through the good hand of God, to whom be all the glory and praise. This week I had a case of amputation of the leg for gangrene of three months' standing. I felt uncertain of the result at first, but, through God's blessing, it has done well.

"We had two baptisms among the patients last Sunday. One of them is an educated youth, and was typically anti-Christian when he came into the hospital; but his heart has been touched, and he gives evidence of a saving change. The second man has lupus on the face very badly. His friends are well off, but despise him, and have given him the cold shoulder; he seems genuine. When he went home, after his first stay in the hospital last year, he gave up worshipping idols, feeling convinced it was wrong."

It was not wonderful to those who followed with prayer and thanksgiving the progress of the medical work in Tientsin, that, as the months and years passed on, the name of "Lu Tai-fu," or Dr. Roberts, became as widely known as that of his lamented predecessor's. Men who had recovered under his skilful treatment, from diseases supposed by the Chinese to be incurable, went forth to distant parts of the province, and even into Shantung and Manchuria, and told of the skill and kindness of the Western physician.

"During the past year," he writes to his father, in January 1890, "the medical work has increased considerably in one branch, i.e. the dispensary. Over 18,000 visits were paid, i.e. 3000 more than last year, and 900 more cases treated."

"God's blessing is resting upon the hospital very abundantly," he writes to his sister Annie. "The patients come in crowds daily, and our wards have been full-up for weeks. Many we have had to turn away, who would like to come in if we had room. This is all because of the gracious smile of God resting on His own work; the earnest prayers of many loving hearts are being thus answered."

To the little daughter of his sister Lily, who constantly cheered his heart with the subscriptions she collected for his work, the doctor wrote: "The hospital is very full, and has been for some weeks. As you know, we have only forty-five beds, but there are fifty-one or more resident in the wards. What do the six extra do? They sleep on the floor. . . . Why do you take in more than you have beds for? you ask. Because, when a man has come a long distance, and has no friends in the city, we don't feel it possible to tell him to wait or go elsewhere. Moreover, he will get a chance of learning something about the one true God, our Heavenly Father, and about Jesus our Saviour; and who knows but one day he may become a Christian?"

To the Foreign Secretary of the London Missionary Society he wrote: "As regards the hospital work, I am almost daily reminded that there are many loving hearts pleading for us, and for these poor, burdened souls that daily crowd our dispensary and wards for healing. The patients are more numerous than we can accommodate. Must we send them away? We can't. Many come from long distances, and we rejoice to take them in, even though we can offer many of them no better accommodation than a wooden floor. Best of all, some of the inmates are daily receiving with deep interest Christian instruction, and are seeking admission into the Church.

"You will be pleased to hear the Foreign Community of Tientsin have given $350 for furnishing a ward, to be called the Mackenzie Memorial Ward. The money is the surplus of a sum raised to put up a monument to Dr. Mackenzie in the English cemetery."

Not only did the number of patients attending the hospital continue to increase, but many of them were of a class that one might have expected would prefer to attend the newly-erected Viceroy's hospital.

"Almost the whole of one ward," writes the doctor, "is filled with soldiers from a large camp of 13,000 men situated about thirty miles from here. They have come to us for various diseases, though they are the Viceroy's soldiers, and should by rights go to his hospital."

"One man, who came into the hospital for dysentery, is a soldier. The means taken for his recovery have been greatly blessed. He is rapidly improving in every respect. He attended the service in our Chinese chapel twice to-day. But it is hard for a man to become an avowed Christian when all his friends are heathen, and hate the Christian faith," he writes to his little niece. "You remember what Jesus said about the daily cross His disciples have to carry. The cross is a heavy one in China. One soldier told me only to-day, that when he was one day learning his Catechism, the general of the camp passed by, and asked him what he was reading. Hearing it was a Christian book, he said, 'You are a long-haired rebel,' and dismissed him on the spot. The man replied that he was not a rebel, but that the book spoke of One who died for the sins of the world on the cross. After a while the mandarin relented, but the soldier has still to suffer persecution for Jesus' sake. Pray for him. His name is Chao Kuei-king. He is a drill-sergeant.

"Many of the soldiers among the hospital patients have improved in their language and manners since admittance. This is a small matter; but it cheers me on, for they are very rough and hard to manage. Two soldiers I heard of the other day, who first heard the gospel some months ago in our hospital. They are often very much occupied in the camp on Sunday, but they still come regularly to the services."

It is no uncommon thing for patients attending a foreign hospital, while warm in their expressions of gratitude for recovery from serious diseases, to declare that they will "chuan ming," or publish abroad his fame.

That this was done by Dr. Roberts' patients, is proved by the fact that large numbers constantly came from districts at great distances, to which single patients had returned healed. "Ten men came this week from one district," he writes, "three of them being brothers, suffering from different diseases." But though it was always a great joy to him to be instrumental in relieving pain, it was a far greater source of thankfulness to see fruit springing up after many days, showing that his labour was not in vain in the Lord. Only when the heavenly harvest is gathered in, and sowers and reapers rejoice together, will the full results of Dr. Roberts' faithful labours be revealed; yet the sheaves that were gathered during his lifetime were sufficient to fill his own heart and those of his fellow-labourers with grateful joy. A few instances only, from the many noted in his letters, can be mentioned here:—

"One man, Liu Wei-hsien, has come back to Tientsin, after an absence of one and a half years. He was baptized as a patient; and, going home, stood fire, all alone, for the gospel's sake. One day this spring he was at death's door, and his friends all taunted him, saying that his sickness was owing to his strange religion (his faith in Jesus Christ); but he replied that, even if he died, he would never return to idolatry, or give up faith in his Saviour.

"One man who left us in the spring, thought by the native hospital assistants to be a hypocrite, has turned out A 1. He has burnt his idols, and got four men in his village to destroy theirs, and is giving testimony to many. Altogether, there are now eight inquirers in the neighbourhood of his home. Oh, praise the Lord! not unto us, but to Thy name be the glory.

"It means so much to a Chinaman to become a Christian," he writes to his sister Annie. "The home, once peaceful, will soon be all in an uproar when they forsake the vain worship of idols, and follow Jesus, 'the foreign saint,' as they call Him—if they do not use some much worse name. But I can say that God's grace is proving all-sufficient when He is trusted implicitly. Praise the Lord for helping Chen Hsiao-cheng to hold on. He is a young man of twenty, who was baptized two years ago. Returning home, his relatives, chiefly his mother and elder brother, who were his only near relatives, began to persecute him; and, finding no cause of just complaint, falsely accused him in the court of law of following an insurrectionary sect known as the 'White Lily Society.' The mandarin or official before whom he was brought, asked him if this were true. He was only a young and inexperienced Christian, and surrounded by an unsympathetic heathen audience, but he replied, 'No, I am a Christian, a follower of Jesus.' 'What kind of a religion is that?' inquired the mandarin. 'A holy one,' replied the accused. 'May I tell you some of the truths we are exhorted to believe, and which we strive to follow in our lives?' The judge gave permission, and the young man repeated the Ten Commandments, and then practically preached the gospel within the walls of the Chinese law court. The official was much impressed, and, turning to the relatives, said, 'He is a good man, and the Jesus sect must be a good sect,' and thereupon dismissed the case. Still his friends persecuted him, but he remained steadfast. Lately they have twice tried to burn down his house over his head. He arrived in Tientsin the other day, much worn in body, but not one iota shaken in his faith. His idea was to start a small business in Tientsin. I have thought we might make a theological student of him. The only drawback is, that his throat is husky. May God guide. Pray the Lord very earnestly to restore him, and make him a great power in the Church. He has some education, and will make a useful worker."

"Poor fellows," he writes to another friend; "the patients, many of them, grasp the great truths of the gospel of Christ very slowly and imperfectly, yet they are very different from the heathen. On Tuesday last, after pleading with the patients to take Jesus as their Saviour, one of them came up after the meeting, and, with true feeling and sincerity stamped upon his face, said, 'I want to believe in Jesus, and become one of His disciples.' He was moved to gratitude because his disease, through God's blessing, had been cured, and he recognised in this the loving-kindness of the Heavenly Father. I went home from that meeting very full of joy, I assure you. It was fruit, after much sowing and no reaping. The Lord bless and keep him, and make him strong in faith.

"Another man, named Chen Pao-lin, came to me the other day with a curious question. Every time he prayed, he said, he had a palpitation and throbbing in the centre of his forehead. 'Was it of any consequence?' he asked. I expect his idea was, that the Spirit entered his body at that spot whenever he prayed, and caused some commotion there. I was able to assure him, much to his relief, that it was of no consequence, and his face lit up with smiles.'

This man, after his return to his native place, was instrumental in leading many others to Christ; and when Dr. Smith visited his home at Ta Liu Fen, he found an encouraging Christian work going on there.

Writing about the Chinese New Year time, he says: "About twelve patients are spending the New Year in the wards. As I was sitting chatting with them on New Year's Eve, one of them said, 'We are all great sinners.' 'How do you know that?' I asked. 'Why, if we were not, we should never be here in the hospital, sick, at this time of the year.' He was alluding to the belief that such calamities are a special judgment from heaven, making them out as worse than their neighbours. I explained the meaning of sickness to them, and was pleased to find how warm a corner in their hearts some had for the gospel. The wife and children of one of the men were living over 3000 miles away, in the south of China. He is paralysed, and was left with us some three months ago by his sailor comrades. 'When I look at that picture of Jesus going to the cross,' he remarked, looking up at one of the coloured illustrations on the walls, 'it brings the tears to my eyes to think of His sufferings.' This man professes faith in Christ, and, I think, knows something of the power and influence of the Holy Spirit."

"One man, who I thought was dying two or three days ago," he writes to his sister, Mrs. Windsor, "said he was going to heaven, and would there wait at the gate for me, to welcome me in some day. As I sat at his bedside, I could not but feel moved at the sight of this Chinaman, but a few weeks ago quite ignorant of the gospel, and now truly peaceful in the hour of apparent death. To-day he is better, and there is more hope of his life; but he seems disappointed, and asked, 'Would I not give him some medicine to send him to heaven at once?' So you see they need teaching, Lily, even after the gospel has become precious to them. Of course we explained matters to him, and tried to show him that the Christian must learn to say, 'Not my will, but Thine be done,' in everything, even the hour of departure."

"A humiliating scene took place in the hospital the other day," he writes; for he ever tried to give a faithful picture of the difficulties, as well as the causes for rejoicing, in his work. "Two inquirers had what was practically a fight; and why? Just for the simple reason that one of them was cold-hearted, and proposed going out to the street to make purchases while the evangelist was preaching. The other man reprimanded him so severely for his conduct in not wishing to remain and listen to the preacher, that at last they came to blows. One patient, who came to us some months ago, while I was away in Yen Shan, told Dr. Smith he despaired of ever regaining his sight, and if we would not take him in, he would throw himself into the river, and put an end to his life, which had become unbearable, since poverty stared him in the face. He was taken in, and occupied one of the free beds, and leaves us today with restored sight, and also an inquirer desiring baptism."

In the summer of 1893 he writes: "This year has been very hot and exceptionally trying, both to Chinese and foreigners. Cholera has broken out, and both Dr. Smith and I have had a bad case on hand this week. Mine was a Chinese colporteur, whose case was so serious that I was up all night with him. For four hours I had no hope of his recovery, and had even said to him, 'Chao, are you afraid to die?' 'No,' he replied; 'why should I be, when I am trusting in the Lord? He is with me now.' This man is now well, thank God; for he had a blind wife and two little children dependent upon him for support."

Roberts does not tell, what is related by his colleagues, how, through the stifling summer night, while himself exhausted with the malarious Tientsin summer, he worked indefatigably, trying one remedy after another, applying them himself when he saw his helpers' efforts flagging, because they considered the exertions useless. But it made a deep impression upon the Chinese, in whose opinion the man, by almost superhuman efforts, had, with God's blessing, been brought back from the gates of death.

Another case which was full of interest was that of a man named Wang. He is about fifty years of age, and, as a lad, was educated by the wife of an American missionary named Holmes, stationed in the Shantung province. Her husband and another missionary, while going out to parley with the rebels, in the hope that they would listen to their proposals of peace, and that so much bloodshed would be prevented, were cruelly murdered. As years passed by, Mrs. Holmes returned with her children to the United States, while the lad, equipped for the battle of life, through her kind interest was employed in the great mercantile firm of Jardine, Matheson, & Co. Hearing one day that his boyhood's benefactor was in pecuniary straits, he drew from the bank a sum of money, amounting to about £200, and sent it to her. Two or three years ago he gave Tls. 300 for the Famine Fund. Sad to relate, this man had fallen a victim to the opium habit. Being a man of strong will, and feeling the injurious effects of the drug upon him, he determined to break off the use of it. For nearly a month he suffered very severe pain, and at last determined to enter the hospital. He benefited greatly under Dr. Roberts' treatment, and gained strength daily. Wang speaks and writes English well; and one day, when the doctor unexpectedly looked in upon him, he found him engaged in reading his English Bible, and the patient told him he was in the habit of reading a chapter every day, though not a professing Christian.

"Pray for him, please, that his stay in the hospital may result in blessing in future days," the doctor wrote to his sister. "He will need your prayers, for he has from three to four hundred coolies or dock labourers under him, in the shipping office with which he is connected." Upon leaving the hospital, this man not only presented a thank-offering of $100, but showed, by his after life, that his residence there had been of great benefit to him spiritually.

It will be seen that the work of the Tientsin hospital was too heavy for one medical man, without qualified helpers, to undertake alone. Dr. Roberts had heartily welcomed the assistance he had received from his friend Dr. Smith, during his few months' stay in Tientsin before he proceeded to Mongolia, where he had been appointed. But he rejoiced that Gilmour was at last to obtain a medical colleague. As time passed on, however, the lonely life undermined Dr. Smith's health; and his wife's sudden death from cholera at Chefoo, just as she was preparing to accompany him, and work among the women of Mongolia, proved an overwhelming sorrow. Dr. Roberts felt that it was absolutely necessary that his friend should seek restored health in England, and he came home for a short furlough. While in England, Dr. Smith offered to return to China as a partially self-supporting missionary, on the understanding that he should be sent out as a colleague to his friend; and this arrangement was agreed to by the Society. It was a source of great comfort and joy to Dr. Roberts, and is repeatedly referred to in his home-letters, and in his communications with the Society.

Some time before, he had written very hopefully with reference to the possibilities of extending the medical work.

Now these hopes seemed in a fair way to be realised, for Dr. Smith was appointed to assist Dr. Roberts in the Tientsin hospital during the heavy work of the summer season, and to superintend the extension of medical work in the country districts.

"I am eagerly awaiting the arrival of Dr. Smith," he wrote; "he will be an unspeakable help. We are full of hope for the extension of Christ's kingdom into the many towns and villages of Chihli, and that in the near future." Dr. Smith returned to China in the spring of 1892. "He is a great comfort to me in my daily work," he remarks. "I literally thank God upon every remembrance of him." To the Foreign Secretary he wrote: "Dr. Smith and I are very happy together in our work. I do not think we could possibly be happier."

Many who had no intimate acquaintance with Dr. Roberts, have expressed surprise that, with a colleague so devoted to him as was Dr. Smith, his last illness should have found him so exhausted with over-work.

But, as it has been well said: "Dr. Roberts was one of those who could not be restrained in the expenditure of energy in the work of life, and into his Chinese career of seven years he put the work of twenty-five." The relief the presence of Dr. Smith gave him in the hospital, only allowed him to turn his energies to the evangelistic work, ever so dear to his heart.

"Dr. Smith's presence is of unspeakable value," he writes. "My afternoons are now free for evangelistic work, chatting with the indoor patients, etc.; and the evenings, for teaching the inquirers to read the Bible. Many of them are unable to read even one character."

I have written especially of the poorer patients who sought help and healing at the hands of the young foreign doctor, but there were also not a few instances of wealthy men who, attracted by his fame, came to seek relief. On one occasion, during the absence from Tientsin of his usual foreign medical attendant, the tutor of the children of the Viceroy, Li Hung-chang, became seriously ill, and he at once despatched a messenger to inquire if Dr. Roberts would come and see him. Some people might have hesitated at complying with such a request, but not one of the Christ-like spirit of Dr. Roberts, and he made several visits to the yamen, doing all he could to relieve the patient till the return of Dr. Irwin.

"Yesterday and the day before," he writes at another time, "I was called in to see a very rich man in the city, a heavy opium smoker. He was recovering from dysentery; but flatulence had set in, and he thought he was dying. When I entered the room, I found the patient reclining on a square, handsomely-carved wooden bedstead, with his opium pipe in his mouth, and the little spirit lamp used for melting the opium burning by his side." They offered the doctor refreshments, and treated him with much politeness. "I hope they will become interested in the truth," he writes; "but it is very hard to win a rich Chinaman for Christ. It means much persecution, and most likely poverty in addition, and the Chinese, like all of us, are slow to take up the cross, and follow Christ." On another occasion, the principal city official sent for Dr. Roberts to attend his sick child, who was suffering from fever, and he was able to relieve him.

People of rank and wealth were less ready to come to the hospital as in-patients, since, though all were received kindly, and the highest medical skill and careful nursing was lavished upon them, they did not receive greater deference than the poor around them. Dr. Roberts considered that, since the treatment was all gratuitous, it was not right to treat one patient, on account of his rank, with greater respect than another.

Still, there were some cases of men of superior rank entering the wards.

"We have a man in the hospital now," writes the doctor in the summer of 1893, "who is the son of a military official presiding over a camp of 500 men. He has led a wild life in the past, and, in consequence, his health is suffering severely. I think he is penitent, and learning the way of life.

"In one of the small wards there is a rich farmer, possessing 300 Chinese acres of land, who has become a candidate for baptism, and has some knowledge of the truth. He is not here as a patient, but in attendance on his son, who, I fear, will never be strong."

But it was the need that drew out Dr. Roberts' sympathies for his patients, and made his name so loved and revered among them. Whether in the hospital wards, in the homes of the wealthy, or the mud huts of the poor, he ever held himself in readiness to go at once to their succour.

Mr. Stephen Massey, of Manchester, accompanied him on one such visit to a patient's home in Tientsin in the spring of 1893, and I give the account of it in his own words: " It was an afternoon in March of last year; Dr. Roberts had been busy in the hospital since eight o'clock, when he, as usual, had commenced his work there with a small Bible class and prayer-meeting with the Chinese Christians in the operating-room. One of the dust-storms which are common in North China was blowing, and, though comparatively a light one, it had completely blotted out the sun, which just before had been shining with dazzling brightness; but, undeterred by this, he was going to see a patient at his own home, and I gladly took the opportunity, otherwise unattainable, of seeing a Chinese heathen family in their house. The patient was a man of some little rank, advanced in life, who had formerly been a soldier, and was decorated with a special button for services in the Tai-ping rebellion. Some disease or injury to the leg had been so maltreated by native doctors, that it had endangered his life; and when at last, in despair, he had sent to beg Dr. Roberts to come to him, as he was too old and ill to come to the hospital, he feared that, at the least, the limb would be amputated. Happily, however, this was avoided; the leg was now nearly healed, and the patient likely to be able to walk ere long. Nor was the bodily cure the only one which was going on. The gentle, patient, sympathetic care of this skilful Christian doctor, who was spending his time in a dirty Chinese house, when he might have surrounded himself with the refinements of a cultured English home, and who sat there on the side of the k'ang, chatting pleasantly with the patient, and about a dozen of his relations and neighbours crowded round the door, was winning its way into the heart of at least one: the sick man had spontaneously put away his idols, and was diligently studying a little elementary book of Christian teaching, specially prepared for the instruction of the heathen. And to hear him tell his wife and friends, not only about the one God and the incarnation and death of the Lord, but about the Holy Ghost and His work in the human heart, made me realise more clearly than before that

God is not far from these strange Chinamen, and that they also are His offspring. The man had not yet found his Saviour, but seemed to be feeling after Him. May we not hope and pray that, even if still in the darkness, the death of his kind and able doctor may be used by the Holy Ghost to reveal Christ to him ?"

CHAPTER X

FAMINE, FLOOD, AND REBELLION.

> "When wilt Thou save the people?
>   O God of mercy, when?
> Not kings and lords, but nations!
> Not thrones and crowns, but men!
> Flowers of Thy heart, O God, are they;
> Let them not pass, like weeds, away—
> Their heritage a sunless day.
>   God save the people."
>   EBENEZER ELLIOTT.

DURING the summer of 1890 the country around Tientsin was visited by a more than usually heavy rainfall. The river rose rapidly, and, after a time, burst its banks. Thousands of persons in the low-lying districts, in the neighbourhood of the Great Plain, lost their all, escaping only with their lives.

Writing at this time, Dr. Roberts says: "There is great poverty and suffering all around us. Large numbers have had to flee from their homes, or they would have been buried in the ruins or swept away. They are now crowded together in poor mat sheds. Their farms, cattle, and grain are all swept away, and, with winter staring them in the face, their lot is sad indeed. The plain of Chihli is converted into an inland sea—boats take the place of carts. There is water as far as the eye can reach, and far, far beyond. The sun rises and sets upon a watery horizon. Think what this will mean in the winter!"

When the cold season came on, the destitution became more severe, and there were numerous cases of absolute starvation. The Chinese Government made an attempt to relieve the sufferers, but only a very small portion of the large sums contributed, by Chinese merchants and others, ever reached the starving people, so heavily was the fund taxed by the officials through whose hands it passed.

Officers from the yamens went round the famine-stricken districts, and dealt out to starving families the sum of about one shilling, with which to face the winter. After this they refused to receive any delegates from flooded districts, dismissing them with the reply, " You have already received help."

The foreign merchants of Tientsin, touched by the destitution which prevailed on every side, started a relief fund, deciding to keep it in their own hands and distribute it themselves, that they might be certain the money really reached those they desired to relieve. They undertook to provide, throughout the whole winter, for fifteen villages. During these seasons of bitter destitution, many an English merchant, guided by the missionaries, went as a messenger of mercy to the wretched mat sheds of the refugees in the city of Tientsin and the villages of the neighbouring plain.

" Every family receives about eighteen pence a month," wrote Dr. Roberts, " and this will probably keep them alive, in many villages, through the whole of the severe winter."

But when spring arrived, the condition of the famine-stricken was not greatly improved; for on the flooded country no crops could be sown, and there was therefore no harvest in prospect. Touched by his letters, describing the wretched condition of the poor around him, and the state of semi-starvation in which many patients appeared at the dispensary, Dr. Roberts' friends sent him funds for the relief of the sufferers. To those who contributed he sent the following account of the way in which the funds had been distributed :—

" On Friday, April 10th, the Rev. T. Bryson of the L.M.S. and myself started to distribute £50, in a village called Wang San Tsuang Tzu, situated twenty miles north of Tientsin. We had heard of the distress existing in this place through a former patient in the hospital, whose home was in that village till the floods came and carried away his house. This man, named Fu, is a Christian, and we were glad to have him to act as our guide to the place. It was blowing hard when we went on board our boat, which was to take us to Wang San; and I must confess that some misgivings came over me as I looked at the crowd that had collected around us, all knowing that we were going to 'fang chen,' distribute relief. The more inquisitive of them had made doubly sure by asking us if this was not the case. Some of them, as my colleague remarked, looked as if they would not mind attacking us in the night to get the money in our possession.

"I said we 'went on board,' a term that sounds over-respectful, to my mind; for the boat was more like a small canal-barge than anything else, and at one end a small piece of matting was suspended—this was our bedroom for the night! Travelling in China is a different thing from travelling in England, for it took us till between 1 and 2 A.M. to reach our destination. Next morning, looking out from under our shed, we could see the village, about two miles away, and were told a cart was on its way to conduct us there. Being somewhat cold after our night's experiences, we preferred to walk. On our way, we saw more than one village still surrounded with flood water. It had only just receded from our pathway to the village of Wang San. Approaching the place, we noticed one of the temples in ruins. A pile of bricks, from the fallen wall of the shrine, rested upon the head of one idol, the hair of a second was blown about by the breeze, and a third bore evident signs of having suffered from the elements.

"Why did the Chinese leave them in this condition? We were in the heart of the famine district, where the people were face to face with the problem how to keep body and soul together, and starving folk do not trouble themselves about repairing temples. Most of the houses of the village had been stripped bare of the thatch and wood which once roofed them, the inhabitants having been reduced to using it for fuel during the bitter winter. Other houses were in a ruined condition. What will the people do when the heavy rains of July come?

"We were conducted to a temple, which was placed at our disposal in order that we might distribute the money. We learned that, during the past ten months, since the floods came, this village had only received help in money from the Government once. Every man and woman had received about one shilling and sixpence, every child got ninepence. As a matter of fact, many were given considerably less than they were supposed to receive. In addition to this money, the Government, last year, gave them half a pound of millet every eight days, and half that quantity for every child; latterly, they have been giving one pound every twelve days. This ration is what a bird could manage to eat in the same time, or less. We found the people living upon the husks of the millet, which they ground into powder and made up into cakes. I saw a little child of two years nibbling at one of these cakes; its pale, thin cheeks told a tale of woe and abject poverty. Most of the people managed to get one poor meal a day; in the worst cases, one in two or three days. Upon examining the official case-book, we found there were over five hundred families. The money we had brought, though only sufficient to give to the adults, would keep them in comfort for one month, and enable each man and woman to buy one and a half bushels of rice of inferior quality.

"We then went from house to house, giving more or less according to the distress, and truly there were many sights which made me feel for the poor sufferers. Many were sick; others, we learned, had died of starvation; others, again, had left the place, to seek help in Tientsin or elsewhere. Deep poverty was stamped on most faces. The money having thus been all disposed of, we returned to the temple, and gave suitable tracts away. Before leaving, Mr. Bryson addressed the people from the temple steps, and turned their thoughts to the one true God, who had thus supplied their wants, and put it into the hearts of Christians to send money for them. He reminded them of the folly of worshipping idols, and trusting in them. Some of the elders of the place then escorted us to the outskirts of the village, where, getting into the long Eastern cart, drawn by two mules, which was waiting for us, we were soon on our way back to the boat. We both felt that the money had been well spent, and were thankful to God for permitting us to share in the blessed work of feeding the poor. The expressions of gratitude, and the pleasure seen on many countenances, when they received the money, was very real, and would have more than repaid for any self-denial; better still, the smile of God rests upon us when we in any measure seek to fulfil His great command of love."

Notwithstanding the well-known fact that China is a land of great mineral wealth and possessed of a fertile soil, she sees probably a larger proportion of her population than any other country in the world living ever on the brink of starvation; for her resources are to a large extent undeveloped.

Throughout a large extent of many of her provinces the people suffer from a chronic condition of famine, caused by the floods. Large sums are continually voted by Government to mend the breaches in the river-banks; but before the money reaches its destination it has dwindled down to a small fraction of the original sum, through the exactions of those in authority.

People in Western lands grow weary of the constant appeals of friends in China to help the famine-stricken, and give it up as a hopeless task, feeling there is no satisfaction in contributing money to relieve a state of affairs which a wise and righteous Government in China itself could soon put an end to.

But the missionaries, who constantly come in contact with the people, and see the bitter sufferings of the poor and downtrodden Chinese peasantry, find it difficult to take this philosophical view of the case. The sad facts of the terrible distress are brought so near to them that they cast theories to the winds, and feel there is no other course but to do their utmost to assist these brothers and sisters in their hour of desperate need.

Two years after the visit just recorded, Dr. Roberts wrote home: "Thousands will die of starvation this winter. A large area of the country is flooded; and with no prospect of further help from foreign nations, and still less of adequate relief from the Chinese Government, great numbers are face to face with death in the near future. Many of these are Christians, who have lost all in the floods, and who, but for the help given by the native Christians in Pekin and Tientsin, would meet with the same fate. What is the cause? The bursting of the mud banks of one of the northern rivers. Every year, during the heavy rains, this is liable to occur; and yet the Government refrain from making the river embankments proof against such contingencies. The fact is, that to do the work efficiently would, as things stand at present, cost a fabulous sum. The undertaking would have to pass through several hands, and every person interested would have to make his fortune out of the affair through 'squeezing,' as it is called out here. Poor China, she sadly needs the saving power of Christ in her Government, and in every part of the realm. And the work of evangelising the land is slow indeed; for men are steeped in the grossest darkness and superstition, and the moral decay of centuries has eaten like a deadly cancer into the vitals of the nation, till now China is worse morally than she has ever been, and nothing but a divine salvation—nationally, socially, and personally—can be of any avail. Let us rejoice that the leaven of Christ's gospel is in China, almost in every province, and that mighty upheavals are taking place, and will yet take place on a far mightier scale than in the past."

In January 1893, Dr. Roberts paid another visit to distribute famine relief. "I went this time in company with Mr. Cousins, agent of the Indo-China Steamship Company, and Mr. Annand of the National Bible Society of Scotland," he writes.

"We started at 8 A.M., clothed in skin coats, so that, spite of the hard frost, we were quite warm. Our conveyances consisted of sledges, driven by one man standing on the end at the back of the passenger. Each of us had his own sledge; the driver propels it by means of a long spiked pole, which he works between his legs as he stands on the sledge.

"We went at the rate of five or six miles an hour; sometimes, for short distances, much faster. Our route lay along the frozen Chen Tung-ho, a small river which flows into the Pei-ho, on which Tientsin stands. On our way we passed several sledges piled up with firing—a great commodity just now, for it is scarce on account of the floods. It consists of long rushes called 'wei tzu,' which serve the double purpose of cooking the food and heating the brick erection which, in Chinese houses, corresponds to our bedsteads.

"After we had gone some six miles, we altered our course. Dragging the sledge over the embankment, we found ourselves on the flooded plains of Chihli, where, as far

as the eye could reach, stretched a frozen sheet of water.
Across this we were driven at a great rate, although the ice
was somewhat rough. You would have been amazed to see
the fishermen we passed on our way. Nothing daunted by
the fact that the ice was 18 inches thick, they were making
large holes in it by means of thick spears worked in a
circular fashion till they had cut out a lump; then at a
distance from this another hole was made, big enough to sink
all the nets, which were then drawn through the water,
under the ice, by means of long ropes pulled by many
fishermen.

"Here were groups of fishermen dividing the spoil. They
had several baskets full of perch and other fresh-water fish,
and were packing them up for sale in the towns.

"After five hours we reached a place not far from our
destination, to which we were escorted on a cart by the
village elders. We could see the villagers eagerly watching
for our arrival. For three years they had seen no harvest,
on account of locusts and floods, and had received but little
help from the Government. Several had already died of
starvation during the winter, and many were reduced to
the last extremity. The sights were such as made us feel
the money was indeed well spent. The food of the people
was the husks of the parable, a dark-brown mixture made
into little cakes. We gave them enough to keep them alive
till the warm weather came; and some of the worst cases
we helped more generously. The most touching cases were
those in which the husband had died of starvation, or some
poor infant had been born into the world only to die in a
few days of famine. One such case died while I was there.
Other people were homeless, and stood upon the ruins of
their houses to receive relief.

"We stopped our distribution at 8 P.M., as it was dark,
and, returning to our inn, spent a quiet evening. We read
the Parable of the Prodigal Son together, and never had we
so well understood the scene before. Partaking of our meal,
we thanked God for food and plenty. Next day we finished
our work after two hours; and, returning to the inn, distributed
some Christian books, and spoke a few words to the people
assembled round the cart. We exhorted them to believe
in the God of heaven and earth, and turn from idols;

for we noticed in many houses, incense-sticks and shrines, notwithstanding the great poverty."

During the winter of 1891–92, North China and the Mongolian border was disturbed by a rebellion which broke out in that district. It was believed to be well organised, and commanded by a famous lama priest. During their first encounters with the Imperialist troops, the rebels were victorious. Large numbers of Roman Catholic Christians were massacred; and a letter written by a native priest residing in the district where the rebels were strongest, gave terrible details of the outrages which had been perpetrated upon the Christian community. China is honeycombed with secret sects; and dissatisfaction with the present Government is widely prevalent, though usually in a passive form. Pekin was thrown into a state of panic; and in the foreign settlement of Tientsin a defence committee was formed for the protection of the lives of the residents, should the rebels succeed in reaching the capital. Li Hung-chang, the Viceroy of Chihli, despatched 6000 of his picked troops from Tientsin to quell the rebellion. They travelled by rail: but before they could reach the scene of warfare the chief Mongolian station of the London Missionary Society was in the hands of the rebels. At the time, Gilmour's young colleague and successor, the Rev. J. Parker, was holding the fort alone. The missionary had remained at his post, cheering the hearts of the little band of Christians, till long after all the wealthier residents, with their wives and children, had left the city. At midnight on the 13th November 1891, he was disturbed by the sound of firing, cries inciting the soldiers to murder the populace, and the blaze of a burning Mongol temple. There was no time for making any preparations; so the missionary and his faithful servant joined the stream of terror-stricken inhabitants which crowded out of the city gates. For several weeks Mr. Parker and his Chinese servant wandered among the mountains, for it was impossible for them to obtain carts to travel with. Walking along the high-roads was not very practicable, since the inns were all closed, and every traveller fully armed. But they determined to try and make their way on foot, till at last their advance was checked by the news that the city just ahead of them was in the hands of another band of rebels.

Sitting down on the brick bedstead of the inn, the Chinese Christian exclaimed, "We have no road now—eastward there are rebels, westward there are rebels, and north and south there are the mountains only!" "There is yet one way open—the way above," replied the missionary. "But we have no cart," exclaimed the puzzled Chinaman. "Perhaps the Lord will send us His fire-cart," was the reply. "Ah, yes," exclaimed the Christian Chinaman, as the meaning dawned upon him. "That way is always open, and we are ready to take it."

Making their way back to the dirty inn outside Ping-fangerh, whose master took them in for Gilmour's sake, they stayed, in hunger and weariness, with rumours of massacres, brought in by refugees, constantly ringing in their ears, for ten days. Then news came that the rebels had been driven out of Chao-yang by the Chinese troops, so they determined to try to return. A terrible sight the city presented—outside the gates lay piles of headless bodies, in process of being devoured by the pariah dogs, which infest every Eastern city. Chao-yang was like a place of death: shops were closed and barricaded, and the busy market-place—where, not so long before, Gilmour had pitched his blue tent, and the news had come to Roberts of Mackenzie's death, and with it the call to leave Mongolia—was deserted and silent. The Christians were constantly being pointed at in the streets as followers of an unauthorised religion, and men were calling upon each other to arrest them. Mr. Parker had no money, for the banks were closed; and it was impossible to get bills cashed in the terror-stricken city. Then his servant, one of Gilmour's converts, who in his absence would be left without means of support, came up and earnestly pressed him to leave, pointing out that by remaining, he, as a foreigner, was endangering his life. "Never mind about me; you go, pastor," said the brave fellow: "the Lord will help me, don't fear; I am trusting in Him." Another poor Christian, knowing that the missionary's larder was bare, came in and silently left six eggs upon the table.

This was the state of affairs in the Mongol Mission that winter; and those who know how reports are exaggerated in Eastern lands, will understand that, when the facts were so startling, the reports which reached Tientsin were terrible indeed; and that the missionaries there were filled with constant anxiety for their lonely colleague. "Mr. Parker is in the thick of the fight," writes Dr. Roberts to his mother; "all we can do is to pray day and night for him."

Then, as the days passed by, it was felt that continued inaction was an impossibility, and that something must be done to obtain news of Mr. Parker. Repeated appeals were made to the Consul for permission for a missionary to travel to the seat of war, to render help to their missing colleague if his life had been spared, and to gather news of him if he had perished. It would be a perilous journey, everyone knew; but when at last the authorities consented to give a passport, on the understanding that the missionary travelled at his own risk, the difficulty lay in deciding who should go, since all were eager to undertake the mission. Dr. Roberts strongly urged his own claims, and was very unwilling to yield. "I am an unmarried man," he said, "and if I lose my life the matter is not so serious as in the case of a man with wife and family. I am certainly the one who should be chosen. Moreover, though I have not had the advantage of the years of experience with Chinese officials which some of my colleagues have enjoyed, yet, from having lived in Chao-yang, I know the district well, and many of the Christians know me."

Each of the missionaries urged his own claim to be sent, and it was difficult to see how the matter would be decided by so small a committee. Suddenly a distracted Chinaman burst into the mission-house, his face white with terror. It was the gate-keeper of the mission compound. "Mr. Parker has arrived!" he exclaimed: "Mr. Parker or his spirit—I can't say which!"

And so the meeting for anxious deliberation was turned into one of joyful thanksgiving to the Lord, who had heard the prayers of His people, and, through hunger, weariness, and scenes of bloodshed, brought His servant to a haven of refuge.

And one of the happy moments in Dr. Roberts' life was that in which he heard how nobly the Christians he had learned to love in Mongolia, had gathered around their lonely missionary, and, in a time of serious personal danger, exhibited so much courage, self-denial, and faith in God.

CHAPTER XI

WORK IN THE COUNTRY DISTRICTS

"Those whose bright faith makes feeble hearts grow stronger,
And sends fresh warriors to the great campaign,
Bids the lone convert feel alone no longer,
And wins the sundered to be one again."

"Beside all waters sow,
The highway furrows stock—
Drop it where thorns and thistles grow,
Scatter it on the rock."
J. MONTGOMERY.

VERY early in his life in China, Dr. Roberts had become impressed with the importance of work in the country districts. On his appointment to foreign service, he had looked forward to a life on the desolate plains of Mongolia. Yet when he was called by God to take up work in the crowded city, and to the charge of the large hospital there, as we have seen, he readily followed the course indicated by the guiding Hand. Nowhere, probably, could he have found wider opportunities of usefulness, or lived a life fuller of happy service, than in the city of Tientsin. He recognised this himself, and rejoiced that the Master had called him to such a post.

"Great is the honour of working for the Lord in a district like Mongolia, far from all foreign influences, in the midst of the natives," he wrote. "On the other hand, one must not forget that Tientsin is the port of the capital, and thus very important to win for Christ."

But it was not only townspeople who found their way to the hospital; sufferers from the country districts heard rumours of the wonderful skill of the foreign doctor, and travelled, some as far as from 150 to 200 miles, in search of healing.

Dr. Roberts soon found that many of these men were really seekers after truth, and that, as a rule, the simple countryman listened more readily to the gospel story than the dwellers in cities, whose frequent reply was, that they "had not time to think of anything but their daily tasks." This experience is no new thing in Christian work. It was not the chief men of the proud cities of Judea who readily received into their hearts our Lord's teaching, but the fishermen and peasants of Galilee.

A careful record of the patients who became Christians while in the wards was kept; and these men were remembered by rotation, in groups of six or eight, at the weekly prayer-meeting of hospital workers.

In very many cases these young converts left Tientsin with but limited knowledge of the Word of God, and many of them were unable to read. It is a wonderful proof of the living power of the Holy Spirit in Chinese hearts, that, amid bitter persecution, and without the strength and help which comes from fellowship with other Christians, many of these men not only remain faithful to their Lord, but are the means of bringing others to a knowledge of the world's Redeemer. Far and wide over the broad plains of Northern China, travellers have found little groups of believers who have gathered round single patients from our mission hospital.

But surely we are failing in duty to our Master if we do not, by increasing our staff of workers, make it possible for them to pay frequent visits to these scattered converts, "confirming and establishing them in the faith," as did the apostles in ancient days.

So deeply did Dr. Roberts feel the need there was for superintending these lonely Christians, that he always advised converts returning to the country districts, to connect themselves with other missions if they had stations nearer to their homes, instead of uniting with the London Missionary Society's Church in Tientsin. For his one aim in mission work was the glory of his Divine Master, and his longing desire for the converts was that they should grow strong spiritually, and be valiant soldiers of Jesus Christ.

His interest in the country work was deepened by the frequent visits made to these districts by his sister.

WORK IN THE COUNTRY DISTRICTS

In the spring of 1892, the appointment of his friend Dr. G. P. Smith to be his colleague in Tientsin, enabled Dr. Roberts to accomplish his heart's desire, and to visit at intervals the towns and villages of the Yen Shan (Salt Hill) district.

In a letter to his parents, he gives the following account of some of their experiences on one of these journeys:—

"It was a true joy to be able to accompany Mary to visit the interesting and growing work of the L.M.S. in the Yen Shan district, situated about 100 miles S.-W. from Tientsin. We started on Monday, 21st March, engaging two boats—one for ourselves, and one for the Bible-woman and the wife of our dispenser, who accompanied us, the latter returning on a visit to her native place. It was a gloomy morning to set out upon—one of those days when one needs to draw the sunshine from higher regions than the sky, and, by simple faith, fall back upon the familiar promises of God's Word. The text in *Daily Light* for the day was inspiring: 'Fear not, for I am with thee; neither be dismayed, for I am thy God.' As we passed the various bridges on the river, it was very Chinese-like to find the men in charge asking for what is called 'wine money.' Without giving this present, it might have been difficult for us to pass on. The next day, at 6.30, we dropped anchor in the Grand Canal at Tu-Liu, where there is the promise of a prosperous work. Dr. Smith has already been there on medical mission work with his evangelist. There are eight Christian families, five miles from the town, some of them former patients in Tientsin. The place is noted for its manufacture of vinegar, almost as pure as the foreign article.

"On the next day I was awoke, about 5.45, by the helmsman calling, in much distress, to my servant to ask for some 'throat medicine'—'he could not swallow, he was choking,' etc. We did our best for him, and by God's blessing he was well in the evening. As we proceeded, it was sad to notice the extensive floods to the west, the villages rising like islands out of the calm but muddy waters. By 10 A.M. we passed the large town of Ching-Hai-hsien, where no Christian work has yet been done. 4 P.M. brought us to another large town, also unevangelised; its sick, especially those with eye diseases, getting worse and worse, because there is no one to help them, while dark souls are sinking into the grave, ignorant of the name of Jesus.

"Taking a walk by the side of the river, before we anchored for the night, while Mary rested in the boat, too tired for a stroll, I came across an old watchman in a fuel-yard. His left eye was lost, from pure negligence, and his other was fast following it. Borrowing a native forceps from one of the small crowd of bystanders who always follow a foreigner in China, I removed some in-growing eyelashes, which were the cause of the trouble, and ordered him some eye lotion. Reaching the outskirts of a village, I was soon surrounded by a larger crowd. One man with a comical face, quite a character for Dickens, pretended to be greatly impressed by the fact that I—a young man apparently—should possess a beard. 'How old might you be?' inquired the man; 'forty at least, I suppose?' There was a general laugh when I replied that my age was thirty; and some jocular remarks were made upon two Chinamen in the crowd, who were about forty-five and had little hair upon their faces. There was a unanimous assent to my remarks upon the Christian religion and the folly of idolatry, and I then spoke to them of God's gift to sinful man. The belief in idols is shallow. A man often becomes a priest because the temple he officiates in has a plot of land, the proceeds of which keep him in comfortable circumstances. The number of temples needing repair is conspicuously great.

"On Saturday, 25th, we reached Tsang-chow, a busy centre, where we hope before long to plant a mission, when men and money are forthcoming. Here we left the boat, and, getting packed into our carts, passed through the main thoroughfare—by a large brick Mohammedan temple, for Tsang-chow is one of the strongholds of this sect in China. An hour later we passed a city in ruins. It was once the capital of a petty kingdom, before the year A.D. 800, when many States became consolidated into one Empire. We saw the ruins of its once fine wall. Within the large enclosure there are now only a few mud huts in one corner; all the rest is a howling wilderness—here an unburied coffin, and there a grave.

"The Tai-ping rebellion and a severe Mohammedan struggle in this region were the causes which brought about

WORK IN THE COUNTRY DISTRICTS

the desolation of this city, once teeming with busy life, and the seat of princely power."

For some hours afterwards, the travellers' course lay through a barren plain, destitute of rivers, trees, or hills, with hardly a blade of grass to relieve the monotony. "This is a robber-infested district, and by night travelling is unsafe. So the carters hurried on, at the rate of three and a half miles an hour, with frequent fearful glances at the western horizon, till they reached, before darkness fell, the western gate of Yen Shan city. It is a place which has seen better days. The Yamen might be taken for a prison house, dilapidated and destitute of paint. The L.M.S. quarters are a credit to the Society, and an oasis in the desert."

The story of Dr. Roberts and his sister's visits to Yen Shan and the large district connected with it, is one of strenuous, unwearying labour. His presence there relieved the pains of many a sufferer, and brought hope and joy into many a home.

Crowds thronged to him for healing from morning to night; and when he went out upon the streets, frequent invitations to "Come in and drink tea," "to enter and rest for a while," took the place of the sneers at the foreigner, and shouts of "Foreign devil" with which missionaries and all travellers in China are so familiar. Others beside the little band of Christians came in to daily prayers, and were struck with the earnestness with which the Christian doctor urged upon his hearers the importance of such subjects as "Laying up Treasures in Heaven," "Leaving the first Principles, let us press on to Perfection," "A Living Sacrifice," etc. Dr. Roberts' medical skill, and the kindliness of his manner, which always attracted Chinamen, won for him an entrance into many homes, and gained the affection as well as the respect of the people. While doing all in his power to strengthen the Christians, and help them on in the life of faith, he was very kind and thoughtful in his attitude towards those who were the worshippers of false gods; and many a time his earnest, loving sympathy proved a beacon light to those who sat in darkness, guiding them to the Saviour he rejoiced to serve.

One afternoon, on his way to a village a few miles distant, Dr. Roberts passed by a fine willow tree, the bark of which had been stripped off in large quantities. It had a great reputation in the neighbourhood for its healing properties. The bark was used as a decoction, and taken regularly by persons suffering from various rheumatic diseases.

In front of the tree was a small shrine in honour of the spirit of a snake, which it was believed resided there, and, in answer to prayer, healed disease. A large number of small paper flags of various colours were fixed in the ground in front of the shrine, grateful offerings from people who had recovered from their sicknesses. Referring to this incident and his conversation with the people, Dr. Roberts writes:—

"Salicin must be the active property of the tree I saw, along with tannic acid. The white and black willow trees have been, and still are, used in England in the treatment of various diseases. Salicin, which in one form or another is used in rheumatic fever, is obtained from various species of the willow, and these drugs are, by the ignorant natives, supposed to be spirits."

Passing through the suburb of a small town, the doctor found that theatricals in the open air, as is usual in China, were going on. One of the leading men of the city had been seriously ill, and the inhabitants had made a vow to the idol, that if he recovered they would pay what was for them a considerable sum, and have a day given up entirely to theatrical performances in honour of the god.

At another place, the doctor notes in his diary a conversation with a man who had become an earnest Christian. "I asked him," he writes, "if in days gone by he had felt comfort and peace when worshipping the idols. He replied by saying that on one occasion, when a little brother of eleven years of age was apparently dying, they had called in a Buddhist nun, after which the child recovered in what seemed to them a miraculous manner."

Many of the people who belong to the numerous religious sects of North China are attracted to the Christian religion. In course of conversation, Dr. Roberts learnt many things about their faith.

"They do not worship idols, but an unknown god whom they call the 'Ancient Father.'"

"One of their forms of prayer is: 'The disciples of Lao Yeh worship him. We beseech thee, have compassion upon us.'

"Their hopes seem to be all centred on the next life. Their belief is a compound mixture of many faiths. They hope, by transmigration, to be born into the world again as rich and influential people. The leaders of the sect, upon the death of one of its members, frequently name the part of the world in which the rebirth has taken place. Apparently, however, they always name some region far distant from that in which their friends reside."

While holding a service in one of these numerous towns which dot the region around Yen Shan, Dr. Roberts found in the congregation a large number who were not Christians. Before they engaged in prayer, he explained to them the meaning of that act, asking that, if willing to unite in the worship of the true God, they would bow the knee as the Christians did. But they all took fright and left the building *en masse*, with the exception of the little band of believers in Jesus.

One woman who came to see Miss Roberts was a Buddhist nun, who had under her instruction a number of young girls. She was training them, at her own expense, to be nuns like herself. This woman freely admitted that she had no faith in idols—they were false gods. "But what am I to do?" she asked pathetically. "My father and mother sent me to the temple as a child, and now there is no help for it: no other course is open to me."

"I had an interesting talk to-day with two men," the doctor writes, "on the difference between Christ's command and that of Confucius. The Saviour said, 'Whatsoever ye would that men should do to you, do ye also so to them'; while Confucius remarked to his disciples, 'Don't give to others what you do not wish to have given to you.' I was conscious of help as I spoke at evening prayer; probably they were remembering us at the prayer-meeting in Tientsin."

As he passed on from town to town and village after village of this large district, Dr. Roberts rested at many places, where, with no settled native preacher, a little band of Christians was struggling on alone among much outward opposition, having provided themselves with a place of worship, though it was often poor and barn-like.

"Mr. Li has prepared two rooms for our accommodation, and is anxious to erect a tent in which we can preach to the crowds willing to hear," he writes of one influential Christian.

"There is a chapel here," he writes of another village. "It is a room lent by one of the Christians. Forty of them assembled to meet with us for worship."

In another town, he speaks of "a three-roomed building, lent by a warm-hearted Christian for use as a chapel. The place is much too small for the growing cause."

"At San Yün Ho," he continues, "an old man has lent two of his rooms for a chapel. On the bare mud walls some tracts are nailed; and on one side the Imperial proclamation, declaring that the Emperor protects Christians, and their religion is not unlawful, as many suppose. Near to it, hanging from a nail driven into the wall, is a small tin trumpet, used to call the Christians to the services. The chief Christian of the place—the deacon—is a very earnest man; he can read and sing pretty well: it is he who conducts the services." Some of the little band of believers who met together in this primitive place of worship greatly interested the doctor. One was a man of fifty-seven—a Christian of but one year's standing, who had to endure severe persecution from his family for coming to the services. Another was "an old woman with steel-white hair, said to be a warm-hearted believer. They sung heartily some of the translations of Sankey's hymns, with strange variations and additional notes in the tunes. It was a very happy evening I spent there," adds the doctor; "it did my heart good to see how they enjoyed the service."

At Ma-Wo, which consists of three villages in one, the leading Christian, named Wu, had fitted up a chapel for the services. There were eight Christian families in this place, and one of them had sent their cart to help the missionary on his way.

"Riding on the cart, I was cheered to listen to the earnest interest with which the converts discussed Church matters. Among others, they spoke of one warm-hearted Christian, a young wife, who had been bitterly persecuted by her mother-in-law, but through it all was showing a spirit of patience and gentleness."

But there were disappointments and trials to be encountered, as well as the cheer which comes with the joy of harvest. "I had a busy day in Chou-chia-tsai," he writes in his diary. "I found a young man who was at one time a helper of Dr. Mackenzie's. He is now a comparatively wealthy man, owning 120 Chinese acres of land; but has become cold-hearted, and, spiritually, seems almost dead. Another, formerly an active Christian, is in the same unsatisfactory condition." After seeing patients all day long, the doctor, with his native assistant, as usual conducted a service in this place, which was well attended. "I spoke on 'Faith without works is dead'; and Ting followed on the same lines, pointing out their dead condition to them. After service, it was cheering to find the words had not been spoken in vain. Some thanked us, saying they felt ashamed, were 'cut to the heart,' and hoped for better things in the future. Two of the leading men made up a quarrel which had separated them, and came to me together next morning, begging that a native preacher might be allowed to visit them occasionally."

At the Yen Shan station there were also troubles to try the patience of the missionary, and jealousies and disputes to be settled. Dr. Roberts had the happy gift of winning the confidence of the native Christians; though he had, as one of his colleagues has said, "a strong sense of righteousness," his bearing towards them was always so brotherly and sympathetic, that his influence over them was very great.

There are many notes in his diaries of quiet talks with Christians of which there is no other earthly record. It was his custom, after earnest prayer for blessing, to ask the erring Christian to walk with him to any neighbouring town or village where a service was to be held. "I had a long talk with Chang," he writes on one occasion, "and was much helped. I impressed on him the great mistake of getting into debt. He is in debt for the new chapel at Yang-chia-tsai, and has not a cash in hand. I showed him the necessity of paying down at once all monies received from Tientsin for the Yen Shan work, to avoid suspicion on the part of the people. I also told him how Ting (the other assistant) was feeling his cold behaviour towards him, and feared he must leave the place, even though he was so earnest a worker. I advised him to be always kind and considerate, and, whenever possible, to have prayer in private together. Chang took what I said very well. Soon after our return, Ting came in on business with a happy face, and said the trouble between himself and Chang was now quite settled; all was right again, and they would be able to work happily together. Thus peace came after storm, and joy after sorrow. We magnify the name of the Lord for grace and help given under trying circumstances."

But it was not only the care of the numerous little churches that came upon him daily. It was the deep longing of his heart that each individual Christian should daily grow in likeness to the Master. The field was in many districts white unto harvest, and the earnest worker felt he could not leave untaught those who were asking for instruction.

The extracts from his diary, brief and pregnant with meaning, are heart-rending to those who knew and loved him, giving as they do such a picture of unceasing labour, the service so joyfully rendered that the worker was rarely conscious of the mental and physical overstrain incurred. May the story of his life serve as a call to others to go to the help of those who, in this and other harvest-fields, are working beyond their strength because the labourers are so few.

"Saw patients through the day," he writes; "then service—subject, 'The Call of Matthew.' I experienced much help in speaking. Afterwards, till 11 P.M., went over the Catechism with them, to which all listened with attention."

Another day the entry in the diary runs thus: "Saw sick till sundown; supper at 6; then, from 6.30 to 8 P.M., talk upon the fundamental truths of the gospel, and was much helped in speaking; evening meeting from 8 to 9—subject, Matt. v. 1-16. Li and Chang both led in prayer helpfully, as if touched. Praise the Lord, O my soul! After this, some of the Christians came into the room in which I sleep, in the old chapel, saying, 'It's only now and again we see you—let us stay and have a chat. Sometimes, when Mr. Ting (the native preacher) comes, we sit up till near daybreak. We can sit up talking of the things of God all night long and not feel wearied next day.' This was a lively prospect after a long day's work," adds the doctor; " but I felt more than cheered that they cared to talk of these things, and were so friendly. When at last they left, I turned in to rest. There was no bolt to the door, and the place is in a lonely situation; but I pushed a form against it, and fell asleep, remembering, 'I will both lay me down in peace and sleep, for Thou only makest me to dwell in safety.'"

The same thing continued day after day, as the doctor passed from one to another of the scattered stations, where little groups of Christians met for worship; while his sister remained teaching the women and children at the older station of Yen Shan. Here he saw patients morning and afternoon; and then journeyed on to Liang Chang tsuang tzu—where he was able to comfort and cheer some persecuted Christians—afterwards addressing the crowds that thronged the courtyard.

"I felt very weak," runs the diary. "It was late before I could turn in for the night. One gets no seclusion in these districts, unless one makes it; and then we appear rude in the eyes of the people. As soon as it was light the Christians were knocking at my door. There is no such thing as retirement; all one's theories on the subject are nonplussed."

Reaching Yen Shan once again, after the long round of visits, patients streamed in to meet him from the surrounding country—some coming in carts from a distance of ten to twenty miles. "The courtyard was full of people at 9 P.M. They spent the night singing hymns, talking, and sleeping, alternately."

The next day was a gala day for the Christians in the Yen Shan district; for it had been decided to have a feast and general meeting in honour of the visit of the doctor and his sister. "The cost of the feast was entirely defrayed by voluntary subscriptions of the Chinese Christians; and there was a surplus of about £2, which was devoted to the support of a Christian school teacher in one of the poorer villages. The feast consisted of chicken, pork, bean-curd, bread, native soup, and tea.

"By 10 A.M. the courtyard was crowded with Chinese Christians—their donkeys, mules, and oxen (which are all used as beasts of burden) making a lively picture. Shortly before eleven o'clock they met in a tent erected for the purpose with poles and matting, and a service was held.

"It was a sight which will long live in my memory. Forms had been borrowed to fill the tent, and every corner and seat was occupied, and fully 350 Christians, baptized and inquirers, were assembled together. Only 50 were women, the rest were (many of them) men whom I had met in my journeyings from station to station. It was the first time I had been privileged to address so many Christians at once. Great was the honour and great the responsibility. I took as my subject Acts i. 8: 'Ye shall receive power, after that the Holy Ghost has come upon you: and ye shall be My witnesses, both in Jerusalem and in all Judea, and Samaria, and unto the uttermost parts of the earth.' 1st, the promise; 2nd, the condition of receiving the promise; 3rd, the result—power and ability to be witnesses. The people listened very attentively, which, I trust, was an indication of interest in the theme."

The work among the towns and villages of this great North China plain has been largely self-propagating. One case only can be given as an instance of how the truth spreads. At the time when the Yen Shan chapel was being built, a few years ago, among the bricklayers there was a man named Chao Chi-jen, of about thirty years of age. The native preacher was anxious that these workmen, while building the house of God, should become interested in the gospel. In the evenings he invited them to come and smoke and talk in his house; but this they refused to do, knowing he was a Christian teacher. So, finding they would not come to him, he went to them; and, sitting down night after night in the poor mud hut, which was their temporary lodging, he so won their confidence that, after a while, they accepted his invitation, and came in to morning and evening prayers. Before the building was completed, five of the men became inquirers, and eventually accepted Christ as their Saviour. One of these, on account of his faith, was disowned by his parents and wife. Another of these men was the above-mentioned Chao. Returning home, he told the neighbours of the new religion he had heard of and embraced at Yen Shan, adding, " If you wish to hear more you must go to Yen Shan yourselves and learn, for I am only a beginner and know little."

Many persons followed his advice, and afterwards became Christians. Later on, Ting, the native evangelist, visited the place. There are now in this district nearly seventy inquirers. One of them is a literary man, a B.A.; another a wealthy farmer; while a third, who is in very good circumstances, has been indefatigable in spreading the gospel news in the surrounding districts.

Though well aware of the poverty of the people, Dr. Roberts was always a strong advocate for self-support among the native Christians, and strengthened their own desires in this direction by the story of the London Missionary Society's mission in Amoy, and the large numbers of poor villages which in that district, by rice collections and various other means, choose, call, and support their own native pastors.

At the close of one of these visits—for many were paid, though a sketch of the incidents of one only has been given above—Dr. Roberts wrote:—

"We have seen, during the past month, in Yen Shan district, much of God's presence, and experienced not a little of His grace and help, for which we magnify His name. I have seen in all 1500 patients; had about 20 operations, mostly on the eye. The elders have dispersed after the meetings in peace, and good friends, notwithstanding our inability to accede to all their wishes. The head workers have settled their differences, and are good friends."

In a letter home he writes: "Baptized patients from the hospital are resident in no less than thirty towns of the province of Chihli alone. Some of these towns are large and important cities, and in none of them is medical work being carried on by any Society. In all of them we have an open door for medical and evangelistic work. When shall we be able to garner in the 'harvest which whitens o'er the plain'? The labourers are few indeed, and the work utterly beyond our present power to cope with."

CHAPTER XII

DR. ROBERTS AS A FRIEND

"In my heart
    An image then began to dwell of One
Who among men was man, yet perfectly
Did manifest the Word of God; and left
These words to us : Lo I remain with you
Always, to the world's end. And I began
To feel Him with us, and to live and move
As in His sight, and to be glad of it,
Though ignorantly. But this sense I caught
From Ugo, from my master ; for himself
So shadowed forth in every look and act
Our Lord, without whose name he seldom spoke,
One could not live beside him and forget."
                        E. HAMILTON KING.

"I ask Thee for the thoughtful love,
   Through constant watching wise,
To meet the glad with joyful smiles,
   And wipe the weeping eyes ;
A heart at leisure from itself,
   To soothe and sympathise."
                A. L. WARING.

"Friend, on your grave in my heart
Grow flowers you planted when living :
Memories that cannot depart,
Faith in life's holier part,
Love, all of your giving.
And Hope climbing higher is surer
To reach you as life grows purer."
            ARTHUR O'SHAUGHNESSY
            (From *Songs of a Worker*).

A MAN may be, and often is, a most earnest and devoted Christian worker, yet at the same time the strength and determination of his character make it difficult for him to work with others without occasional friction. He finds it hard to deal gently with the failings of his colleagues, and is often out of harmony with their plans.

This was not the case with Frederick Roberts. He was not only an enthusiastic and wholly consecrated Christian worker, but at the same time a friend strong and tender.

He won the affection of his fellow-students in college days, and the same thing occurred when he entered upon his life-work in the mission field.

"Sympathy was deeply woven into his character, and took men captive," wrote one of his brothers. "He always saw the best side of every one's character, and never spoke about the weaknesses of others," remarks his sister Mary. "He was staunchly true to his friends, and would never allow the least word said against them."

He had drunk so deeply of the spirit of Christ, that, in a very marked way, he manifested in his life the meekness and gentleness of his Divine Master.

Dr. Horton, in his *Cartoons of St. Mark*, observes: "You might almost know what a man is if you know how he feels to children and what he thinks of money. One may be a good man, and yet, from some fault of temperament, may not be attractive to little children; but it is very doubtful whether you can be a good man if little children are not attractive to you." Dr. Roberts was certainly in a marked degree a lover of children, whether Chinese or English; and the little ones returned his affection, with interest.

His love for his nephews and nieces in England was very deep, as the frequent letters he found time to write them in his busy life plainly show; and the texts some of these children gave him at parting were treasured as precious recollections. "There are splendid ponies here in Mongolia," he writes in one of his early letters. "The people ride them without a saddle. In some parts of the country these ponies are wild, and are caught by good riders chasing them on horseback and throwing a long noose over their heads. Tell the dear children that's what Uncle Fred is going to try and do, in another sense, to catch the Mongols and take them to Jesus. I hope they will pray that I may be able to catch a great many, and learn to throw the noose well."

To one of his nieces he wrote:—

"My dear Hilda,—We are very grateful to you, dear, for working so hard to get money for the poor Chinese, that their pains and aches may be cured, and that they may hear of Jesus Christ, the Saviour of the Chinese as well as the English.

"I think, if you could stand by my side some morning, and see some of the Chinese who come to the dispensary, you would feel even more than you do now that the money goes to make many happy. I have got a bed called the 'Lynwood Bed,' where all the year round one and another will be cared for and treated for nothing. Sometimes patients come over 100 miles to the hospital, walking all the way, and so poor that they have spent all on the road. When we are able to do them good, we take them in; and it is such cases as these that mostly occupy your 'Lynwood Bed.' . . . .

"I had such a bonny wee pet of a patient, a boy five years old, to-day. He had been before, and was much better. As he liked the medicine, he thought the prescription also would be good; and I find he rolled it up, put it into some water, and swallowed it, with no bad effects! There are idols in most of the homes of Tientsin, and in temples, where the people go and bow down to them, knocking their heads against the floor, and seeking riches or happiness from them. But there are many homes where the people worship God, and are taught about Him.

"Now, dear, take care of dear mother, and then we shall call you 'Nurse Hilda'; and do what she wants you to, Hilda, even though you may not always know why you should.—With much love, in which Aunt Mary joins, your affectionate uncle, F. C. Roberts."

When he arrived in China, he soon won the affection of the children in our mission circle; and as he often lived for many weeks together in the house with them, his brief seasons of recreation were generally spent in their company.

When he came in to the evening meal, the children would be on the watch, and greet him with delighted welcomes. He was always ready to listen to their accounts of the day's doings, to laugh over their toy "nonsense" books, such as *Alice in Wonderland*, or to tell them stories of the days when he was a boy. He interested them so much in his little Chinese patients, that they were always anxious to do something for them also. One brave little lad, who came from one of the famine districts in the hope of earning his living in Tientsin, injured his thumb badly while working for the shoemaker to whom he had engaged himself. He was compelled to work on, while suffering intense pain, till, hearing one day a customer speak of the kindness of the doctor at the Mission Hospital, and his great skill, he determined to make his way there. Dr. Roberts took him in, and quite won the boy's affection, as he did that of all his patients. The thumb had to be amputated, to prevent further mischief. The doctor's little English friends supplied the lad with a new suit of clothing out of their pocket-money. It was amusing to see him, on his way to the Sunday school, how he followed the doctor with most admiring eyes, always keeping as near to him as possible. After some months' stay in the hospital, he left for his distant home; we hope, to carry the news of the love of Jesus into a district where no missionary resided.

Many toys from the English nursery found their way over to the hospital, to the beds of Dr. Roberts' little protegees; while quilts to make wadded Chinese coverlets were sewn by busy little fingers, delighted to do something for the men in whom "the doctor" was so interested.

Fifth of November, Chinese New Year's Day, and the Feast of Lanterns, were gala days for the mission children. Dr. Roberts was always ready to stir up the bonfire, let off the fire-crackers, and light the lanterns. Snow rarely falls very heavily in Tientsin—the climate is too dry; but whenever it did, there were always grand snowballing times with Dr. Roberts. The young folks would lie in wait for him on his way to and from the hospital, sure that he would never be too busy for a few minutes' frolic with them. Christmas Day was always given up to the children, and the evening spent in merry romps with them—the doctor being one of the happiest of the party.

During the hottest weeks of several summers it was necessary to take our children away from the malarial atmosphere of Tientsin.

On these occasions Dr. Roberts took several of his brief,

rare holidays, and always laid himself out to add to their pleasure; not as a task, but it seemed to increase his own enjoyment, for, as his sister writes, "these children were his delight." Expeditions were made in rough flat-bottomed Chinese boats, to find something approaching to a bit of beach on the swampy foreshore of Taku. Then he would wade with them, pick up shells, and talk of some of the wonders of the shore. Another year he paid several visits of a few days to the Tong Shan district, which is slightly hilly. Here he joined in the children's rambles, climbing the grassy slopes. He was more helpful than anyone else at the picnics—fixing up swings in the trees, searching for wild flowers, pulling down the high branches of flowering shrubs for the little ones to gather themselves, and in numberless ways trying to add to everyone's pleasure.

At least two of these children owed, under God, their lives to his skill and unwearying devotion. With one little lad he went down, as it were, into the Valley of the Shadow of Death, tending him through a most serious illness. The crisis was barely past before Dr. Roberts himself fell ill with malarial fever; but almost every day he sent cheery and loving letters to his little patient, who was nursed in a room connected with his house.

"MY DEAR ALEC,—Thank you for your nice letter. I am not so very ill, and hope to be better soon. Auntie does not play with me, but she sings to me, and this morning she read the Bible to me. I think our verse was: 'Whether we live or die, we are the Lord's.' No sickness can come to us unless Jesus allows it, because we are His property. Dear mother will tell you what that means. I like your text, Alec, very much; but I don't think it's any easier to obey than the one I wrote about yesterday. The fact is, our hearts are such poor sinful things, that we can't do any of the good things the Bible says we ought to do unless Someone helps us. I will not tell you who that Someone is. You must try and think who the Bible says He is. Auntie sends, with me, ever so much love, and I am, your loving friend, F. C. ROBERTS."

"MY DEAR ALEC,—You may put up the toy telephone if you like, only it must be burned after you get well. I am glad you say I got on better in the boat-race game to-day, and that the boat you called mine won. I thought from what you said before, I must be a bad racer. I am so sorry I am not yet able to come round and play with you, dear.

"What a nice verse you had for to-day! I was reading this morning about Jesus, that He did not please Himself; and the great Apostle Paul says we ought not to please ourselves, but ought always to try and please God by our words and actions. This is very easy to talk about, Alec, but very difficult to do; and let us very earnestly ask Jesus Christ to help us not to please ourselves, and not to do what self would have us do, but what He would have us do."

Another day he wrote:—

"I also heard the gong last night. I am afraid if it rains much more we shall have a great flood. We can see the rising water from my window. The plain is like a large lake, and men are sailing on rafts across it. Here and there are houses like islands standing out of the water; the people have left them and gone to live somewhere else. Auntie has been hearing from Mrs. Liu of so much suffering among the poor Chinese because of the floods, and she has been giving them money to help them to buy food. This is what Jesus Christ likes us to do, but what Satan tries to get us not to do. He says to us, 'Don't you give your money to the poor. Keep it all for yourself, to make yourself happy!' Let us ask Jesus, Alec, to make us kind to the poor, and all around us. The verses I was thinking of this morning were about 'being of one mind towards one another.' Now, you won't know what that means, Alec; but it's something like a lot of boys who all wish to play the same game. We say they have one wish, and grown-up people call this having one mind. Well, the Bible says grown-up people should be like brothers and sisters, all thinking the same and wishing the same about pleasing our Saviour. It means we should not quarrel, but love one another; let us try and do that to-day. Good-bye, my little patient. Your loving doctor,
F. C. ROBERTS."

In order to have friends, we must show ourselves friendly, is a truism, and certainly Frederick Roberts cultivated as few do the art of friendliness.

I have heard him remark sometimes, "that God gave us Christian friends in order that we might, in a very real way, be helpers of one another's faith. For himself," he said, "conversation and united prayer with his friends was a great source of stimulus and spiritual refreshment. The friendship of those who were not in Christ must always, if they only thought about it, have a shadow over it; but Christian friendships would endure for ever, since they could never suffer more than a temporary shortlived break, with the certain hope of reunion by and by." He thought "God gave us here, in the society of Christian friends, much happiness, yet the fulness of the blessing would only be discovered in the presence of the Lord through the endless ages of eternity." "We ought to pray unwearyingly," he used to say, "for those members of our Lord's body who were specially tried and tempted. Desiring (as we must do) that God should be glorified in the lives of all His people, instead of criticising and commenting upon the weaknesses of Christian friends, we should carry them in prayer to the Master, crying to Him to heal them." He thought "we ought not simply to pray and think with sympathy of those who were bound to us by special ties of love, and then imagine that we were fulfilling the new commandment because we loved those we could not help loving. Those who were not followers of Jesus found it an easy matter to love those who loved them. The Christian was commanded to love those to whom, naturally, he would not feel attracted—to love when he did not like, for Jesus' sake. Many people," he believed, "felt troubled lest they should love their friends too much; he had sometimes shared in the fear that arises of allowing human love to enter the holiest inner recesses of the heart. Yet, seeing the Lord Himself felt a special affection for the inmates of the home in Bethany and 'John the Beloved,' and even in the agony of the Garden craved for the sympathy and love of His disciples, it was clear that the closest and holiest human love might endure in His presence."

He thought "we ought not to be selfish in our friendships, but ever willing to share the things which brought special joy and brightness into our own lives with others. We ought to be glad for others to share in the Christian intercourse which gave a zest and savour to our own lives, even while we thanked the Lord for it as a special gift to us. So, by sharing our blessings with lonely Christians, our joy became doubled, because heightened by a knowledge of our Lord's approval."

These were his theories upon the subject of Christian friendship; and they were practically carried out in his life, which was full of brightness and sunshine, while crowded with constant work.

"I am very happy," he wrote to his mother soon after his arrival in Tientsin; "the Lord has already made up to me a hundredfold, according to His word. I see the fulfilment of Mark x. 30." . . .

Later, he wrote: "I would not change places with —— or anyone else, on any score whatever. Truly, with dear Mary, I have a goodly heritage, and our cup runneth over. I wish it would run over so as to bless the patients who are so dark and unspeakably ignorant of God and His laws."

The latter period of Dr. Roberts' life in Tientsin gained an added brightness from the arrival of his friend of college days, Dr. G. P. Smith, who was appointed his colleague by the L.M.S., for the work had increased far beyond the power of one man to compass. "I am eagerly awaiting the arrival of Dr. Smith," he wrote to Rev. R. Wardlaw Thompson early in 1892. "We are full of hope for the farther extension of Christ's kingdom into the many towns and villages of Chihli, and that in the near future." "Dr. Smith and I are very happy in our work," he wrote later. "I don't think we could be happier."

Few men, working as untiringly and conscientiously as Dr. Roberts did, could have found time to keep in touch with absent friends by frequent letters. He had the pleasant gift of a ready pen; and his friendly epistles, dashed off rapidly, were the expression of his own earnest, affectionate nature, and often rich in spiritual thought. In times of sickness or special anxiety, his friends were constantly borne upon his heart in prayer, and the letters he wrote to some of them at these times were "as streams of water in a dry and thirsty land."

To a young fellow-worker of the London Missionary

Society, who under his care and skill had recovered from a trying illness, but on his return to Mongolia suffered a serious relapse, he wrote :—

"MY DEAR WILL,—Lack-a-day, and so you are down once more with the old enemy. How we did all feel for you when your letter was read. . . .

"Spiritually, what does it mean? The school of stern discipline and trial, always calculated to be helpful to us—*cæteris paribus*. By the way, have you not more than once said in my hearing, that you thought you would have been so and so if you had experienced more suffering in your life? Yes, there's no such thing as luck in God's universe—the knowledge of our every thought, the numbering of the hairs of our head, seem to state it in so many words. Cheer up then, Will: it's 'hard lines,' as we say; but it's all right, and will end all right." . . .

At another time he writes: "Your wish about the time for being alone with God for two months, I thoroughly sympathised with. You did not get it! Just as our Lord of old failed to get His, when with His disciples He departed privately into a desert place. For my part, Will, I am beginning to learn that life out here does not give much facility for such delightful times. The brief seasons of daily prayer are all that we can get. May God help us to make the most of them, and with all our hearts to believe in the efficacy of private prayer. . . .

"It goes without saying that we must all be conquered by germs one day, till this mortal has put on immortality. But, Will, that time has not come for you, thank God, as we think; it's not even in the distant future. . . . I wonder whether the Tientsin climate and Chao-yang are the same these days. It's dangerous weather for souls pilgrimaging to heaven! If one doesn't look out, one can stray into all manner of bypaths, such as quick temper and irritability. This I find, to my shame and humiliation, at times. I think, at a Keswick Convention in Tientsin in July, the penitent forms would be full daily. Love; best wishes. Look up. Hold on. Your loving friend, F. C. ROBERTS."

From a series of letters addressed to the writer during

brief absences from Tientsin, and afterwards while in England on furlough, I select a few extracts. They are fair specimens of his correspondence, and show how love to Christ and implicit obedience to His commands was the keynote of his life.

"MY DEAR MRS. BRYSON,—So many thanks for your letter, which, without a doubt, it did one good to get. Thanks also for your kind invitation to Tong-Shan 'Convalescent Home.' No; I fear I can't have the pleasure. Your arguments are weighty (it's very good of you to argue the point), but one thought outweighs them all. I can't see my way. You know the strange sense of guidance one gets sometimes, which leaves no alternative but to follow in the path God appoints. Now, I am in the midst of Koch's fluid experiments, and can't leave them, can I?—even for the pleasure of a visit to Tong-Shan.

"The last I paid was the happiest I ever spent there. Why? Because God gave me some work to do, and helped me to do it. . . . Lord help us to drink deeper of these wells of joy. Ah! one has only sipped as yet of the water that He gives.

"Thanks very much for your prayers for the hospital. God is working in some hearts; but it is very trying to wait and wait, and see hearts still unmoved by the gospel. And yet why am I not more moved myself? One look back at the early apostles, and what some of them underwent for Christ's sake, and then one honest look at oneself—ah! This is the way to humble oneself, and shut one's mouth with a true sense of unworthiness. But what then—is that all? No; there must be the daily endeavour to follow Christ in the path which He has marked out. It is the path in which I can, trusting in Him, glorify Him—by heart-submission in all things. Bringing—oh, what a divine word!—every thought into captivity. Quick to detect every unsanctified thought which tends to death; quick to discern the presence of God to help.

"May we ever experience this sense of union with Him, and victory over the world, the flesh, and the devil through His indwelling power.

"'Greater is He that is for us, than all they that are

against us.' Ah! I think we often underestimate the Master's strength, and, stagnating our souls, lean on our own strength, which is weakness.

"I think, perhaps, three weeks hence, Mary and I will have the pleasure of another week-end with our dear sister at Tong-Shan and the chicks. Good-bye; pray much for the hospital, hospital workers, and hospital physician and evangelist, who remains always, your loving brother,
"FRED. C. ROBERTS."

At another time he wrote: "We learn almost more under the cloud than in the sunshine, don't you think? Few of us can maintain close communion with God for long together when everything is calm, and as we would naturally have it. The Lord will be with you and restore you speedily, we trust; but, anyway, our lives and moments are in His safe and tender keeping." . . .

Later, he wrote: "Mary and I feel grieved that you have had such times of trial and sickness since your arrival in England, and that intervening oceans have hindered us from offering any help it might have been in our power to render; but all is well, and misfortune a word of but very limited application in the Christian's vocabulary. . . . When one looks on from afar, it is easier than for those in the midst of the smoke of the battlefield to know how things lie. You seem to have been set adrift on a stormy sea alone—seem, only seem; for with all your trials and difficulties God is intimately acquainted, and they have all come with a passport from Him, and come as sanctifying and ennobling influences sent to teach you the secrets of the gospel of His love, which are hard to learn, even theoretically, when all things are smooth, bright, and fair. Think of John in the prison, discouraged like yourself, and finding it hard to reconcile the love of the omniscient Saviour with his protracted imprisonment, and comfort yourself with the thought that to allow John to continue in prison till the will of the Lord had been accomplished was a far greater honour than to have sent a legion of angels to his immediate rescue. So, when the holy divine will of the never-erring Master lengthens the months of deferred hope till the heart groans under the strain, it is only that we may learn the better to say, 'I can do all things through Christ, who strengtheneth me,' and 'My flesh and my heart faileth, but God is the strength of my heart and my portion for ever.' He will not allow your faith and patience to be strained too severely. Has He not promised us in His own Word? I feel how easy it is to sit down and remind you of these old familiar truths, yet be of no more use than Eliphaz and his other friends were to Job—to 'chiang' the 'tao-li'[1] of the thing is easy, but to suffer patiently hard. We can only pray that you may be kept calm and peaceful, and rest in the assurance that all things are working together for good, whichever way we look at the matter. . . .

"May you have a speedy recovery, and more of Heaven's sunshine than I am enjoying; more, also, of transforming communion with the risen Saviour, through faith and the Holy Spirit, with more experiences of the reality of those things which many doubt, but which are real to those whose vision is clear, through His illumining presence."

But Dr. Roberts' friendship and sympathy was not confined to the inner circle of his own colleagues of the London Missionary Society. "He was very broad in his sympathies," writes a member of the Methodist Mission. "He took an earnest interest in all missions. He was singularly free from all sectarian narrowness, and always rejoiced greatly in the progress of God's work in any part of the field. He will be missed by men representing many forms of Christian effort in China."

Lonely workers were specially laid upon his heart; he always rejoiced to welcome them to his home, when passing through Tientsin, and constantly made time to see them on board their boat or steamer, and give them a brotherly Godspeed.

"Dr. Roberts was a public man of whom every Christian in China was proud," writes Mr. Charles Studd of the China Inland Mission. " . . . There has never yet been a man or woman from the coast but had a word about and for him."

"My friendship with Dr. Roberts extended over six years," writes Mr. Stanley Smith. "He had a most winning

[1] Preach the doctrine.

presence and manner; and one became attracted to him at once by his transparency of character, warm-heartedness, and utter absence of all unreality. . . . I had a long walk and most profitable talk with him, on one occasion, on the possibilities of union with Christ. It stands out in my memory, that in this conversation I had talked with a man who was living in experimental enjoyment of this union. . . . Fred was the last man who would have listened to, or acquiesced in, human praise. No one, it seemed to me, had got a tighter hold of that most salutary truth: that in us there is no native good, and that what is good in us comes from a Higher Source than ourselves. Still, many praise the Lord for the graces of the Redeemer which shone out so brightly in our dear friend, and we among them. His cheerfulness and humility, his generous kindness and thoughtful sympathy, his loyalty to God's Word, and his love for souls, will constitute an unending memorial to our God and Saviour, in whose presence he is now for ever satisfied."

"My heart was much drawn to him," writes Mr. Archibald Orr-Ewing; "he did love the brethren, and counted no service he could render a trouble. His frank manner was calculated to inspire confidence in all his patients; and the decided way in which he expressed his opinion carried with it a great deal of weight, and tended to convince those consulting him that he was right. . . . He was known as a peacemaker, and sought most truly to wear the badge of discipleship given by our Lord—'By this shall all men know that ye are My disciples, if ye have love one to another.'"

"Truly he redeemed the time; his was, indeed, a beautiful life," writes Mr. Tomalin of Ning-hai. "I always think of him as a saint of God. He was holy in all manner of conversation. His loyalty to Jesus was thorough, his devotion intense. The way in which he addressed Christ as 'Master' in his prayers was to me thrilling, so full of reverence, and yet of the warmest and most unreserved love. Every memory of him is helpful and fragrant with Christian graces."

"We felt intensely the Home-call of our dear friend Dr. Roberts," writes Rev. J. A. Stevenson, Deputy Director

of the China Inland Mission. "I have seen a great deal of
him at various times, and was deeply impressed by his
intense earnestness and desire for the salvation of souls. I
shall not soon forget our last talk here, and his remarks
upon a text I have in my office—'The Lord shall guide thee
continually.' As I look at that text I am reminded of
him. No one could be in his presence long without
feeling convinced that he was a consecrated and spiritually-
minded man—an ideal missionary."

"There are few men," writes Dr. Shrubshall of the
Methodist Mission, "who, in the anxiety and strain attached
to medical work in a foreign country, and especially when
that work happens to be on a larger scale than ordinarily
falls to the lot of one man, would retain the even temperament, the ready and willing ear to listen to unexpected
calls and interruptions, and the bright smile so characteristic
of Dr. Roberts. In his case, the cause was the ever-
present help of a Divine Burden-Bearer, whose power and
aid he experimentally knew. But the hard work was at
times more than his physical strength could sustain. Once,
when he spent a few days' rest at Tong-Shan, we were
talking about the necessity for recreation; and I told him
it had been said that he would not accept an invitation
unless to the house of a missionary, or where there was a
decided Christian influence. 'Why, my dear Shrubshall,'
he exclaimed, 'I would go to other houses; but I must take
every opportunity to speak for Christ, and I don't think I
should be invited again. I would not shut myself off
from others—they would shut me out.' No man believed
more truly, or tried more fully to exemplify, the words of
Christ, 'Ye are My witnesses.' But the witness, so un-
mistakable in his clearness, has been called to his reward,
while to us the need of his presence and help seems great as
ever."

One who was for some time a member of the Tientsin
Foreign Community writes: "I could enumerate numberless instances of Dr. Roberts' kindly thoughtfulness to
individuals which came under my own notice. He was in
the world, but not of it, and loved by all who knew him—
Europeans and Chinese alike. He was my ideal of a
Christian man, in every sense of the term. I never knew a

more consistent man. His life was a constant denial of self. He was always following in the footsteps of his Master—'going about doing good.' He was a helper of the fallen, and always tried to raise them to the higher plane of the Christian life on which he lived; and was truly a witness to the fact that Jesus does live to-day, in the hearts and lives of His people."

CHAPTER XIII

PERSONAL CHARACTERISTICS AND GLIMPSES OF INNER LIFE

" If our love were but more simple,
  We should take Him at His word;
And our lives would be all sunshine,
  In the sweetness of our Lord."
                              FABER.

" How can I, Lord, withhold
    Life's brightest hour
  From Thee, or gathered gold,
    Or any power?
Why should I keep one precious thing from Thee,
When Thou hast given Thine own dear self to me?"
                              C. E. MUDIE.

DR. ROBERTS' term of service in China was short—only about seven years; but the work he accomplished in that period, many of his older colleagues maintain, might well have been spread over the lifetime of any ordinary man. It seemed as if the words of our blessed Lord, "The night cometh, when no man can work," were ever ringing in his ears. Yet he performed his varied duties with the most joyous self-abandonment. It was no task for him to work for his Master; he rejoiced that he was counted worthy of the honour of serving in a field where labourers are still so few.

There was nothing morose or sad about his life: his voice could often be heard, from the room in which he studied, ringing out clearly and joyously in some hymn-tune that had caught his fancy. His love for children has been touched upon before. The beauties of nature were also a constant source of enjoyment to him. Probably there are few places upon the earth's surface more destitute of natural beauty than the desolate, treeless plain of Tientsin. Yet every twig and leaf and flower seemed to speak to him of a Father's love and care.

It was a real pleasure for anyone to share his walks—he was usually so exuberantly happy.

"Look at that fellow," he would say, watching the upward flight of some Chinese songster till almost out of sight in cloudland. "Isn't he praising his Creator?"

"Tientsin is very interesting just now," he writes to a friend. "First, the cloudland is grand: I never saw anything like it at home. There are high massive clouds of all imaginable shapes — dark clouds in front, then white columnar clouds behind, and in the background the distant blue of the sky. It makes a picture you should see, if you wish to appreciate cloudland."

"The winter is passed," he writes again, "and already the warm spring days have arrived; a few more days will see the wild geese and the ducks winging their distant flight to the quiet moors of the North, while already the flocks of crows, evidently hastening to their summer rookeries, cheer one with the thought that welcome spring will soon be here, as it is already in the Chinese calendar and noonday sun."

"I went for a stroll to-night, in the light of the setting sun. The heavens looked lovely. The evening star shone out clear and bright. The willows, still beautiful with their autumn-tinted leaves, stood out black and sombre against the pale-blue sunset sky."

But although Dr. Roberts delighted in all the good gifts of God,—in birds and flowers, the joy of friendship and the gambols of little children,—the secret of the brightness and joyousness, which everyone noticed as one of his striking characteristics, lay far below the surface in a heart at perfect peace with God, which had enthroned the Saviour as its Lord and King, and taken His Word for its constant guide.

He was accustomed to talk very freely about spiritual things to those who had the privilege of his closest friendship. I frequently noted down afterwards some of his remarks which struck me as specially helpful; and from this record shall make a few extracts, since they seem to give, better than any description of his character, brief glimpses into his inner life.

One day Dr. Roberts was speaking of our Lord's charge to His disciples: "As the Father hath sent Me, even so send I you." He said he thought "it was most important for us to remember these words were addressed to us as much as to the disciples. Jesus had sent us, just as He Himself had been sent by the Father, to represent Him to the dark souls around us. Many of them were quite unable to understand much about the doctrines of Christianity; but they could all feel the influence of a life. So we should make it our constant aim to live Christ before them. If they see us easily annoyed by trivial things, irritated by the overcharge of a few cash in our accounts, worried by the failings of servants or the stupidity of patients and coolies, can we expect the Chinese to believe that, in reality, our thoughts and hopes are all centred in heaven, and that here we have no abiding city? Souls are of more value that all the world. How careful, then, ought we to be, lest we exercise an influence over them not for good.

"It is so easy for us to lose control over ourselves in a hot climate, or during the long dry season. I can distinctly feel its effect upon myself," he continued, "making me inclined to be irritable and impatient. But all this only means that we must draw more constantly upon the strength laid up for us in Christ. He has promised grace sufficient for our needs—the greater the need, the more abundant the grace.

"Of course our great Enemy will try to tempt us in all sorts of ways. He will tell us everybody gets irritable in a hot climate, and we must make allowances for ourselves. If we are always so meek and mild (as he calls it), we shall never get Chinamen to pay any attention to our wishes, since they are quite accustomed to receive orders from foreigners in a rough tone of voice, and do not feel troubled by it, as we might."

"I am quite certain these are all suggestions of the Evil One. Did not our blessed Lord encounter similar trials to those which meet us at every turn? and yet we remember 'the meekness and gentleness of Christ.'"

On one occasion I remember reading aloud an article from our *Chinese Missionary Journal*, the writer of which was greatly discouraged because he saw daily large crowds of Chinese flocking to him for medicines, while the majority of them were quite indifferent to their far deeper spiritual need. Dr. Roberts remarked: "I do not think, at any rate in the present stage of our work, we can expect to see crowds hastening to listen to the gospel as they do to gain relief from physical pain. It is the difference between appreciation of temporal and spiritual blessings, things seen and things invisible. We must have the husbandman's long patience: results are not with us. The ploughing and the sowing are ours. Our work just now is to live for Jesus, and tell His message of love to all who will hear it."

One of Dr. Roberts' favourite texts was Hebrews xii. 1. He used to say he thought "weights" were clearly distinct from sins: "something that we felt to be a drag or hindrance to our progress in the Christian life, like extra clothing to the athlete, or the carrying of a burden, however light. Since, therefore, we had decided that the most important thing for us was to use our lives in the Lord's service, it was certainly the wise thing, through communion with Him, to discover even the smallest thing that hindered our upward progress; so that, by laying it aside, we might run the race more easily and happily. One thing, however, we should always guard against; and that was, judging others, who may not feel the weights that press upon us. Let us be willing always to follow our Lord's will as revealed to ourselves; but it is a serious hindrance to our growth in the divine life when we begin to criticise other Christians, and think harshly of those whom the Lord is also guiding — though, perhaps, by a different path to that in which He is leading us."

Talking one day over several passages,—among them, "Ye are the light of the world,"—Dr. Roberts said that sometimes in the past he had felt greatly troubled on account of the difficulty he experienced in introducing religious topics when in the company of those who were not Christians. It had been a positive cross to him at times, and he had often wished that he could speak as readily as some Christians he knew, of the things he felt to be so all-important. He regarded it as a great failing in his character, which the Lord alone, by filling with His Spirit, could enable him to overcome.

At another time, he said he had "lately been much impressed with the conviction that it was not the Master's will that we should always be attacking people on the subject of religion—feeling it a burden to speak, yet driven to do so. While seeking our Lord's guidance in the minutest details of daily life, we could trust Him to show us His will in this matter. It was better to talk little with those out of Christ on directly spiritual topics, unless clearly guided to do so. Yet let us be specially careful always to live Christ, to let our light shine; but unconscious shining is the best." With reference to this subject, he spoke at another time of a great tree he had seen at the edge of a cliff while in the Highlands of Scotland. After a severe storm a portion of the cliff fell, and left the roots all exposed to view. It was then seen that this fine spreading tree, towering high in the air, had an equally far-spreading strength of root and fibre down below. So, he said, he thought "it should ever be with our Christian life. We ought to have a far deeper experience of the verities of the spiritual life than we ever gave expression to. It was very helpful to talk often one to another upon these things, as the Christians of old did; but we must never go beyond our own experience. Let the roots of our spiritual life strike down far more deeply than the spreading branches of the outward manifestations of that life."

In connection with the subject of freewill offerings, Dr. Roberts said, one day, he thought, while with regard to some things we had our Lord's clear command, which if we failed to obey we must suffer the sorrow of broken communion, yet other matters were left for our own decision. Some people would tell us certain things would be useful "for polishing our weapons to be used in the Lord's service," as Miss Havergal puts it, thus making them more effective for His use. As an instance, he mentioned the temptation he sometimes felt, when there were specially interesting or uncommon cases in the wards, to give up all his spare time for professional study. He recognised it as his clear duty to give necessary time to the consideration of every case, so that he might do the best possible for each patient. But then, he said, I might easily go a step beyond that, and yield to the temptation that comes to me, as a professional man, to study closely cases rarely seen in England, with a view to special proficiency. If to do this I must neglect Chinese study and spiritual work in the wards, then life is not long enough for everything. So he preferred to fill up his time with work which seemed most likely to hasten the coming of his Master's kingdom, laying these possibilities of greater professional efficiency at the Lord's feet as freewill offerings of love. He said he thought all Christians felt at times a longing to let others see that the followers of Jesus could successfully compete with worldly people in various spheres of work. There was nothing absolutely wrong in this desire; yet he thought "if we were only willing to give up, for the Lord's sake, possibilities of success in other fields than those which tended directly to the advancement of His kingdom, He would give us a very real sense of His approval and acceptance of such freewill offerings. Jesus might Himself have entered upon His work as the world's Redeemer possessed of all the prestige which wealth and rank and culture would give. He chose instead the lot of a Nazarene peasant, and, for most of His followers, men who were lightly esteemed by the world."

At one time he thought deeply upon the subject of spiritual thirst and its satisfaction. Referring to a remark made by an earnest Christian, a leader in missionary work in China, whom Dr. Roberts greatly admired and loved, that the promise, "He that believeth on Me shall never thirst," was intended to have its fulfilment in this life, and that for some years he had felt such complete satisfaction in Christ that the feeling of thirst could barely arise before it was satisfied—Dr. Roberts said he had not in his own experience attained to that.

The verse, "Blessed are they which do hunger and thirst after righteousness, for they shall be filled," being quoted, and the lines—

> "Then raise and quench the sacred thirst
> Which never pains again"

"Yes," he said, "but I am still not clear that these promises do not point to a fuller and more blessed fulfilment than any we ever dream of, in the land where, in the presence of the Lord, all spiritual desires are for ever satisfied.

But I think," he added, "that many things which are not plain to us at one period of our Christian life become clearer as we proceed—following our Lord very closely, just searching His Word for Christ's own ideal of the Christian life, and then very simply going on to attain it."

He thought and talked often upon this and other passages relating to this subject, especially John vii. 38, and eventually worked the result of his meditations up into a week-night address at the Union Church in Tientsin. His addresses were usually the result of long meditation, over certain passages of Scripture, which, from study and prayer, he felt he had gained some light upon. The passage last mentioned impressed him much, because he felt it gave such a far-reaching and fruitful idea of what the Christian's influence should be. He said: "Through the Spirit's power abiding in us, we ought to be far greater blessings to all who came in contact with us. Our lives should be like the beneficent course of a river, bringing gladness and beauty to the land through which it flowed. Had we such an outpouring of the Spirit as we might claim, we should be far more fruitful in life and work. Our friends in the Foreign Communities who might not yet have been attracted to Christ, would feel there was some real power in our lives, and then God might use us to help and bless them. The Chinese converts would feel it too, and be strengthened and led on to a higher plane of spiritual life. The heathen in the preaching halls and the hospital wards would be influenced too, and we might expect such rich blessing to follow as we had never known before."

One day Dr. Roberts said he had noticed times of special anxiety, sickness, and weariness were often rich in spiritual blessing. We might be under the cloud; but if it was with Jesus, we were only drawn closer to Him by outward trials. The disciples feared as they entered into the cloud on the Mount of Transfiguration, but the fear melted away in the joy of more intimate communion.

Sometimes he thought we longed, like the disciples, to stay on the Mount of Blessing, and lengthen the " brief bright hours of fellowship" with our Lord, feeling, with Peter, it is good to be here. " But these seasons of special blessing only come to strengthen us for seasons of special service. Here are the poor Chinese, bound in soul and often diseased in body, waiting for us to go and carry to them tidings of healing and blessing, just like the poor distracted father with his lunatic son at the foot of the Mount of Transfiguration. We want to stay up in our little Mount of Blessing, but Jesus calls us, and, answering His call, following the leading of His Spirit, we go right down into the valley, and find the service waiting for us, the needs of the people appealing to us more loudly than ever before to work for our Master. Yet we can take the quiet rest upon the mount from His hand as well as the service. But these happy times are only a foretaste to cheer us on. The rest that remaineth will come with the service, without sin, when life's work is over."

In reading aloud the memoir of a medical missionary one day, I came to the passage, "He never performed any serious operation without first seeking help and direction from God." Dr. Roberts interrupted me with the remark, "Any serious operation!—I should think any operation, serious or slight, one would hesitate to undertake without the Lord's help."

Everyone who knew Dr. Roberts well was impressed by the way in which he carried every minute detail of his life to his Master for guidance. He would be uncertain about a matter at one time; and perhaps some hours after, he would state clearly the course he thought the best. "The Lord has made it clear to me," he would say simply. While other people were distressed and perplexed on account of the absence of advisers in whom they trusted, he carried every matter to his omniscient Saviour, and never failed to get clear guidance. When he saw any of his friends perplexed or in doubt, he would say, with his bright smile, "Let us have a few words of prayer together for guidance." His prayers always seemed to carry his friends into the very presence of the Lord, and they rose from their knees with "lightened cheer."

He often said he "believed that implicit obedience to our Lord's command was the condition of progress in the divine life. Through the Spirit, Jesus Christ is made to us wisdom, righteousness, sanctification, and redemption; but if we allow anything in our lives which blunts or disturbs our communion with our Saviour, it is always fatal to growth in grace. If we will but yield ourselves entirely, Christ will give us all of strength we need to tread the upward path. We must be very severe with ourselves, but never judge others. The more we know of Jesus, the more we shall feel how utterly unlike Him we are, and the better we can estimate the wonderful possibilities of the life we have taken from His strong and loving hand. Prayer and watchfulness, and faith in God, would enable us to gain the victory over every besetting sin." He had great faith in the virtue of plodding in the Christian life—not being too utterly cast down by failures. "Despair," he used to say, "was one of the weapons used against Christian by Apollyon in the Valley of the Shadow of Death. The right thing is to go on hopefully, sure that, since we are on the upward path in Christ's strength, we must overcome. We must never lower our ideal, but, by constant watchfulness and prayer, press onward towards it."

"In times of temptation," he said one day, "we must resist the devil. We dare not drift or sleep at any time, for no man ever became a saint in his sleep. We were Satan's servants once, now we are bound to be entirely the Lord's. Satan tempts us just as he tempted our Master, with the world's prizes, its schemes and plans for doing the Lord's work. We don't like to be considered, with St. Paul, fools for Christ's sake. At other times, when in God's strength we have overcome some sore temptation, Satan comes to us and tries to make us think we are really wonderful Christians, for we can pass through temptations and not be harmed by them, as some poor weak souls would be. We are living so near to Jesus, that is why He succours us. And then he suggests that we can easily relax watchfulness for a time. Ah, but it is in Christ's name alone that we can overcome these most subtle temptations; if left for a moment to ourselves, we fail utterly."

Dr. Roberts had a stronger feeling than most Christian people I have known about the body being, as it were, a barrier to complete and full communion with our Saviour. Sometimes he seemed to look forward as eagerly as St. Paul to the time when, released from this frail tabernacle of clay, he should see his Lord face to face. Once he said: "While here in this world, we can never lay our armour aside for a single moment; our life here is to be a constant warfare against the world, the flesh, and the devil—all three." He thought that temptations hedged us round on every hand, and that often the nearer we pressed to Christ the fiercer they became. While we all thought him so holy in life and character, he never so regarded himself. He used to say that all possibilities of sin lay in every heart, though he admitted that the temptations that appealed strongly to some people did not disturb others.

One day, after I had read an article the writer of which maintained that "the blood of Jesus Christ, His Son, cleanseth us from all sin," referred to unconscious sin, Dr. Roberts remarked sadly: "Ah, but I think it covers far more than that; as far as I am concerned, I know I often sin consciously, yet, thank God, I know that He applies the cleansing blood." Dr. Roberts' busy life left little time for general reading, and he was often utterly wearied out when the day's work was over. Yet, apart from medical reading and Chinese study, which were included in the day's work, he greatly enjoyed devotional books, as well as occasionally some bearing on Chinese matters, which he thought would enable him better to understand the people to whom he had devoted his life.

He liked to have his sister or a friend gather from these books the most salient points or striking passages, and read them to him. In this way we went through many of Andrew Murray's books; also Moule's and Meyer's and Goulburn's *Thoughts on the Spiritual Life*, which appealed to him strongly. He was much impressed with Stalker's *Imago Christi*, and some of the chapters touched him very deeply, especially that entitled "Christ as a Man of Prayer." "See," he said, "when texts are gathered together, how much there is to show the great dependence our Lord placed on prayer. His days were filled with the ceaseless toil of preaching, teaching, and healing, under very trying conditions. None of us have the day's work He had, yet He rose often a great while before day, to obtain some quiet hours of communion with His Father, which He felt so absolutely needful. How much more necessary, then, must such quiet hours be for us?" Afterwards he studied the book with much delight, and many passages in his copy of it are deeply underlined and

GLIMPSES OF INNER LIFE

commented upon. I have heard him say he believed that the feeling of irritation and annoyance which sometimes rises in our hearts, when people act contrary to our wishes, was as displeasing in our Lord's eyes as violent outbreaks of temper. He thought it was possible to attain to our Lord's ideal, and have peace ruling in our hearts. Once, when in a Chinese house-boat outside the Taku forts, our boatmen were exceedingly trying. They determined to take a different course to that which we had decided upon, because the tide was against us. They are accustomed to be shouted at in a tone of command by foreigners generally; and seeing that Dr. Roberts spoke to them in his usual kind way, they thought they might easily take their own course and disregard his orders. Their obstinacy and impudence tried him sorely, but he did not speak an angry word. After a while the men quietly altered their course, and went in the direction he desired.

"Fred had the gentlest and sweetest of natures," writes his sister Mary; "he was rarely ruffled. I could count the times in his life when I saw him vexed: twice it was with Chinese servants, because he thought them wanting in politeness when answering my questions. Once, and once only in his life, I saw him really angry; it was during a discussion on the subject of Faith-healing, a matter which will probably distress the minds of many of the Lord's followers till He comes who shall make all things plain.

"It was at the conclusion of our monthly missionary prayer-meeting in Tientsin, and Fred and a missionary who had been in China two or three years began to speak on various topics connected with mission work; and after a time it drifted to Faith-healing. My brother contended, first, that those who use medicines depend as much upon God's almighty power to heal them as those who do not use means. Also that God could heal with or without means, if He so chose; but the facts and experiences of everyday life showed that He was willing to bless His own appointed means, and that it was not showing want of faith to use what God had provided. He added, that he did not think that any Faith-healer could honestly say that the cures of to-day, brought about by God without the use of medicines, were the same as those performed by our Lord Jesus Christ while on earth, or by His disciples after His death. He did not question the fact that there had been wonderful cures, but they were generally of diseases affecting the nerves, where faith had proved undoubtedly a most helpful means to a speedy recovery.

"The argument was provoked by the other missionary remarking that he considered it wrong to use drugs which, given in large doses, would prove poisonous. In the course of this discussion Fred became very angry, and so did his friend, and they parted, both of the same opinion as before.

"My brother and I walked home in silence through the mission compound, but I saw he was intensely grieved. 'Mary, I ought not to have spoken as I did,' he said as he bade me a sad 'good-night,' and went at once to his room. Next morning he told me how utterly miserable he had been till, turning up the passage in *Daily Light*, he read, 'Though he fall he shall not be utterly cast down,' which gave him much comfort. That morning he wrote to the missionary with whom he had carried on the discussion the night before, asking his forgiveness for the unchristian way in which he had argued. They are now both in that land of perfect love where earth's mysteries are made clear."

The discussion thus referred to is mentioned in the recollections of another friend, Mr. G. W. Clarke of the China Inland Mission, Tientsin. "Dr. Roberts was a man of prayer," he writes; "he walked with God, and constantly prayed over his work. His frequent remark after prescribing was, 'With God's blessing, I hope it will do good.' He was a man of faith and works. After one of our united missionary prayer-meetings, a Swedish friend, who was a strong advocate of Faith-healing, made some disparaging remarks about using medicines, in the presence of four missionary doctors. It is needless to say there was a warm discussion, at the close of which dear Roberts spoke plainly. A beautiful phase of his character was a tender regard for the feelings of others. He knew he was right in his statements, yet, fearing that he had offended, he wrote a very kind letter, apologising to the brother with whom he had carried on the discussion."

Dr. Roberts felt very strongly that the deepest need of our spiritual life was that it should be daily nourished by reading and meditation upon the Word of God, and communion with the risen Lord. He thought the best time for Bible study was the early morning, before the rush of the day's work came on. This was his own plan; but he used to say: "We cannot lay down rules for others. Doubtless the Lord will make up to those who are prevented from seeking Him in the early morning by a special blessing and sense of nearness at another time."

Yet, often when the work was very heavy in the hospital, and he had been watching over serious cases till a late hour, and through the long strain of the hot summer days, he could not always rise as early as he desired. "My difficulty just now," he writes to his sister Annie, "is early rising. I don't deny myself sleep in the morning in order to have more time to draw near to God. I could write a book on the subject, so fully have I looked round it; but to rise before 6.30 A.M. is at present beyond me—6 A.M. is the time I am due to get up. I should value your prayers on this score for me, Annie."

He used to speak sometimes of how other Christian workers had, in answer to prayer, been able to rise very early to obtain time for the study of the Word of God. When he spoke in this way, he often looked pale and worn from overwork. He assented sometimes to the remark, that when the Lord saw we could not obtain all the time we desired for communion with Him, He could give us, in a short space of time, grace sufficient for the day's needs. Yet he was always very fearful of allowing his spiritual nature to suffer for the sake of sparing his health and strength.

In *Bowen's Meditations,* a book which he found very helpful, he marked, among other passages: "The people of God deny themselves, for the good of others, of property, ease, friends, *health*; whatsoever they do, they do for the glory of Christ." The word health was deeply underlined. "If few love the Lord, there is the more need that I should love Him to the utmost of my capacity"; "A man that diligently seeks God has renounced the search of other things"; "What we do without the Lord, we do disobediently," were other sentences in the same book which he marked and commented upon with special approbation.

He admitted, however, that duties never clashed in reality.

Speaking one Sunday night, he remarked : " There is a serious case I have now in the wards; it will be necessary for me to rise early, do some professional reading, and think and pray over the case. It would not be right for me to be reading my Bible when another duty is clearly waiting for me. It would be wrong for me to-morrow to omit the necessary professional reading in order that I might gain for myself the strength of the quiet morning hour."

Among Dr. Roberts' private papers, intended for no other eye than his own, are many notes upon passages of Scripture, and meditations upon life's pathway. The former he made, because he thought, when studying the Scriptures, we ought to use every available help to banish wandering thoughts; for it was easy to read constantly and regularly, and yet receive little spiritual blessing, if we were unable by the Spirit's power to concentrate our thoughts on the passages we read.

On the last night of the last year of his life, Dr. Roberts thus sums up the failures and causes for thanksgiving of the past year:—

"31st December 1893.

"Often have you been proud, vain, puffed-up—thank God you know it, in a measure. You have been more concerned about the material success of the hospital than the salvation of souls.

" You have been envious and jealous in some things. . . . Humble yourself before God for these sins.

"You have manifestly neglected prayer and private communion this year. Is it going to be the same in 1894 —your last year of work for Jesus in China before your furlough home ?

"You have not studied God's Word as regularly and prayerfully as you ought to have done. Hence your growth in grace has been hindered. Your love for Jesus Christ is not very powerful, very controlling, and constraining. Your zeal is small in degree. Earthly thoughts occupy a more prominent place in your heart and mind, heavenly things a less prominent place.

"O my soul! when will you learn that life and power spring from death and cross-bearing ? Deny yourself; take up your cross, and follow Jesus. Jesus denied Himself sleep for you—can't you deny yourself one hour more of sleep in the morning, in order to think what a cross He bore for you? Draw near the throne and learn of Him.

"Causes of thanksgiving for 1893:—

"I praise Thee, Lord, for health and strength given, for money sent in sufficient for hospital needs, for all loved ones in China and in England, for Mary, for the prayers of Thy people, for George[1] and the division of work, for all the help and success granted in the work in Tientsin and Yen Shan, because I still look heavenward for all the comforts of life, for peace outward and inward, for joy and cheerful spirits, for a sure and living hope, because the medical work is a growing one, for my calling and its many opportunities of glorifying Thee, for its far-reaching influence over the inhabitants of Chihli. To Thee be all the honour, power, and glory.

"*1st January* 1894.

"Lord, help me this day, and every day, to please Thee. Help me to deny myself extra sleep in the morning, in order that I may have extra time for special private prayer, to love Thy holy Word more, and to search it more diligently, and to think, speak, work, and live only for Thee. To deny myself worldly and fleshly lusts, that I may be more fully consecrated to Thee. To live more in Thy presence, and more in the power of the Holy Spirit. To be humble and meek and gentle, wise and patient. Give us the joy of real harvest among the patients this year, if it please Thee. Help me to study my medical work, to keep abreast of the times, and to prepare for the M.D."

A few selections from the many letters Dr. Roberts wrote to relatives and friends in England, show how the whole current of his life ever tended heavenward, and that humility of spirit was one of his striking characteristics.

Writing to his sister Annie, he says: "You refer in your last letter to a great blessing recently received with reference to being cleansed from indwelling sin. I should like to chat with you and Mr. M. on the subject, which is not so clear to my mind as it seems to be to yours and his. I have much to learn which you seem to have learned already, and am often amazed at the difficulty of the

[1] His colleague, Dr. G. P. Smith.

Christian life, and the alarming rapidity with which one may fall into sin of so many kinds. I do ask your earnest prayers that I may grow into Christ in all things, learn what it is to die daily and only live to glorify Him. I am very conscious of the great need of more of the Holy Spirit's presence in my heart and the work which the Lord, in unspeakable condescension, has given me to do. May He hearken and bless and sanctify, wholly for His name's sake. May you, dear, scale higher and higher, and ever receive grace to watch and pray ; for on the sunny heights of full trust in Jesus there are dangers which you know of, there are precipices which one can easily fall over, there is spiritual wickedness and the power of Satan on every side, even in the heavenlies."

In a later letter he writes : " The dangers accompanying lofty attainments in the divine life to which you refer, may you ever, by His grace, be saved from, dear sister. Many, scared by the spiritual disasters following such experiences in the unwatchful, shrink from pressing onward and upward. 'He that is down need fear no fall,' seems to be their motto. The truth on the subject of Christian holiness would, to my seeing at present, be well expressed in these words : ' I am black, but comely'—comely through the Lord our righteousness, black in my original nature, which, at best, one can only reckon as dead. Even the most holy from time to time are black through sins of ignorance, if not of a worse nature. The truth that some seem to have lost sight of, is that self does not die in an hour ; and one is constantly waking to the fact that thoughts and aspirations, it may be, which we once regarded as signs of grace, become, in the growing light of the rising Sun of Righteousness, mere ugly excrescences of self. Examples of this will at once occur to you. . . . They point me to the possibility, in myself and others, of falling from the height of spiritual experiences in Christ Jesus. Not, for my part, that I have already reached any such dangerously high standing-ground, but I trust one is on the upward march, however slowly."

To another sister he writes, during a season of severe sickness : " Can I be sure that this is the will of God for me ? you may have asked yourself. Why am I chosen to suffer again and again ? Is it only misfortune, as those who are strangers to God, and call Him only Creator and not Father, might say, or is it really of God? Yes, dear, as you think over these things, you can and must believe that God knows all about your troubles, your desires, and your cross, and that He is with you. Now, here's a verse; think over it, and rejoice over it: 'I will be with him in trouble,' Ps. xci. 15. That is written for you; take it, and claim the promise every moment. Would you not rather be with God in trouble, than without Him without trouble?"

In a later letter he writes: "I am sometimes sadly amazed at my own shallowness of belief in spiritual things, and at that of the average Christian. May the Lord graciously help us to live up to the mark of our high calling in Christ Jesus. Let's have more reverential, humble faith in the Three-One God, and let us hold it fast, for there is nothing that slips out of our grasp more easily than faith. All one needs to do is to become careless or lazy in prayer and meditation upon the Word of God, and then our faith, which, to begin with, was divine, loses its vital power, which was Christ, and becomes nothing more nor less than an empty shell—the husk, the echo, the imitation of something real which we once had."

Later on he writes, with regard to one of his nieces: "We long to hear that dear H. is taking a stand for her Saviour in school, and is growing more and more like Christ. She has many talents—valuable gifts, especially when accompanied by spiritual gifts to sanctify these natural powers. It is, I am sure, hard for you to bring her up for Christ and His service. But, dear, be restful with nothing short of this. Oh, by your prayers and Christian life and words teach her to see the reality of the Christian faith when unmarred by a worldly spirit, and that the only life worth living is the one after the pattern of Jesus Christ, however disfigured by failure and temporary weakness the copy may be at first. I imagine, dear, your saying to yourself, 'Yes, but Fred does not know how hard it is.' Don't I? I think I know somewhat; but if I do not, Jesus Christ, who has called us to this life, does, and we know that He possesses unlimited power. The impossibility lies in our limited faith, which at times is more like credulity than honest, genuine faith. I am convinced we need to deepen the roots of our faith before there can be vigorous growth and abundant fruit."

With reference to another niece, Dr. Roberts wrote: "The Lord bless E., is our prayer, and accept her for His service as a missionary anywhere He pleases. Wouldn't we rejoice if that should be China? We need women full of the Holy Ghost and with many natural gifts, for China. A good temper, loving heart, and not over-sensitive constitution, are great qualifications,—given, of course, the source of all true spiritual power."

Respecting a nephew he wrote: " I think if B. wants to be a medical missionary, it would be a great mistake to send him to Cambridge. Edinburgh is the place *par excellence*. Life in Cambridge would be a poor introduction to life in China, dear. If he could get under Dr. Fry of the Medical Missionary Home, Edinburgh (paying his own expenses), and work among the poor of Edinburgh in his spare time, I think it would prove invaluable. Or he could live in private lodgings and work with them as I did, which would do quite as well."

To a fellow-student of days gone by, Dr. Roberts wrote: " Hurrah for your appointment! . . . I am more pleased than I can tell. My best wishes that you may be an honour to . . ., to your speciality, and to your Alma Mater; and may you take the standing of a true, consistent, genuine Christian physician. First in Science, first also in your Christian profession—let there be no doubt which side you are on. Dear old . . . is a noble type of a cultured Christian scientist, minus that cant and patronising spirit which some men in eminent positions display in religion, to the universal disgust of onlookers, whether Christians or not. Far be it from us to make any man our pattern, except in general principles. Our great example is the Great Physician. Yet, while I rejoice truly in your success, I do so with trembling ; for success, while it often makes a man and develops him, has sometimes a deteriorating effect, as you and I know full well. Which will it have in your case ? Time will show.

" It is my privilege to write to you with perfect freedom and candour ; but if the above lines sound too sermon-like, or grandfather-like, or goody-goody, don't on that account laugh at the possibility they imply, but hold fast what you have, and go on to perfection in every worthy pursuit, especially the pursuit of divine truth."

In a letter to his sister Ala, Dr. Roberts says: "If you were here you would say, How is it with your soul, Fred? Are you in communion with Jesus Christ? Now, I don't believe in pulling up the roots to see how they are getting on; and yet one should examine oneself, though some experiences are not so good to talk about as to meditate upon, so as to be more watchful in the future. But I am thankful to report some progress heavenward. God has shown me this year, more than ever before, what stuff I am made of by nature, what utter helplessness is mine; and this is progress. China is very trying for the spiritual life of God's servants; and every day we need to be unceasingly on our guard lest we should lose patience with the natives, who are certainly exasperating at times. Then another danger is that arising from heavy work. I refer to the danger of falling away from close communion with the risen Lord. Strange, but true, that we need to be reminded constantly of the glorious fact of His resurrection and ascension. The lapse of long years, particularly in a heathen land, is apt to obscure the sight, as in a thick fog; and the Christian worker finds himself sailing along in an accustomed channel, but yet in the dark, and running the risk of departing from Him who alone is the source of life, peace, and power. I tell you these things, Ala, that you may know how to pray for me.

"It is being laid upon me more than usual these days," he writes later, "how much I need a baptism of the Holy Spirit. But He will satisfy, and I am happy in His promises."

"I have just been reading Ps. cxviii. 1, 6, 7, 14, telling what the Lord is to His chosen people; and I can truly say that all that the Psalmist states is true, and far more. He is our strength, our helper, and salvation from hour to hour. He is with us, and is blessing us and making us channels of blessing to others. Your account of your visit to Keswick Convention was refreshing. It must be like heaven upon earth to visit Keswick, if only one is in the Spirit and looking up to God alone to speak through His servants."

It has been seen that, at the death of Dr. Mackenzie, the high Chinese officials withdrew their support from the hospital. It would have been a sore trial to Dr. Roberts to feel that the pecuniary responsibility connected with it must be entirely thrown upon the London Missionary Society. At the same time he shrank from soliciting funds for carrying on the work from gentlemen, whether foreigners or Chinese, whom he knew to be out of sympathy with it as a Christian agency. But he carried this matter, as he did all his other anxieties, to the Lord in prayer. The result was startling to those whose faith was weak; for by far the larger portion of the funds needed to defray expenses were received by him as freewill offerings from the Lord's people in England and China. Not that his faith was never sorely tested.

"He was very careful about the expenditure of money upon himself," writes his sister Mary; "and loved to save, that he might help others. He never would put by any money he received as salary from the L.M.S., but paid it over to the hospital funds. The medical work was maintained by voluntary contributions, and occasionally the funds fell very low; and once, I remember, he had come to the last dollar. He said nothing about it at the time; but I found out afterwards, that for two months he had supported it entirely himself."

Writing in the early days after he took charge of the work, Dr. Roberts says: "With reference to a remark made about the necessity of getting the natives to support the hospital, it is more difficult than you would think. First, we have very few rich patients, and without exception they have been given an opportunity to subscribe. Some have given the equivalent of £1, or 10s., but are afraid to give more because it would be supporting a Christian institution."

"On one occasion," he writes, "we had been praying together and in private for some weeks for money to come in, but none —none—none came; and to-day we were only a week from the next monthly account for hospital, with only £4 to meet it with. Imagine then the joy with which we welcomed your kind gift!"

"I can't tell you how it has cheered me," he writes to one of his sisters, "to receive your loving, generous gift; truly it has come from the Lord. This you will easily gather from the fact that I had not enough money left for next month's hospital account; and as I never go into debt for the medical work, humanly speaking, I should have been compelled to fall back on the L.M.S., which I am naturally reluctant to do, as they have so many expenses. Yet I must say the Society has always been very kind in matters of money, and kept always to their promises. The sum sent will pay for all the general working expenses for some months, also for the Glenn Bed and the Lynwood Bed. It is such a joy to receive consecrated money for the hospital. Truly it makes one 'happy all over,' as the Salvation Army puts it; and have you not found that when we do our best in the matter of giving, the Lord comes to our rescue and saves us from an adverse balance? I have watched His gracious dealings with me in regard to the hospital funds with much comfort, and not a little strength to faith."

Dr. Roberts was specially touched by one contribution to the hospital funds, which came very regularly year after year. It was raised by a band of Leicestershire villagers, for whose spiritual welfare the doctor's sister worked unwearyingly. They thus became interested in Foreign Mission work. The means they used to raise funds for the support of the hospital are thus described in the *Chronicle* of the London Missionary Society: "For some time the men, women, and children in this village have been supporting a bed in my brother's hospital in North China; but about fifteen months ago one man said that he felt enough was not being done. It was then proposed that a plot of ground should be obtained, to be tilled by the men and lads in their spare time. Little by little the work has grown; and now we are looking out for a third plot, so many are the offers of workers. Those who felt unable to do garden work have been busy with other odd jobs after the day's work was over; and the pence thus earned have been added to the rest, with the result that £10 was sent to the hospital last April, and this month we hope to send £10 more. As the potato crop was not quite as good as usual this year, the workers felt that something else must be done, so as to send more money rather than less to China. Accordingly, those having musical talent are getting up a service of song, the proceeds of which will be added to our mission fund. The women have helped, by sewing, etc., and by doing weeding and such-like work for the mission plots. In addition to this, we have a monthly missionary prayer-meeting, at which we give accounts of interesting mission work going on in different parts of the world; and every Sunday morning we remember the dear workers abroad at our half-past seven prayer-meeting."

Help of a similar kind was sent regularly from classes conducted by another sister of Dr. Roberts. After a time letters were written by these bands of workers in England to the Chinese hospital workers, who sent letters to them in reply. All this tended to strengthen the bond between them, and to make them feel they were fellow-workers under the same Master.

"I have just finished reading *The Story of the China Inland Mission*, by Miss Guinness," Dr. Roberts writes after his last Chinese New Year's holiday, "and a great treat it has been. I have noticed in my own experience, connected with the hospital work, that the Lord's hand has been present stirring up His stewards to remember the needs of the work, quite apart from any request from me. He has never yet failed me. In nothing do I feel more at rest than in the matter of the hospital funds—when one has all one's treasure on the altar, then we can safely throw the responsibility of the support on the loving Father. This year, when I need more money than usual for private use, He has correspondingly already sent me in more money from other sources. Nothing gives me more joy to contemplate than this. I wish other things were as easy to surrender as one's purse."

If the large circle of those who knew and loved Dr. Roberts, both in England and China, were asked to name what they considered the central idea of his life, the controlling desire to which all else was subordinate, they would each reply, I think, "that it was to win souls for Christ."

The present chapter has dealt more largely with the devout spirit which longed intensely after personal holiness, and whose deep desire it was to show forth in daily life the image of the Master.

But the other side of his character was not less remarkable. It has been said that supernatural beliefs demand supernatural lives. People have sometimes remarked that if we truly realised the wonderful power of the religion we profess, our constant desire would be to allure others to the same heritage of joy, which, amid life's stress and storm, fills our hearts with hopes which baffle all expression in the speech of mortals.

Certain it is that Frederick Roberts always felt he had been saved to save, and ever strove to induce others to share with him the Heavenly manna which had satisfied the deepest longings of his soul.

Early in his missionary career he had written truly: "I see clearly that love alone can win men's hearts to God." It was by his unfailing courtesy, his kindly consideration for everyone, whether Chinese or foreigner, that he gained opportunities of speaking for his Master.

"He did not go much into society, except that of missionaries," writes his sister Mary. "His one excuse for not doing so was, 'I have not time.' It was not that he thought it wrong to do so; on the contrary, he would have said that the ideal thing for a Christian man to do, if he could,—and he would lay stress upon that,—was to go in and out among all classes of society as our Lord did, sowing the seed of the kingdom broadcast over all ground. But he felt he had been called to a specific work, which brought him into the society of the poor and degraded. He knew that the longest life is but short, and he wanted, for Christ's sake and in His strength, to influence them specially. It was as if he had received the burden of Chinese souls from the Lord Himself; and as he stooped to lift it he realised that it would need the concentration of every God-given power of body and soul to do it. And in the power of the Holy Spirit, which is not of man, but of God, he did this."

He had always a cheery remark and kindly smile for the coolies on the bund. He usually put some simple tracts into his pocket whenever he went for a walk on the plain; and would make opportunities for conversation with passers-by, and, after a little general talk, speak of the religion of Jesus. A missionary of another Society, taking a short stroll with Dr. Roberts one day, was much impressed, as they stood at an angle of the wall looking over the densely-populated city of Tientsin, by the intense longing in his face, even more than the words, "Oh, when will the time come when this great city shall be won for Christ?" He took a deep interest in the young Chinese medical men trained by his predecessor; and whenever they were in Tientsin, or passing through that port, he welcomed any who were inclined to come, to his home. He prayed much that those who had accepted Christ might be kept faithful in their difficult positions.

The sailors on the gunboats which wintered in Tientsin, among whom his sister constantly worked, were always welcome at the doctor's table; and he usually made time in his busy life to come down for a while to the evangelistic service held on Sunday evenings in the Temperance Hall, and speak a few words at the close. Some of his short addresses given at these times were remarkable for the simple yet forcible way in which he presented the offer of salvation through Jesus Christ, and they must have touched many hearts.

His last Christmas Eve was spent by the deathbed of a member of the little Foreign Community at Taku. "It was the most solemn Christmas I ever spent," he wrote. "At the request of Dr. Fraser, I went down to treat Mr. P., one of the pilots, who was seriously ill with a stroke resulting from apoplexy. I found him in a precarious condition, practically hopeless, with very laboured breathing. His mind becoming somewhat clear before he passed away, we were able to speak to him and draw from him some expression of faith in Jesus as his 'Pilot across the bar'—which was comforting to the distracted widow in her great sorrow. That Sunday he gradually sank, and at 3.30 P.M. on Christmas Eve passed away. At 6 P.M. we had a Sunday evening service, truly a most solemn time, in which I had an opportunity of speaking from the words, 'Be ye also ready, for at such a time as ye think not, the Son of Man cometh,' and also on the first advent of Jesus Christ and His mission to mankind."

Writing after Dr. Roberts' death, a missionary of another Society says: "I was at Taku recently, and saw the profound impression made upon the little community by the early call of one who had ministered to them so well and spoken so faithfully."

During the doctor's rare holidays, his thoughts were

filled with possibilities of service. Out on a Chinese junk, across the Taku bar to the lightship, one summer day, while the rest of us were quietly enjoying the fresh sea breeze, Dr. Roberts was in the stern, speaking to the rough Chinese boatmen of Jesus the Saviour. Later on in the day I saw one of the men diligently spelling out the simple Chinese Catechism he had received. Walking round the Taku forts, he won the respectful attention of the usually rough Chinese soldiery by his Chinese courtesy. They brought out chairs and asked us to rest, listening attentively as he spoke of the Heavenly Father's love in sending Jesus to die for them.

His short trips by steamer to Japan and Chefoo were looked upon, not merely as health trips, but as opportunities for helping others on the heavenward way.

Writing from the Taku bar, when just starting on one of these trips, he says: "I am very happy, and look forward to my trip, full of hope and expectation—of much blessing in many respects. How good it was of God to give me a foretaste of it yesterday. First, in the train I enjoyed a very profitable talk with Mr. C. on the relation of the Chinese to Christianity, and the reason for their present hostile position. Then on the tugboat, going out to the steamer, the Lord opened up the way to have a very free talk on spiritual things with a gentleman on board, who thought that coming out openly for Christ would injure his business prospects."

"We are in the narrow part of the inland sea," he writes later, "with blue sky above, blue waters below, and hills hemming us in on every side. These hills are mostly covered with pines; but near the shore there are terraces, where the spring wheat is ready for the sickle. What a delightful contrast to our Tientsin scenery! and yet our river-bank, crowded with living and immortal souls, is in a sense a more attractive spot. The dear old Chinese faces, too, I can see no longer; but in their place the round-headed, close-cropped, short-statured Japs."

Spending a Sunday in one of these Japanese towns, Dr. Roberts took a service in the consular prison, and afterwards spoke at a Sailors' Meeting. "I have had some plain talks," he wrote, "with the ship's doctor and some of the passengers;

but I seem to be only just learning how much I need of the Holy Spirit's teaching." He afterwards spent some days in the company of a young Englishman, much run down in health, suffering from religious melancholia. "I trust he will be saved, physically and spiritually," he wrote. "It does seem as if this were some work the Lord had for me to do here; and I feel glad to have come, for this if for no other reason."

Some of the sights of Japan reminded Dr. Roberts of England. "It was so like our beloved native land, must I confess that a sigh half escaped me for the old country, and a desire to be back there for a season? It was but a thought; for we are where God has placed us, and where we delight to be for His sake. Great is the honour and great the joy—is it not, dear sister? The prayers that are being offered on my behalf are being graciously answered, and I am daily having the honour of testifying for God and the Truth to foreigners. In some cases it is truly remarkable to notice the guiding hand of God—it adds a joy to my trip."

Dr. Roberts was constantly cheered by the remembrance of the prayers and offerings of friends in England. "Mary and I often talk about our privilege in having so many beloved relations whose hearts are truly in the work, and who constantly pray for us, and think of us, and thus support us in the work."

At the same time, in view of the great need of China, his heart was often stirred within him at the apathy of many English Christians who show no interest in Foreign Missions, and by whom our Lord's last command of love is totally disregarded. His prayers for the awakening of the Churches of England were like those of some young prophet of ancient days, who had seen, as in a vision, the burden of the Lord.

The news of the commencement of the Forward Movement filled his heart and mouth with joyful thanksgivings. "We are unspeakably rejoiced," he writes to the Foreign Secretary of the London Missionary Society, "to hear of the Forward Movement and Self-Denial Week; and the news has a most helpful effect upon us and our work."

To a friend he writes: "We have just been celebrating Self-Denial Week; and I am glad to say that, on the score of eating, we were able to deny ourselves very little—we live simply, but lack no essential. Tientsin sends about £30 to the fund—not bad, is it?"

Then, as the months passed by, mail after mail brought out the news that the Churches were halting, and some had even called a retreat. This tidings was received in Tientsin, and indeed through all the mission stations in every land, with grief and disappointment.

"We are much interested in the Forward Movement of the L.M.S.," he writes; "but some have sounded a retreat, and others are dismayed. Will not the Churches rise, and, in the strength of God, meet the difficulty, and gladly give liberally what God first gave to them?"

"Talk about self-denial," he writes to a friend; "it is not to be measured by giving up superfluities for a week, but by how much we keep back. The L.M.S. is approaching a crisis. Our great hope is in the outpouring of the Spirit of God on our wealthy Churches, and then the money will flow in."

In another letter he speaks of a visit he paid to a lightship on the Taku bar, nearly eight miles out at sea, manned by three Europeans and eight Chinese: "I could not help thinking—What won't men deny themselves of for the sake of money, compared with denial for Christ? Here are these men, nine months out of the year (very few days excepted), living in a boathouse, shut off from communication with the shore. Then think what a lot of fuss is made about a little sacrifice of time or strength for Christ!"

Some of Dr. Roberts' last letters to Rev. R. Wardlaw Thompson show how deeply his heart was touched by the news of retreat, and the dishonour he felt it brought upon his Master's name. "May we be saved," he writes, "from becoming the laughing-stock of those at ease in Zion, and those who are without her walls. It is our earnest and constant prayer that the goal which the Directors and Churches have set before them, in connection with the Forward Movement, may be reached by 1895, and all the money be forthcoming. Oh, how easy, if hearts were touched, to give in proportion to that of the widow who gave her all, her last coin—should we not say, her last absolutely necessary coin? Sometimes, with a sad heart, I think of the lives of many dear Christians at home, surrounded by every comfort they could wish, or nearly so, and then I remember the great need of God's work at home and abroad. I cannot but say to myself, 'Do they indeed know what whole-hearted consecration for Jesus means ? But the spirit of the widow comes from God, and not from man; neither can the appeal of man stir up one soul to practically deny itself, and take up its cross daily and follow Jesus.'"

CHAPTER XIV

THE LAST MONTHS

"By this time the Pilgrims were entering into the country of Beulah, whose air was very sweet and pleasant. In this country the sun shineth night and day. . . . It was upon the borders of Heaven."—BUNYAN'S *Pilgrim's Progress.*

"Peace, perfect peace, by thronging duties pressed!
To do the will of Jesus, this is rest."
E. H. BICKERSTETH.

THE New Year 1894 dawned brightly upon the little company of London Missionary Society workers in Tientsin. The Week of Prayer was, as usual, observed by the native churches of all the missions, in company with Christians the wide world over.

The meetings were largely attended, and were succeeded by a series of evangelistic services, lasting for more than a fortnight. They were conducted by Rev. Mr. Pike of the American Methodist Episcopal Mission, though missionaries of other Societies took part in them,—the result being, that a wave of spiritual blessing passed over the Tientsin native church.

"January has been ushered in this year," writes Dr. Roberts, "with a promise of brighter days. Never in my experience have such meetings been held among the Chinese Christians as are taking place every night at present. Sinners are daily being convicted of sin, and seeking forgiveness; backsliders are being restored. We hope that a time of great revival of spiritual life has come, and that Tientsin has been moved by the power of the Holy Spirit.

"I have felt it laid upon me to attend every meeting. I never heard the doxology sung so heartily as on Friday night by about one hundred native Christians. After the meeting, some of them came forward and shook hands with us, a mark of great fervour and warmth on a Chinaman's part, as they usually merely bow. Some wept for mercy, and others showed by their faces that the religion of Jesus was a real joy to them—something living, and not dead, like their own faiths. I would not have missed these meetings for a great deal. They have strengthened my faith in the gospel of Jesus and the Person and work of the Holy Spirit, in convincing men of sin, of righteousness, and judgment. The reality and possibility of a Chinaman being convicted of sin, after the experience of the last few days, not to speak of past years, is for me impossible.

"One patient went home from the meetings, and prayed in deep anxiety, in the ward, for salvation; he is now a believer. The ward-workers are being stirred up greatly, and I myself am conscious that God has been in our midst."

To the Foreign Secretary of the London Missionary Society he wrote: "You have doubtless heard of the impetus given to the Tientsin native church, from a series of revival services in which all the missionaries took an active part. Many have been truly stirred of God, and a deep sense of sin was present. It did one good to see Chinamen deeply moved by God's Spirit, and in earnest private and public prayer seeking His pardoning grace. One practical outcome of the meetings is the inauguration of the Christian Endeavour Society."

The work within the hospital wards and the dispensary was also full of encouragement. "The sick crowd to us in larger numbers than ever before. Without any exaggeration, the work is growing, people come about us freely, and regard the hospital as a home and refuge in time of sickness."

Dr. Roberts was an enthusiast in his profession, though the consuming passion of his life was the desire to win souls for Christ. Even while bearing the heavy burden of the hospital work alone, and studying for the three examinations in Chinese which the London Missionary Society expects missionaries to pass, he was always anxious, as he expressed it, "to keep abreast of the times."

In reply to a letter from his father upon the subject, he writes, early in 1894: "I am keeping the M.D. in view, and am preparing a thesis on Dysentery, a very important and common complaint here, which it is necessary to be well up in. The careful study of the subject in all its aspects will be accompanied with much profit to the patients and to myself. I regret that time does not permit me to devote more than one brief year to the subject, and only the spare moments of each day in that year."

At the Chinese New Year season, when all business is suspended and dispensaries are closed (for few Chinese care to leave their homes, even to have serious diseases healed, at such a time), Dr. Roberts, with his colleague Dr. Smith, took a health-trip of a few days to Shan-hai-kwan, the present terminus of the Chinese Imperial Railway. Dr. Young of the Scottish Presbyterian Mission, a fellow-student of Edinburgh days, accompanied them.

"The train started at 9.40 A.M.," writes Dr. Roberts, "and proceeded at the rate of 30 miles an hour. When we reached Tong-ku, we had a pleasant walk on the platform, and a cup of coffee. The river was still frozen over. By 3 P.M. we reached Lan-chow, prettily situated among the hills, on a large river called the Lan. Mr. Cox, the engineer, has succeeded in erecting the largest bridge in China over the river; it is 2200 feet long and 60 feet high, and has 18 stone pillars supporting it." They made their way to the premises of the American Mission, where they learnt from the chapel-keeper that a series of services, similar to those which had been followed with such blessing in Tientsin, had been carried on by Mr. Pike in this lonely station, and attended with similar results. The fifty or sixty converts present were all moved to tears, and about thirty followed each other in prayer. This time of self-conviction was succeeded by a season of great peace and joy. "We had a little meeting with the Christians after supper and also in the morning," he writes. "At this station there are no settled foreign missionaries."

Another railway journey of six hours brought the travellers to Shan-hai-kwan. "The line skirts the long chain of hills separating North China from Mongolia of former days. In the distance we could see the turrets of the far-famed and justly-renowned Great Wall of China. Many a long century have they stood there—since fully 200 years B.C. It was amusing to watch the crowds at the various stations who had come to see the engine—a great wonder in their eyes. The line is a great success,—crowds go by it every day,—but the Chinese directors 'squeeze' the profits. I am very sorry to say that the progress of the line towards Kirin (Manchuria) has been checked, owing to the diversion of £200,000 towards the Empress of China's sixtieth birthday celebration, which takes place in 1894.

"We sat on the seashore where the Wall dips into the sea. It is built of large hewn blocks of granite, a yard, a yard and a half, or even more, thick. The largest blocks form the foundation. I selected a piece looking very ancient, and hope to show it to you next spring. It was an interesting sight looking seaward, for winter is not yet gone. Huge blocks of frozen breakers lined the shore as far as the eye could see. Farther out at sea a great stretch of ice was visible—all that remained of the frost-bound gulf of a few weeks before. Above us was a cloudless sky and warm sun. We chatted pleasantly with our comrade of former student-days in Edinburgh. What changes have taken place since then! . . . About 12.30 we said 'Good-bye' to Dr. Young, as he rode off in the direction of his distant home (if a Chinese inn can be called by such a name). He expected to reach it after three weeks' travelling."

Early in March—leaving the hospital in charge of his devoted colleague, Dr. Smith—the doctor, with his sister, and their fellow-worker, Rev. D. Murray, paid his last visit to Yen Shan, the hopeful country district where interest in the gospel was so widespread and workers so urgently needed.

A graphic glimpse of his life in Yen Shan is given by Dr. Roberts, in a letter written at this time to Mrs. Gregory, wife of his former pastor at Augustine Church, Edinburgh. "Pen and paper," he writes, "can give but a meagre idea of what a day at a country station means. Before daylight the Christians hang about our door seeking admission; reminding one how our Saviour when on earth, if He wanted time to be alone with God in prayer, had to take it when others were asleep, or fail to get it at all. Morning prayers with the Christians over, tickets are distributed to the patients. On a busy day they will come in an incessant stream from morning to night, leaving one only time for food between—to get which one has to ask the inquisitive crowd to retire outside for a few minutes. The patients come in cart-loads from one or another of the nine hundred villages governed by the Yen Shan city. The carts are drawn by three or four animals—either mules, oxen, or donkeys, according to the affluence of the owner. They all come in their best attire; if young people, in bright-coloured garments—blue, red, green, and purple. . . . Who can tell all the tales of woe that one brief day spent among them records? A father brings his daughter,—who is stone-blind, and has been so for years,—in the hope that the foreigner may have some panacea, and so be the means of restoring sight and lighting up anew the expressionless features of his child. A husband brings his wife, for two years bedridden—the cart is her bed for the day, as she comes with the crowd to consult the Western doctor. Again and again do we meet with those whose sight might have been saved had there only been a medical missionary in the district years ago. Why was there not one? Echo answers, Why? How painful is the thought that many a young Christian doctor is seeking and making his fortune in England, lining his nest and laying up treasures on earth, while these poor souls, and thousands more, are losing sight, hearing, and health, when, had he been present, they might have been saved.

"The day wears on, as I have described, and at night we have a service with all who care to come. What a different meaning attaches to that word in China to what we understand by it at home! Everything is strange to the people—you have to begin at the beginning, and try and show them that there is but one God. This is no easy matter, for a Chinaman's gods are legion. He inherits his grandparents' thoughts about religion; and all his ancestors down through the centuries thought the same. He readily owns that to worship idols is foolish; and yet he continues to do so, because it is fashionable and he would be laughed at if he did not. Then one advances to speak of sin. Here

Chinamen are lamentably in the dark. "What is sin?" you ask a patient. He points to his wounds, it may be, in reply. But beyond a vague idea that he must, somehow or other, have offended the gods, and they are punishing him, he cannot go. His sins do not trouble him—even the best Chinamen tell lies quite comfortably; and as for bad ones, their native atmosphere is falsehood.

"And yet, thank God, His Spirit does quicken them. I have seen the natives bend the head with shame as the word has gone home like an arrow to their hearts. In Yen Shan we have many earnest native Christians—men born of God, I believe, who delight in spiritual things. Oh, how great is the need for more labourers, and how slow we are to take in the meaning of those words of Jesus, 'The field is the world,' and to see that it is white unto harvest!

"We are so often more intent upon buying the wherewithal to make ourselves comfortable, than upon lifting up our eyes to the multitude in every land who are seeking the gracious Teacher if haply they may find Him, or those who, in the dark, are groping towards the light. My heart is sad, as I write, at the critical condition of the Forward Movement, and that already some have counselled us to retreat.

"What! Is there not enough wealth in the Congregational body to carry through a humble scheme for sending out a few more missionaries to benighted lands? May Augustine Church take a noble stand in this matter, as I trust it has already done, and be a noble example of faith, love, and self-sacrifice to all the Congregational churches of Scotland."

This sketch, given by Dr. Roberts in the hope of stirring up more interest in mission work, gives a sufficiently graphic picture of the work he did and the life he lived on that great plain of Chihli. It is only an outline, however, and requires to be filled in by the rough notes in his diary, and the words, eloquent with love, in which his Chinese helpers tell of his never-wearying labours among them. When the day's work of healing the sick was over, and most people might have felt the time for well-earned rest had come, he not only conducted services for any willing to attend, but when everyone else had returned to their homes, little companies of twos and threes still remained. They were the more earnest among the Christians, who, feeling the inspiration of his earnest spiritual life, sat till a late hour on his brick bedstead, talking with the young doctor of the deeper secrets of the spiritual life. "We could stay here all night!" some of them were accustomed to say. A few, touched with the evident weariness of the missionary's countenance (though his heart never wearied), would retire; but others remained till the night was far spent.

During this visit the doctor had the joy of finding that an influential man, in whom he had previously felt much interest, was still holding fast to the faith, and anxious that others should find Christ. This person, Li Lien-pei by name, was a leader in a sect whose followers number many thousands in North China, known as the Mi-mi Chiao, or "Secret Society." Many of these societies are suspected of political aims; but in North China, speaking generally, they are almost entirely religious. They abjure idolatry, abstain from opium, spirits, and smoking, and in many cases are really seekers after truth—dissatisfied with their ancient faiths, and, in the darkness, groping towards the light. When these men become Christians they are usually very sincere and earnest in their belief, and anxious to win their former co-religionists to a knowledge of the Saviour of the world.

It was partly his medical skill that gave Dr. Roberts an entrance into the home of this man; but Li Lien-pei had heard from some of his friends that the religion of Jesus seemed to promise more than any other faith of which they had previously heard, and he sent an urgent invitation to the doctor to come and pay him a visit—sending a conveyance in which he could travel.

He was considered a wealthy man in the district, as he owned 150 Chinese acres of good land; he was also an intelligent man of some education.

Upon Dr. Roberts' arrival at his home, he found it a spacious range of buildings with three courtyards. He was soon engaged in conversation with this interesting inquirer, explaining some of the mysteries of the Christian faith. The private apartments, as is the custom in China, were soon crowded with neighbours anxious to see the foreigner; and to these the doctor proclaimed the glad news of salvation.

After tiffin he was asked to see patients, and several hours were spent in healing people sick of many diseases; but before attending to their bodily needs, in the crowded courtyard he preached to them of Jesus, the great Physician of the soul.

During this visit Dr. Roberts discovered, from conversation with his Chinese friend, that he had first heard of the gospel of Jesus from a man who had been treated in the Tientsin hospital, and become an earnest disciple. He expressed a desire for more light; and the ex-patient invited him to travel with him a distance of about fifty Chinese miles to the nearest mission station, where a native evangelist of the London Missionary Society was in charge. So interested did he become in the new religion, that, after talking through the day, he sat up with his host the whole night long, hearing the doctrines of the Christian faith explained. Returning home, he set to work to read a collection of Christian literature which had been given to him by a friend some years before, and laid aside unread—one, in particular, being *The Evidences of the Christian Faith*, by Dr. Martin of Pekin. This man had over 800 followers, scattered about in thirteen surrounding villages. They looked up to him with much respect; and, finding that he had discarded his old faith for the religion of Jesus, they also were very anxious to be instructed in it. "We do not, however, consider them inquirers as yet," continues Dr. Roberts, "until they learn for themselves something of Christianity."

After this last visit the doctor wrote as follows: "Li Lien-pei holds on. Mary and I spent the night in his house, and had a deeply-interesting meeting there with several professed inquirers, in the room where formerly he presided over the meetings of the Secret Society in his district." The result of this visit was an earnest desire on the part of other educated men to embrace the Christian faith. "The medical work in Yen Shan rejoiced my heart much," he continues. "Thank God for the joy He gives in ministering to the suffering, and especially in districts where there is no other foreign doctor."

It was after this season of happy but exhausting labour that Dr. Roberts returned to Tientsin, to find that during his absence his friend and colleague, Dr. Smith, had been attacked with influenza. Though recovering, he was still far from strong, and it seemed imperative that he should take a change before the great pressure of work during the unhealthy summer season came on. Dr. Smith was not at first willing to leave his post; but his friend brought such pressure to bear upon him,—maintaining that it would be for the benefit of both that he should return invigorated for the hard summer campaign,—that at last he yielded, and consented to take a health-trip to Japan. A stronger reason than usual existed that the summer should see his colleague rejoicing in restored health, since it had been arranged that Dr. Roberts and his sister should take their furlough in the autumn, and it would be difficult for one in sole charge of the work to leave Tientsin.

From the date at which his return home for a season of rest was recommended by the Tientsin Committee, Dr. Roberts' letters all show the joyful anticipation with which he looked forward to the meeting with his happy home-circle and dear friends in England. "You have heard the news," he writes to his sister Annie, " that Mary and I are returning in the autumn, as the hospital work is too much for one man to do two summers successively alone. . . . And thus God is Himself arranging for our seeing you all very soon again. Had we had the arranging of it, I am bound to say we should have preferred staying on till the spring; not that we do not long intensely to see you all again, but that we might stay out as long as possible prior to returning for our parents' golden-wedding celebration in the spring. As the thing has turned out other than we wished, and as there is a general feeling we are doing the proper thing, I conclude it is God's guiding hand. It is almost too good to be true, that by the time you get this we shall be within three and a half months of starting home to see you all, to chat together upon things new and old, to refresh each other in the Lord, and to gather new strength for the terrible fight against Satan's kingdom and power in China and in England."

"Hurrah for our re-union (*D.V.*)! an unbroken family in old Ashfield," he writes to another sister. "The thought is transporting; what will the actual experience be! The joy of seeing you all is very real; there are few joys greater—of earthly joys, none. Love is a flower that has grown well in our home. We have not lost the feeling of brothers and sisters. It is as fresh as when we all sat round the table together in dear old Ashfield. Mary and I are very busy from day to day, never an hour hanging heavily; but we constantly think and speak of the happiness before us in seeing you all. May God grant us this joy!"

A friend of another mission, who had decided to study Medicine at home, and meanwhile spent much time in initiatory work in the hospital, writes: "How his expressive eyes would light up at the thought of his expected meeting with his dear ones. I never knew a man who could smile like your brother. He used to make frequent references to this hope, even during the pressure of hospital work. His enthusiasm about his parents was almost boyish." "The last few months," writes one of his colleagues, "he was so happy in the thought of his home-going. We often laughed at his high spirits. We used to tell him that he had become so versed in Chinese etiquette and speech that he would be making some droll mistakes in England."

But with the thought of home there always came the remembrance of the work that awaited him there, in common with other missionaries on furlough; and he longed intensely to be an instrument in the Lord's hands for awaking the churches of England to the great need of the millions in heathen lands who have never heard their Saviour's name.

"May we come in the power of the Holy Spirit to plead for the great heathen world," he writes to a friend. "May I ask your prayers for us in this matter specially? I feel the difficulty of the work that lies before us in the churches of England. Merely to amuse the people is too low a standpoint to take of deputation-work. The churches need arousing; and God is still willing to use the weak things of this world—those who are looked down upon by men (and such are we in Tientsin)—to accomplish His divine will and stir up the home churches. What a joy it will be if, in any humble measure, we are His instruments to accomplish this purpose! The difficulty is to humble oneself to being merely a voice among men, a branch in the Vine, an instrument in the Divine Master-builder's hand. Friends at home often weaken the message of God's servants by unwise praise,—*e.g.* 'How well you spoke!' or, 'How earnest and eloquent you were!' should he happen to be a good speaker,—till, alas! the Holy Spirit is grieved, and, pride puffing up the heart, the speaker loses his anointing with power which comes only through the baptism of the Holy Spirit." To his sister he added, in a letter received after the news of his death: "Pray for us, dear Annie, that we may return to you all in the fulness of the blessing of the gospel of peace—meek, lowly, humble, mighty in the power of the Spirit to testify to the churches those things which God has wrought among the Gentiles in China."

So prayerfully and earnestly did Frederick Roberts anticipate taking his share in the work which he then thought awaited him in England.

It is not wonderful that many who knew him re-echoed the words of his senior colleague, Rev. Jonathan Lees, who said that his first thought upon hearing the news of his death, was regret that the Christians of England would never know the beautiful spirit and whole-hearted consecration of the man who had won so many Chinese hearts for Christ. A friend of another mission, who was the guest of Dr. Roberts and his sister not many months before his Home-call, writes: "I have met few others in China whose lives have spoken to me more distinctly as to the blessed possibility of living a very busy life, and yet of living in the sweetest communion with our Lord and Master."

His life was truly a very busy one; and yet he had always "a heart at leisure from itself to soothe and sympathise," and was ever ready either to comfort the sorrowful or rejoice with the glad. If he heard of any case of serious illness in the Settlement among the Europeans, whose friends were not numerous, he always found time to pay them a cheery, friendly visit.

"I have the most grateful recollections of his kindness to me personally in times of sickness," writes a young business man. "I lay seriously ill once in the Settlement hospital; and notwithstanding the many calls upon his time in the Chinese hospital, his kind care and attention to all my wants, temporal and spiritual, were simply boundless. Of all the friends who visited me, none were so welcome and none so constant. His sunshiny disposition made his very presence, as if by magic, impart fresh life and comfort to me. He used to read the Bible to me daily, and pray that we might become conformed to the image of Christ."

A few extracts from the letters he wrote at intervals to this friend, which serve as a specimen of the words of loving, earnest counsel he sent to many others, run thus :—

"The feeling of utter helplessness on our part to attain to God's ideal of manhood and standard of perfection is our only safeguard, is it not? If only coupled with it there is faith in His existence and omnipotence, then the problem is solved. All said and done, to live up to the Bible standard of perfection is no easy matter; but let us press on, and hope and trust in Jesus and His Spirit, who will accomplish the work for us. . . . The parasitic tendency in all of us is humiliating—we are men-worshippers almost by instinct. . . . Do not be discouraged if friends are few: there is a Friend who sticketh closer than a brother."

Dr. Roberts was always deeply interested in any work he thought likely to increase sympathy with Foreign Missions. He took an active part in the preparation of the memoir of his beloved predecessor, Dr. Mackenzie, reading the manuscript through with the writer, and suggesting many alterations and some additions. " Let us be anxious only for one thing," he used to say—"that it is baptized with prayer;" and he almost always engaged in prayer before or after his work upon it. A short sketch of Gilmour's life was also written with his help. Upon the writer's return to England after its publication, she sent him a copy, and, in acknowledgment, he writes thus :—

"My sister and I have just returned from Yen Shan. One's brain-cells, never very calm, seem all confused after an hour's racing in 'rickshas over the Tientsin streets from the Hsi-kou Wan-tsz, where we landed; but I must send you a few lines, as on my arrival I found a welcome letter from you and a copy of *The Story of James Gilmour*. . . . I am thankful also to get some of dear Gilmour's letters to me in a permanent form. As I glanced over them this evening, how they brought up old times and memories to my mind once more! They brought that sainted veteran in the Lord's army so near to me."

It has often been noticed by those who have been bereaved of their dear ones, that during the last months of their earthly life they were much occupied with thoughts about the land beyond the river, and the life eternal which awaits us there.

To Frederick Roberts the dividing line between the two worlds was never that barrier grim and fearsome it is to many, even of Christian souls. I remember once, after an illness, speaking of the rest of the life beyond. "That is not quite my thought," he replied, smiling in his bright way; and, opening a Bible at Rev. xxii., "'His servants shall serve Him': that is my idea of heaven—active service for our Master, without weariness, and without sin too."

He often dropped remarks to those who knew him best, which made them feel how slight, to his perception, was the veil which separated things seen from things unseen.

As a general rule, however, he always gave one the impression of a man whose life was brimful of gladness and happy work, who had no desire to rest from his labours. "Fred wanted to live to be old like father," writes his sister Mary, "for there seemed so much to be done, and so few to do it." The motto of his life might well have been the lines, applied to another able and active worker—

> "I ask no heaven till earth be Thine,
> Nor glory crown while work of mine
> Remaineth here. When earth shall shine
> Among the stars, her stains wiped out, her captives free,
> Her songs sweet music unto Thee—
> For crown give, Lord, new work to me."

Nevertheless, scattered thickly throughout his letters during the last year of his life, are constant allusions to the world beyond; and his sister tells how, during the last months, he derived great strength and joy from the study of his old professor, Principal Edwards', exposition of the 1st Corinthians, especially the portion referring to the resurrection.

A few months only before his death he wrote, of the passing away of a friend of college-days:—

"Poor J— A—: only poor, though, from our point of view. Doubly blessed from his own standpoint, for he lives 'in

God's sight,' as the original version puts it. 'In God's sight all are alive' (Luke xx. 38). His career has been a short one; but he ran it with the Saviour ever in view, and he has reached the goal before any one of us, his companions. Who will be the next to hear the summons?"

"'Life passes away as a dream', the Chinese say," he writes at a later period. "But we shall awake to find that the future life is the grand consummation of the present, and heaven and its higher service ours in Jesus Christ."

To his sister Lily he wrote: "One day, dear,—when and where we know not, and it matters not very much,—we shall be able to speak face to face of the King, and of His work and His matchless grace in saving us and calling us to His blessed service. Lord grant that in that day we may have no cause to be ashamed in Him. . . .

"Most of us are a good half-way on life's journey, eh! Some farther on still. But as earthly visions and possibilities become more and more confined, what about the heavenly? Will not these seem more real and more within our grasp, and shall we not all feel that we are here only for a brief season, and that the heavenly ties are becoming more numerous year by year?"

To his sister Ala he writes: "It is dawning upon me in all its fulness that man is of few days. Our little story will soon be told, dear, and our race run. What about the laurels, the 'well done' from Jesus' lips, the smile of welcome from Him? This is the sweetest thought of life: that beyond the scenes of this fleeting present there is a hereafter of personal existence, and that in heaven. Pray much that we may be good and faithful servants. What a depth of meaning lies in these words. If His searching eyes can scan our work for Him and call it good, how very good that work needs to be! And then 'faithful,' always at our post, reliable, steadfast,—working for Him as if He were in person visibly at our side. May He graciously give us this portion. We ask no more. Pray, dear, that whether we see the fruit or others see it, we may daily have the heart-conviction that our work is owned as His work and that He is pleased with us. If only He says, 'Well done, good and faithful servant' that is more than enough for me. He will have more than rewarded me. Pray that it may be my burning desire to do His will in everything—there is nothing higher than this in heaven or in earth. . . . I am looking forward to the time when we shall refresh each other again with chats over the sunny days of yore, and the still sunnier days before us in heaven. There is no disguising the fact heaven is becoming more visible on the eastern horizon. It's not a mirage, but a sure and certain hope that one day even our feet shall stand within those pearly gates and join in the song of Moses and the Lamb."

CHAPTER XV

THE BRINK OF THE RIVER

"High honour theirs to prove,
   Still stands redemption's sign ;
Not lost the type of love,
   Nor quenched the martyr line."
                                    ENSOR.

'See, this picture is not Death,
   But risen Life ; another hero-face
Stamped with high victory before he fell :
Triumphant where he fail'd, crown'd on his cross,
   And, like his Lord, self-sentenced to his doom."
                                    E. FURSKE.

IT is recorded of many of the most distinguished of the Lord's servants, that they have expressed a desire to die in harness—that the Master's Home-call should find them in the midst of their labours. This joy was granted to Frederick Roberts in abundant measure. His last letter—written only three days before his last illness—to his beloved parents is a record of loving service.

"I am keeping well, and have any amount of agreeable work," he writes. "This week brought a nice letter from Ala. She says the Enderby Christians were praying for the patients very earnestly, and that they asked for 'showers of blessing.' On the very day the letter arrived, two patients gave in their names as applicants for baptism. I was struck by the coincidence. How much are the prayers of dear friends at home associated with blessing received here! Eternity will reveal many answers to fervent prayers offered by some obscure Christians at home. This last week I had one or two anxious cases in the wards. First, a case of stone in the bladder. The man had been a sufferer for seventeen years. An operation under chloroform was necessary. Under the gracious blessing of God, he is now convalescent. You will, I know, join me in praising God for this mercy. The second serious case was severe fever,—temp. 104°,—which for six days resisted powerful drugs; pushed hard. It being only malarial fever, as I judged, I felt that something active must be done to break the back of the fever, otherwise the man must die. So, giving two very powerful doses of fever and diaphoretic medicine within an hour, I cast the man upon the providential care of God. The result was all we could desire. The man, after enormous perspiration, regained normal temperature, and has been well ever since. I was specially conscious of the goodness of God to him and to me in our hour of extremity. This poor man was far from home; and to have died far away from home and friends would have been very sad for him, and very regrettable in every respect. The third case was the aged, and apparently much-trusted, cashier in the Viceroy's camp (one of the camps in Tientsin). He came in with congestion of the liver, threatening to go on to abscess, very breathless and in great pain, not having slept for many days. Six native doctors had given him up. He said, 'If you heal me, four Taou-tais (high city magistrates) will be most grateful to you.' Poor old man! We took him in, and the first night he was so ill I feared he would pass away in the night. He also is now recovering, I think. We cannot but acknowledge the goodness of God in the matter."

Another letter, of about the same date, was written to his colleague, Mr. Bryson, who had shortly before left on furlough. It was filled with information about the various native helpers and the progress of the different branches of the work, showing how constantly and earnestly he thought and prayed not only for blessing upon the medical department, but the whole work of the mission.

"Our last remembrance of Tientsin," writes his friend, Mr. Stanley Smith, "was Dr. Roberts' loving ministry on behalf of our little son, whose illness has practically come to an end, owing, under God, to his skill. He looked to me much run down, and so much thinner, especially in the face, to what he was before; but just the same bright fellow, full of cheer,—exuberant, I might say,—and yet, running through all his converse, that humility and self-forgetfulness which seemed to have become wrought into the very fibre of his being."

"He had great sympathy with the members of the C.I.M.," writes Mr. G. W. Clarke of Tientsin, "and made special arrangements with the doctors of the Community to attend them in time of sickness."

To many a lonely mission station in the far interior the news of Dr. Roberts' Home-call went as a crushing personal sorrow. One of these solitary workers had been down to Tientsin for medical advice, and under Dr. Roberts' skilful treatment and brotherly kindness was restored to health again. Returning to his lonely outpost, a few weeks brought him the news that his friend had been called to the higher service. His letter is only given as a specimen of many others, telling of loving deeds done, as the outcome of a heart which brimmed over with "love for the brethren":—

"Your letter brought me the saddest of news—dear Dr. Roberts gone. I am staggered, bewildered, and overwhelmed. I went to the only place of comfort, the Throne of Grace . . .

"I am sure those of us who knew Roberts and learned to love him, will never forget him; and that the remembrance of him will ever be an inspiration enabling us to take heart afresh, knowing that a short time only will bring us to Roberts and other kindred spirits.

"He was the last foreigner I saw as I left Tientsin, and I have seen no foreigner since. As I was getting into my jinricksha outside the C.I.M. premises to join my boat above the native city, Dr. Roberts said, 'Here, dear brother, take this,' and placed in my hand a beautiful rose that was almost fully opened. 'Don't be long at a time without taking a change to see someone,' he said, referring to my lonely station. 'Good-bye, and may God give you many stories of conversion to tell.' As my jinricksha sped along, I turned round to take a last look at him. Ah, little did I think it was my last look in this life! The rose he gave me I kept fresh in a cup of water on the road till it fell to pieces, never looking at it without thinking of the giver. I had a letter to write him by this mail of things which he had asked me to let him know about. Now he is where there is no need to know of such things."

The story of Dr. Roberts' last illness is best told in his sorrowing sister's letter to their bereaved parents.

"Fred was quite well a week before he died," she writes, "only looking tired; but I put it down to the fact that he had more work than usual to do in the hospital, Dr. Smith being away for a much-needed change.

"It was only on Tuesday, May 29th, that he felt poorly. That evening we went out to dinner at Mr. Verity's of the American Mission. After dinner Fred went, as usual, to his meeting at the hospital, returning to Mr. Verity's soon after nine o'clock.

"We spent a very helpful evening. Mr. Pike was there, of whom I am sure Fred will have told you in his letters. After we had been singing hymns for a while, he suggested that we might tell some of our Christian experience. I remember a little of Fred's. He said he had recently been thinking much of those words in Jude, 'Kept for Jesus Christ' (R.V.). Then he went on to explain them. How kept—for what? by whom?

"When he had finished his remarks, some one said: 'Why, doctor, that was sufficient for a sermon!' And so it was; but he was always the same. He seemed to live in an atmosphere of heaven, and he could always give you some beautiful thoughts on a passage of Scripture. . . . The morning following the evening spent at Mr. Verity's, I noticed he looked very white, and did not take his breakfast. I asked the reason. He laughed, and said, 'Mary, I do like to see your face when anything is the matter with me.' Then he added, 'I have a little fever, and have not been well in the night.' I insisted that he should not go over to the hospital prayers, but return to his room. This he did, and never got up again. From the first day his illness took a serious form. He could retain no food: even ice, if taken freely, brought on vomiting. The fever was remittent in character, varying from 100° to 105°.

"At the beginning of his illness he said to me, 'This is a great cross to me; but the Lord has sent it, to make me more sympathetic with the patients in the hospital. How many times I have treated men with the same kind of fever. Pray for me, Mary, that I may be patient.' His illness, all through, was very beautiful, notwithstanding that he was in great distress and could not rest. His mind was full of God; and he would be constantly praying or asking me to pray, or repeating passages of Scripture.

"In the evening, when the sun had gone down and the light had almost faded, he sometimes thought he could sleep a little, and would say, 'Mary, sing me to sleep.' Then I would sing softly the hymn father is so fond of, 'Son of my soul, Thou Saviour dear, It is not night if Thou art near.' During his illness he constantly spoke of our going home. Once he said, 'How strange that I should be ill just as they are getting our letters about returning this autumn.'"

Leaving his sister's letter for a time, I turn to the accounts given by others of his colleagues and friends who nursed him through the short, sharp illness that carried him home. "The disease was very mysterious. It seemed as if some virulent fever had struck at once at the life-centres; and he never was quite himself from the beginning of the sickness to the end. Perhaps the general Godward turn of his mind is the sweetest remembrance of those sad days. On the third day of his illness, Dr. Frazer, who was his medical attendant, told Mrs. Dr. King there was no hope, as he had no strength or constitution to resist the fever. The fever had completely left him on the Tuesday, but he had no strength to rally after it. I believe he was completely broken down, shattered by overwork—first of all in Yen Shan, and then during Dr. Smith's absence in Japan. He had gleams of calm during his delirium, in which he spoke so nicely of leaving the castles of iniquity and sin, to go beyond to the many mansions. We all did our best for him, but God considered the harvest of his life ripe, and reaped it."

"On the third day of his last illness I saw him," writes Dr. Shrubshall, an old fellow-student passing through Tientsin at the time; "and though the painful change from health to sickness was so marked, yet all hoped to see him again in the midst of his hospital work. He was filled with gratitude at the kindness of friends, and this led him to express his sense of the wonderful love of God, and in prayer and praise to lead our thoughts to heavenly things. Later, as unconsciousness crept on, still his language was often that of prayer for others, and the wish of his wearied heart to depart and see in His beauty the Master he loved and had so faithfully served."

"Dr. Shrubshall and I sat up with him," writes his colleague, Rev. A. King, "the night the crisis came and consciousness gave way to wild delirium. As the day broke and the sparrows began to twitter, he folded his hands and looked upward, saying, 'The birds teach us a lesson, don't they: as soon as it's daylight they sing praises to God'; and then he prayed that Dr. Shrubshall and I might be used by the Lord to bring many Chinese to the knowledge of the truth. He spoke little about dying; but up to the day before he passed away he followed closely the course of his sickness. He often insisted on seeing the clinical thermometer himself; and at times he felt his own pulse, and then said, 'Well, well!' as if he could not understand it."

"Fred was only unconscious the last day," continues his sister. "It was early Tuesday morning when they called me; and I observed a great change in him from the previous night. He was delirious. He threw his arms round me, and said, 'Mary, I am dying.' I could not speak; but presently, dear Chassy Kerr, thinking of you all at home, whispered to me to try and get some last messages. . . . I said, 'Fred, dear, I am going to write to mother—have you any message?' and this was his reply: 'Yes, give my love, and tell them facts; but, above all, tell them to rejoice—rejoice that this their son was lost and is found; was dead and is alive again for evermore.'

"He lingered on all that day, very delirious; but even in his delirium his words were of Christ, and he literally preached the gospel to those around him. All that night he was very quiet; but I did not go to rest, for we knew the end was near. If he spoke at all, it was sure to be a verse of Scripture. I heard him say, 'In my Father's house are many mansions; if it were not so I would have told you. I go to prepare a place for you.' 'There is no other name under heaven given among men, whereby we may be saved.'"

"A few hours before his death," writes his colleague, Rev. D. Murray, "I asked him if he was resting in Jesus. 'Oh yes,' he replied very readily; 'there is none but Him.' I repeated the first verse of the 46th Psalm, 'God is our refuge and strength.' He immediately went on with the rest of the quotation himself, repeating several verses.

"In his last hours, when his strength was waning and memory failing, it was surprising to note how aptly and correctly he quoted passage after passage of his Lord's words, clearly indicating that they had entered into the very fibre of his life."

"About 1 A.M. I went into his room again, after a short absence," continues his sister. "I sat down by his side and took his hand. He recognised me at once, and seemed surprised to see me at that hour. 'Mary,' he said, 'is that you? who sent you?' I said, 'The doctor.' He smiled sweetly, oh so sweetly! and seemed so glad to see me. I felt I could not trouble him to talk, for he was by this time extremely weak and very distressed.

"I said, 'Fred, dear, Jesus loves you; and he repeated the words, 'Yes, Jesus loves me,' changing the pronoun. I think these were his last words, except a Chinese word which he repeated twice over. Fifteen minutes after, our darling had finished with earth—it was just a gentle falling asleep at last."

"His last word," writes another watcher, "was the Chinese exclamation 'Keo-la—Keo-la!' meaning, 'Enough—enough!' repeated twice over in a loud, strong voice; and then he slept quietly away into peace. His falling asleep made me see a new beauty in the words 'Asleep in Jesus.' The prayer of Jesus prevailed over our prayers, 'Father, I will that they also whom Thou hast given Me be with Me where I am.'"

"For myself, I feel heaven nearer to me since he was called Home," writes a friend of another mission. "I learnt many lessons from the closing hours in that upper room. What a privilege it was to minister to him, and to note his love, faith, and confident hope as he descended the valley. I felt at the time the reality of the unseen, and saw the grace Christ can give to His followers in their last hours. As I stepped out on to the verandah the dawn was beginning to break. It seemed a type of that eternal day into which he had entered; and there came into my heart an earnest longing to be like him, and a desire to catch his spirit. If his dear ones only knew the help his life has been to me and many others, they would be comforted in their sorrow by the thought of his continued influence."

"When the serious nature of Dr. Roberts' illness was known," writes another missionary, "many prayers ascended to God to spare His servant, if it was His will. Dr. Frazer was most anxious about him. 'Roberts is burning away,' he said, 'and he has no fuel. He is a wonder. Most careful in his work, he has done twenty-five years' work in seven years: a man of his nature could not go slow.' He called the disease malignant malarial fever. It was of a strange type—new here. There were only three cases in Tientsin, and all died. Roberts had no stamina, due to long-continued overstrain. You can't reason about such men. It's no use blaming them—they cannot help it. It's no use thinking of them as not having lived to do their work. His life of seven years will tell more than if it had been spread over twenty."

"It is remarkable," writes Mr. G. W. Clarke, "that Dr. Roberts died in the same house as Dr. Mackenzie. Once, near the end, he pointed to a portion of the room as if beholding his beloved predecessor, and said clearly, 'John Kenneth Mackenzie.' It was my privilege to perform some of the last offices for our beloved friend. Just before we placed his body in the coffin, a member who was under discipline, and had been suspended from church-fellowship for a time, called and asked, 'How is Dr. Roberts?' 'The Lord has called him to heaven,' I said. I took him upstairs to see the remains of his kind and faithful friend. Poor man, he burst into tears, and sobbed aloud, saying, 'Oh, my friend—my friend!' We carried the coffin to the Wilton House of the L.M.S. It was covered with wreaths of flowers sent by foreign and native friends, and was carried to the hearse by the native hospital workers."

Sad indeed is the story of how the tidings of the beloved physician's death was received by the sick patients who filled the hospital wards. "Many a lip quivered as the news passed round, 'Lu Tai-fu ssu liao' (Dr. Roberts is dead)," writes one who visited the hospital that morning. "It is not usual to see a Chinaman in tears; but I saw many weeping when they heard they would see him no more. One poor lad, whose arm he had saved, wept bitterly, refusing to be comforted. It was indeed painful to see so much suffering without a physician, and to note the pathetic looks and hopeless manner of those to whom Dr. Roberts had been a ministering angel."

The funeral took place at 5.30 the same day, in the English burying-place in Tientsin,—a sacred spot indeed to those who watch with prayerful hearts the coming of Christ's kingdom in China.

It is on the edge of the bare, desolate plain of Chihli; but loving hands have made this little corner fair with trees and flowering shrubs. There, until the resurrection morning, sleeps, by the side of his well-loved friends, Mackenzie of Tientsin and Gilmour of Mongolia, all that was mortal of Frederick Roberts.

"The funeral service was half in Chinese, conducted by Rev. C. Stanley of the American Mission, in the mortuary chapel, and half in English, by Rev. J. Innocent of the English Methodist Mission, at the grave. A great host of Chinese were there; many weeping—their best friend gone. Before the mourners separated, the sweet, hopeful strains of the Christians' 'Good-Night' floated on the summer air."

He has gone from us; and yet no one who knew and loved him, and had the opportunity of faintly estimating the influence of his consecrated life upon the Chinese, as well as his fellow-workers, can feel for a moment that it was an unfinished or broken life.

"He leaves a fragrant memory here for holiness of life, and a single eye to the glory of God and the service of his fellow-men," writes a colleague. "His humility and strong sense of righteousness, along with a sympathetic bearing in all his dealings with the Chinese, quite won their affection."

"He won the confidence of the Chinese as fully as the affectionate admiration of his colleagues," writes the Rev. J. Lees. "His charming gentleness and unassuming manner, linked with singular firmness and common sense, enabled him to be of great service to the Native Church. Many of his patients bless God for the double cure given to them through his care."

"His was a noble life—a splendid life," writes another colleague. "I wish I could picture it as I saw it and felt it. He came to China as a medical missionary, and no self-interest marred his consecration. I could never enter the hospital wards without seeing a vision of this ministering angel. Would that I could give some adequate idea of the man as he lived—the most saintly, the most laborious, the most efficient missionary! But his was not the saintliness of the desert—he was a man of the people, and lived as a man among men. If humility, gentleness, unselfishness, cheerfulness, devoutness, and charitableness go to make up a saint, then Roberts was one. There was a wonderful completeness and symmetry about his character. He was strong yet tender, diligent but not fretful, able yet humble, unselfish to a degree and liberal, yet conscientious in little things. There were in his life no great bursts of soon-spent enthusiasm, flying before every passing breeze and dying down into a calm, but the steady motion of a steamer, that goes on day and night without stopping, till at last it drops anchor in port, receiving an abundant entrance into the desired haven."

The testimony of other fellow-workers in the North China Mission of the London Missionary Society all tell the same story, of a life beautiful in its Christlikeness and entire devotion. "My impressions are only the general ones—that he was one of the sweetest, noblest characters I ever met," writes one. "His name calls up many happy and sacred memories, and always will," adds another. "He never can go out of my life, if I live to be a hundred years old."

It is not possible to quote more from the many loving tributes to the holy and stimulating influence of Dr. Roberts' life upon his fellow-workers which have come from various parts of the great Chinese Empire. "We thank God that we ever knew him," is repeated over in various ways.

"The grave has been bright with many-coloured flowers," says a recent letter from Tientsin. "Many visit it to reconsecrate their all to the Master's service. I often go."

And the Chinese testimonies to the blessed influence of the life which Frederick Roberts laid down so joyfully on his Lord's altar, for China's redemption, are not less striking.

Even during his lifetime I have more than once known Chinese Christians remark: "We never saw anyone so much like the Lord Jesus as Dr. Roberts is: he dresses our wounds with his own hands; and the poorer a man is, the more care he lavishes upon him." "Lu Tai-fu has gone to heaven, has he?" exclaimed a Chinaman in this country, when the sad news reached him. "Ah, we all used to say he was so like the Lord, and now he has gone to be with Him."

The translation of a Chinese letter, sent by the native hospital workers as a small tribute to his memory, runs thus:—

"Since Dr. Roberts took charge of the hospital, now more than six years ago, his fame as a doctor in saving men has been widely spread abroad. Every day between 80 and 100 out-patients were attended to, and between 40 and 50 indoor patients. The number of those who received relief during the six years must have been very great. Not only were they healed of bodily sickness, but many, trusting in the Lord, were saved in soul, and led to give thanks to God unceasingly for His mercy. The members of the church and the hospital patients, without exception, feel deeply grateful because in his life Dr. Roberts so truly embodied the compassionate spirit of our Saviour. He spent himself in saving others, and shrank from no amount of toil; so that, in tending the sick and preaching the gospel, he hardly seemed, night or day, to give himself a moment's repose. His heart's blood he expended to the last drop. Alas! in the fifth month of the present year he was attacked by a severe sickness, and left the world to return to heaven, and has entered into the great blessing of rest. When the sad news reached the patients and Christians, there was not one who did not mourn his loss, rendering honour to his virtue and recalling the memory of his kindness. We shall never cease to give thanks at the remembrance of his goodness.

"A TRIBUTE FROM THE WORKERS IN THE
L.M.S. HOSPITAL, TIENTSIN."

Extracts from a translation of a letter sent by the Christians of Chi-Chow, one of the country districts of the London Missionary Society, to Dr. Roberts' sorrowing parents, run thus:—

"Dr. Roberts' geniality, goodness, and charity have long been known to us. Now that we hear of his return to God, we all shed tears and are sad-hearted. We wished him to live long, but God wished him to go; and God's will is better than man's. The Bible refers to some men of whom the world was not worthy; and although our hearts are full of grief, still there is joy in it, because God does not wish such good men to live long amid the afflictions of earth, but takes them away to enjoy heaven's delights. . . . You, honoured friends, having heard of your son's death, must be sad, and are weeping and cannot prevent it, owing to feelings of flesh and blood which cannot be described. You will do well to remember that Dr. Roberts in this life was an earnest disciple of Jesus Christ, and in the life to come his reward will be great. We therefore beseech you not to grieve beyond measure, because in all His doings God has an aim and a plan. Our wisdom can never fathom it; therefore let us be restful in Him, and submit to His will. We also think of Miss Roberts on her voyage home. May God constantly protect her, and bring her to you in safety. We write these few words in the hope that you, honoured ones, will receive greatly of the Spirit's comfort. Peace be with you.

"Signed, on behalf of over 300 converts, by
 NINETEEN NATIVE PREACHERS AND DEACONS."

Dr. Roberts took a warm interest in Chinamen of every rank with whom he came in contact. Some of the Chinese doctors who had studied Medicine under his predecessor were much attached to him.

One of these gentlemen writes thus:—

"MY DEAR MRS. BRYSON,—I hope you will excuse me for the delay in replying to your letter asking me to give you a short sketch of my acquaintance with our late dearly-loved mutual friend, Dr. F. C. Roberts. The delay is due to the present war going on between China and Japan. By the death of Dr. Roberts the Chinese have lost a sincere friend. He was liked by all the Chinese. His kind attitude towards the people among whom he worked brought him many friends. His persuasive and sweet manner gave him great opportunities for doing medical missionary work. His immaculate character and noble life inspired great confidence in his preaching when he was not doing medical work. He did five men's work. His professional skill had few equals. His reputation, like that of my late beloved

Dr. Mackenzie, his predecessor, was known throughout every corner of North China. He was a true friend to my people; and he helped me in more than one way, professionally and otherwise. He always had an encouraging word for those who were in trouble. I have seen him trying to comfort those who were in trouble for hours. He was, indeed, a patient man. He was truly a missionary of Jesus Christ. His loss is mourned by both Christians and heathen. I hope this will not reach you too late.—With kind regards, yours very truly, KIN TA-KING."

Another letter says:—
"Words are inexpressible for the great loss we have sustained in the death of Dr. Roberts, in whom we placed much hope for the saving of our countrymen, both in body and soul. We lose—he gains. He has well earned his rest. The Lord reigneth. We mourn that we are temporarily separated from him; but there is a joy to think we shall meet again in our Father's house."

Such are a few of the testimonies coming from sorrowing Chinese hearts of the influence of Dr. Roberts' holy life and work among them. People say that Chinamen are phlegmatic and not easily affected; yet for many a long year to come the name of Dr. Roberts will awaken memories of skilful tenderness and Christlike love in many a Chinese heart.

A missionary connected with the National Bible Society of Scotland relates how, three months after Dr. Roberts' death, after a month's travelling he reached a remote city in the province of Shantung. While selling books and speaking to the people of the truths of the gospel, he was suddenly accosted by a man who strongly recommended the books to the people, advising them to make purchases. He explained that some time before, while on a visit to Tientsin, he had fallen seriously ill, and was induced to enter the Mission hospital. Dr. Roberts not only cured his disease, but quite won his affection by his great kindness. When strong enough to return home, he found himself without funds for the journey; these Dr. Roberts supplied. With many expressions of gratitude he told this story to the curious crowd, winning at once their kindly sympathy for the man who was a countryman of Dr. Roberts. Some difficulty was experienced later on in hiring a barrow (a common mode of conveyance for man and baggage in that district), but Dr. Roberts' Chinese friend came to the rescue. He procured a barrow and two men to push it, adding, " If at daybreak, when you wish to start, either of these men fail you, I will act as your barrow-man myself"—and he did so. " It was a constant pleasure to have him with us," continues the missionary. " Often on the road he persuaded people to buy the books, putting in a word of commendation about them. This is but one case; but there is no doubt that, far and wide over the plains of Northern China, there are very many hearts that think gratefully of Dr. Roberts."

On another occasion, an hospital assistant, travelling in a part of Chihli infested by robbers, was suddenly set upon by a small armed band, and ordered to deliver up all his goods and strip himself of his garments. While preparing to comply with their demands, one of the banditti drew nearer, and, regarding him very closely, exclaimed, " We must not touch this man—he is from the Hall of the Healing in Tientsin. I was there a few months ago, and received free medicine and much kindness from the foreign doctor." The men's threatening attitude changed at once; and they rode off, leaving the hospital assistant to pursue his way in peace.

On the departure of any patient from the hospital who was interested in the truth, it was Dr. Roberts' custom to defer baptism, giving the man the address of the mission station nearest to his home, with whatever Society it might be connected, earnestly advising him to connect himself at once with the Christian Church there. He thought this arrangement better for the convert himself; and his work was ever, not so much for the London Missionary Society (though he was warmly attached to his own Society), as for the Lord and Master who had called him to that service.

A missionary of the Methodist Mission writes:—

" Among our students we have now a bright man, saved, through God's help, by Dr. Roberts from an opium-smoker's grave. He is now a decided Christian, and has given a chapel to our mission. A station on the Grand Canal has also been opened for us by one of Dr. Roberts' ex-patients; and as far north as the Presbyterian Mission in Manchuria, men have become Christians as the result of his life and words."

Frederick Roberts gave himself and all that he possessed to the service of the Master he loved so intensely, to win China for Christ and hasten the coming of the Kingdom in that dark land; and it is not too much to say that his life and his death have brought nearer the day of that great Empire's redemption. Surely there are many young hearts, which have devoted the strength of their youth to the Lord, who will press forward to fill the places so frequently left vacant.

It has been truly said that missions are costly: they always have been—they always will be. "They belong to a costly order of things. They exist to realise the redemptive purposes of God. . . . They cost millions—they cost men; and as the odour from the broken alabaster box of youthful life steals round the world, we admit this ointment might have been sold for a great price and given to the ends of nineteenth-century conservation." Yet surely there is no greater joy in this world to the Christian heart, than that which comes from laying down our best and dearest at the nail-pierced feet of the world's Redeemer—our blessed Lord and Master!

Handsome cloth, large crown 8vo, 3s. 6d. post free,

THE DOMINION OF CHRIST.

The Claims of Foreign Missions in the Light of Modern Religious Thought and a Century of Experience.

By WILLIAM PIERCE,
Minister of New Court Chapel, Tollington Park.

Rev. H. W. Horwill, M.A.—"A masterly book."

Rev. George Cousins in "L.M.S. Chron."—"We direct the attention of our readers to a volume from the facile pen of the Rev. W. Pierce. Lucid in thought, chaste in diction, earnest in spirit, enthusiastic and hopeful in tone, and thoroughly practical in aim, this busy North London pastor passes under review the whole missionary enterprise in general, and the L.M.S. in particular. We heartily commend his book, and desire for it a large circulation."

Times, Weekly Edition.—"The book is in no sense official, and will be none the less valued for that."

Expository Times.—"What sermons can do for us is to light the spark of interest, and Mr. Pierce's sermons are admirably fitted for that indispensable service."

Llanelly Mercury.—"An excellent and timely volume; a careful perusal will stimulate workers in Christ's cause."

Guardian.—"Mr. Pierce writes in the true missionary spirit, and his book is instructive on the vocation of the worker, and the important branch of medical and hospital work, both for men and women."

Bookseller.—"The author is throughout animated by a desire to strengthen the cause of missions."

Medical Missions.

Illustrated with 21 full-page Plates, neat cloth boards, cr. 8vo, 3s. 6d.,

PIONEERING IN MOROCCO.

A Record of Seven Years' Medical Mission Work in the Palace and the Hut.

By DR. ROBERT KERR.

Regions Beyond.—"A simple, unvarnished narrative of work in this unhappy country."

Scotsman.—"Admirably illustrated; one learns a great deal about Morocco and the Moors from within as well as from without."

British Weekly.—"Dr. Kerr's experiences are frankly and simply written, and the get-up of the book reflects much credit on the publisher."

Echo.—"Is a timely work. It might be rather awkward for Dr. Kerr if his book were translated into the vernacular while he himself remained in the land."

Christian Leader.—"There is a twofold interest in this book. It is at once a lively record of travel, and a chronicle of self-denying missionary service in one of the darkest places of the earth. Dr. Kerr's book is well calculated to awaken sympathy; it is brightly written and admirably illustrated."

H. R. ALLENSON, 30 PATERNOSTER ROW, LONDON, E.C.

SECOND EDITION.

Handsome cloth, large crown 8vo, 3s. 6d., with Three Portraits.

JOSEPH SIDNEY HILL,
First Bishop in Western Equatorial Africa.

By ROSE E. FAULKNER.

With an Introduction by the Right Rev. Bishop STUART.

SOME OPINIONS OF THE PRESS.

India's Women.—"So full of stirring scenes and lively anecdotes as to compel the attention of the most casual reader . . . likely to take a high rank among the biographies of English missionaries."

Rev. J. E. Page in "Fellowship."—"What completer proof can we give of the deep interest of this book than this, that we read it straight through at a sitting, and finished it amid tears which would not be held back ?"

Times, Weekly Edition.—"The life of Joseph Sidney Hill was not a long one, but it well deserved the modest space devoted to it in Miss Faulkner's volume."

Literary World.—"Well written and full of interest."

Otago Workman.—"The simple story of an earnest life, devoted to the noblest of callings, and ended amid a halo of glory. We recommend the book to the perusal of every one."

New Zealand Mail.—"The biography is a graceful and sympathetic tribute to the memory of a philanthropic and unselfish man, whose name still remains green in the memory of the citizens of Auckland. . . . Contains capital portraits."

C. M. Gleaner.—"We wish specially and earnestly to recommend the Memoir of Bishop Hill. It is just the book to give away, particularly to young men and boys."

Mr. Eugene Stock in the "C. M. Intelligencer."—"We trust the volume may have a wide circulation, and be used of God to awaken in many a livelier sense of responsibility as regards a world that is lying in the darkness of heathendom. To a young man the story it tells should be an inspiration."

Christian.—"A large number of Christian friends on three continents at least will welcome this biography, and through it our brother being dead will yet speak, calling every reader to the life of happy consecrated service which he lived."

H. R. ALLENSON, 30 PATERNOSTER ROW, LONDON, E.C.

VALUABLE NEW EDITIONS OF PHILLIPS BROOKS' WORKS.

Neat cloth, uniform with Phillips Brooks' Works issued by Messrs. Macmillan, crown 8vo, 5s.,

LECTURES ON PREACHING.

BY THE RIGHT REV. PHILLIPS BROOKS.

Expository Times.—"We have already had more than one edition in this country. But Mr. Allenson has done very well to let us have another, and to publish it in uniformity with the other books by Phillips Brooks which we possess. It is a book of permanent value."

Baptist Magazine.—"They constitute a really great book on preaching. There are some books which men will not willingly let die, and this is indisputably one of them."

Freeman.—"Simply impossible for a sensible man to read these lectures without gaining a new enthusiasm for preaching and new power in it."

Speaker.—"Dr. Phillips Brooks was himself a preacher of uncommon gifts, and readers of these noble and impassioned pages will be at no loss to discover wherein lay the secret of his power."

Uniform with "Lectures on Preaching," crown 8vo, cloth, 5s.,

THE INFLUENCE OF JESUS

ON

The Moral, Social, Emotional, and Intellectual Life of Man.

BY THE RIGHT REV. PHILLIPS BROOKS.

Expository Times.—"'The Influence of Jesus' is theologically the most characteristic of all Bishop Brooks' works. So if one would understand this man, we must read this book. Mr. Allenson has therefore been wise in his generation, and has given us a new and attractive edition of it."

Saturday Review.—"This volume gives us a kind of object lesson to supplement the 'Lectures on Preaching.' Here, indeed, we see what the lecturer meant when he spoke of preaching Christ; here we have the whole range of man's possibilities illustrated in Christ's life."

BOOKLET ADDRESS BY PHILLIPS BROOKS.

Post 8vo, neat artistic wrapper, 28 pp., 6d. net; post free, 7d.,

THE LIFE WITH GOD.

Christian Endeavour.—"The closing address of a series of mission services held in Boston, 1891. With unsurpassed eloquence the preacher emphasises the great truth that the only natural and complete life is the religious life. Endeavourers will be particularly interested in what is said respecting prayer, Bible-reading, and seeking the Church."

Christian World.—"It is almost overwhelming in its power, eloquence, and tender pleading. It is also essentially human as is the religion which it sets forth. The preacher's great point is that the religious is the only natural and complete life. Dealing with the man who urges, 'What room is there for Christianity in such a crowded life as mine?' he says: 'It is as if the engine had said it had no room for the steam; it is as if the tree had said it had no room for the sap; it is as if the ocean had said it had no room for the tide; it is as if the man had no room for his soul.' The sermon altogether, in its range both of thought and of emotion, is at an immeasurable remove from ordinary conventional religious utterance, and will convey needful lessons to preachers, quite as much as to business men."

H. R. ALLENSON, 30 PATERNOSTER ROW, LONDON, E.C.

SOME RECENT VOLUMES OF SERMONS.

Crown 8vo, 3s. 6d.,

BROKEN IDEALS, AND OTHER SERMONS.
BY REV. JAMES THEW, LEICESTER.

Baptist.—"These fresh, out-of-the-way sermons combine the experience of a saint with the wonder of a child... Buy it, and it will make your holidays holy days."
Nottingham Daily Guardian.—"His discourses show a manly common sense."
Literary World.—"Have conspicuous merit. We do not remember to have met Mr. Thew in print before, but we shall be glad to do so again."
British Weekly.—"We welcome this pretty and tasteful little volume of sermons; they are fresh and tender."

3s. 6d. a Volume,

MYRTLE STREET PULPIT. SERMONS.
BY REV. JOHN THOMAS, M.A., LIVERPOOL.

Of Vol. IV., just out, *The Baptist Magazine* says: "We rejoice that there is in the great city on the banks of the Mersey a ministry so able and eloquent."
Of Vol. III., *The Expository Times* says: "There is not a commonplace sermon in it, and it contains some of the finest we have read for a long time."

With additional Sermons and Prayers. Crown 8vo, 404 pp., cloth, 6s.,

SUNDAY MORNINGS AT NORWOOD.
BY REV. S. A. TIPPLE.
NEW EDITION.

Freeman.—"It is twelve years since the first edition of these vigorous and suggestive sermons were published, and no one who knows their value will be at all surprised that their republication should have been urgently called for."
British Weekly.—"There are more original ideas in Mr. Tipple's volume than in many which have rapidly run into nine or ten editions. Both the prayers and the sermons give evidence of a fresh, lucid, and forcible thinker. No connoisseur in sermons can fail to appreciate the fine quality of Mr. Tipple's work."
Brondesbury Chapel Magazine.—"The rare spirituality of these sermons has long been recognised. If you know a dear old saint who is quietly waiting for the lifting of the veil, give her this and she will thank you. If you know a man of business who is all unconsciously becoming hardened and worldly, give him this. It will do him good. The marvel is that Mr. Tipple is not better known. A man who can preach like this would number his hearers by thousands if this were not such a topsy-turvy world."

Large crown 8vo, 6s.,

THE KINGDOM WITHOUT OBSERVATION.
BY THE LATE REV. JOHN DAVIES (of Old Gravel Pit Chapel).

Expository Times.—"There is not a flaunting word nor a catchpenny thought within it. There is reserve, and the staying grace of sincerity, and it will be deeply loved and honoured by those who can discern."
Christian World.—"Tenderly sympathetic, with some affinity with Erskine of Linlathen."

H. R. ALLENSON, 30 PATERNOSTER ROW, LONDON, E.C.

A LIST OF NEW BOOKS
AND ANNOUNCEMENTS OF
H. R. ALLENSON, PUBLISHER AND BOOKSELLER, 30, PATERNOSTER ROW, LONDON, E.C.

Containing—
SPECIAL BOOKS FOR WORKERS AMONG CHILDREN, MISSIONARY WORKS, AND HELPS TO PREACHERS.

Important Forthcoming Volumes of Sermons.

Clifford.—SOCIALISM AND THE KINGDOM OF GOD. Sermons by John Clifford. M.A., D.D. Preparing.

Davies.—THE KINGDOM WITHOUT OBSERVATION and other Sermons, by the late Rev. John Davies, of Brighton. Ready shortly.

Pierce.—THE DOMINION OF CHRIST. Sermons on Foreign Missions, by William Pierce, Minister of New Court Chapel. Ready shortly.

Intended as a contribution towards the Centenary Celebration of the London Missionary Society.

Thew.—BROKEN IDEALS, AND OTHER SERMONS, by Rev. James Thew, Leicester. Preparing.

Tipple.—SUNDAY MORNINGS AT NORWOOD, Sermons by Rev. S. A. Tipple, with additional matter.

Mr. Tipple's book has long been out of print; this new edition with new matter will prove welcome to many old and new friends.

Stevens and Burton.—A HARMONY OF THE GOSPELS, for Historical Study. By Professors Wm. A. Stevens and Ernest de Witt Burton. Small 4to., Cloth, 6s.

An Analytical Synopsis of the Four Gospels in the Version of 1881.

Stevens and Burton.—OUTLINE HANDBOOK OF THE LIFE OF CHRIST. 8vo., Cloth limp, 2s. 6d.

H R. Allenson's List.

Abbott. — How to Become a Christian. By Rev. Lyman Abbott, D.D. Five simple Talks to the Young. 32 pp. 1s.

Barlow. — Endless Being; or, Man made for Eternity. By J. L. Barlow. Crown 8vo. 165 pp. 2s.6d.

"Admirable in tone, free from littleness, calm and earnest in spirit."—*National Baptist.*

Bathgate. — Aunt Janet's Legacy to Her Nieces. Being Recollections of Humble Life in Yarrow in the beginning of the Century. By Mrs. Janet Bathgate, Selkirk. With portrait of the author and four full-page illustrations; Second edition. Crown 8vo. 198 pp. 2s. 6d. net, post free, 2s. 9d. Now Ready.

"Attractive within and without."—*Christian Endeavour*

"We have truly enjoyed "Aunt Janet's" story. It is as fresh as a mountain breeze."—*Life of Faith.*

"Of excellent flavour and moral influence, and shows how the humblest lot may be glorified by godly faith and zeal."—*Word and Work.*

"It will do anyone good to read this faithful record."—*Sword and Trowel.*

Bible Readings, Books of. *See* Needham, Tyson, Wolfe.

Breed. — A History of the Preparation of the World for Christ. With Maps, Charts, and Illustrations. By Rev. David R. Breed, D.D. 2nd Edition, revised and enlarged. Large demy 8vo., Cloth. 483 pp. 7s. 6d.

Brooks. — Influence of Jesus. By Phillips Brooks. Lecture 1.—Influence of Jesus on the Moral Life of Man. Lecture 2.—On the Social Life of Man. Lecture 3.—On the Emotional Life of Man. Lecture 4.—On the Intellectual Life of Man. New Edition. (Uniform with Macmillan's Edition of Phillips Brooks' Sermons). Crown 8vo, Cloth. 5s. Now Ready.

Brooks. — LECTURES ON PREACHING. By Phillips Brooks. New Edition. (Uniform with Macmillan's Edition of Phillips Brooks' Sermons.) Crown 8vo., Cloth. 5s. Now Ready.

Brooks. — THE LIFE WITH GOD. By Phillips Brooks. In artistic wrapper. 28 pp. Post 8vo. 6d. net, post free, 7d. Now Ready.

"It is almost overwhelming in its power, eloquence, and tender pleading. It is also essentially human as is the religion which it sets forth. The preacher's great point is that the religious is the only natural and complete life. Dealing with the man who urges 'What room is there for Christianity in such a crowded life as mine?' he says: 'It is as if the engine had said it had no room for the steam; it is as if the tree had said it had no room for the sap; it is as if the ocean had said it had no room for the tide; it is as if the man had no room for his soul.' The sermon altogether, in its range both of thought and of emotion, is at an immeasurable remove from ordinary conventional religious utterance, and will convey needful lessons to preachers, quite as much as to business men."—*Christian World.*

Bible.—POCKET CONCORDANCE TO THE. By Rev. J. Brown. Smallest handy Concordance in print. Cloth boards, 3 by 5 by ½in. Post free, 1s.

Children's Sermons and Addresses.—*See* under Coyle, Eaton, and Tyndall.

Chudleigh. Devonshire Antiquities.—By John Chudleigh. With Map and Index. Post 8vo. 2s. 6d. net. Second Edition.

Containing Illustrations of eighty Dartmoor Village and Wayside Crosses, Inscribed Stones, Stone Circles, Cromlechs, Clapper Bridges, Tolmens, Kistvaens, Logan Stones, and other objects of interest.

"This is a series of twenty-three illustrated Devonshire walks, chiefly over Dartmoor. The pedestrian antiquary will find the book of some use as a guide. . . . . The book is very cheap."—*Antiquary.*

Clifford.—SOCIALISM AND THE KINGDOM OF GOD. A Series of Sermons by Rev. Dr. John Clifford. Crown 8vo., Cloth. Preparing.

Coyle. — FOUNDATION STONES. Lectures to the Young. By Rev. Robert F. Coyle. Crown 8vo., Cloth. 192 pp. 3s.

Dale. — FINGER POSTS ON THE HIGHWAY OF LIFE. By John F. Dale. Post 8vo., Cloth boards. 400 pp. 3s. 6d.

A splendid gift book for older boys and young men.

Davis. — A SKETCH OF THE LIFE OF JOSEPH HARDY NEESIMA, LL.D. (The Runaway Boy who Founded the First Christian College in Japan), with many Illustrations. By Rev. J. D. Davis, D.D. Crown 8vo., Cloth. 156 pp. 2s. 6d.

"Few books of a biographical nature have ever fallen under my eyes which have so interested and delighted me. The riches of missionary literature more and more increase. No man or woman can read this book without a positive addition to heart-wealth."—REV. A. T. PIERSON, D.D., in *The Missionary Review of the World.*

"Was there ever a more wonderful romance in real life than the story of Joseph Neesima, the Japanese fugitive boy? Providence sent him to a noble New England gentleman, to be educated in our best schools, that he might go back to preach the gospel to his countrymen, and do more than any other Christian in moulding the institutions of the new Japan, which, within the last twenty years, has emerged from the twilight of the Middle Ages."—*The Golden Rule.*

Dawson. — HIGHBURY QUADRANT PULPIT AND CHURCH MAGAZINE. Monthly, 1d. Contains an Address by the Pastor, Rev. W. J. Dawson.

Eaton. — TALKS TO CHILDREN. By Dr. T. T. Eaton. Introduction by Rev. John A. Broadus, D.D. Crown 8vo., Cloth boards, gilt top. 222 pp. 3s. 6d.

"They reproduce Scripture History in the terms of modern life, and give it both a vivid setting before the youthful imagination and a firm grip on the youthful conscience."—*The Independent.*

Elliott. — THE WORKERS' WEAPON. Its perfection, authority, study, and use. By John Henry Elliott. Narrow 16mo., Cloth. 98 pp. 1s. 6d.

Everts. — THE SABBATH. Its Permanence, Promise, and Defence. By W. W. Everts, D.D. Crown 8vo. 278 pp. 3s. 6d.

H. R. Allenson's List. 5

Everts. — THE CHRISTIAN APOSTOLATE. Its Principles, Methods, and Promise in Evangelism, Missions, and Social Progress. By Dr. W. W. Everts. Crown 8vo., Cloth boards. 533 pp. 6s.

Faulkner. — LIFE OF BISHOP JOSEPH SIDNEY HILL (first Bishop in Western Equatorial Africa). By Rose E. Faulkner. With an Introduction by the Right Rev. Bishop Stuart, late of Waiapu. 3 excellent Portraits and a Map. Personal Recollections by the author, Mr. Bennett, W. Hay M. H. Aitken, and Eugene Stock. Large crown 8vo., Cloth. 228 pp. 3s. 6d. Second Edition.

It is hoped that the publication of this book will be looked upon as a suitable and timely memorial, and also be of great interest generally.

"Miss Faulkner has done her work well. A striking likeness of Bishop Hill appears on the title page, also one of Mrs. Hill in the body of the book, and another of the Bishop in his episcopal robes. We strongly advise our readers to purchase the volume, and make all the use they can of it by recommending it to their friends."—*Life of Faith.*

"A large number of Christian friends, on three Continents at least, will welcome the biography of Joseph Sidney Hill. To know him with any degree of intimacy was to love him, and to magnify the grace of God that shone so brightly through his character and life. . . . This volume will, undoubtedly, be a welcome one in many a Christian household, and through it our brother, being dead, will yet speak, calling every reader to the happy consecrated life of service which he lived. . . . The first brief sojourn in Africa, the busy fruitful years spent at the Antipodes, the mission work at home, the return to Africa as peacemaker in the native Niger Church, and the later chapters in the Bishop's life are all described by a vivid and sympathetic pen."—*The Christian.*

"We wish specially and earnestly to recommend the Memoir of Bishop Hill. It is just the book to give away."—*C. M. Gleaner.*

"It is but a short time ago that Joseph Sidney Hill was, if we may so speak a fresh and rising star in the firmament of missionary work and interest, and then, on the eve of launching forth into new and extensive efforts for the spread of the Gospel, he was called up higher, and the star had set on earth; but its light still lingers amongst us, and it glows with warmth and radiance in the pages of this volume, in which his career is sketched by the sympathetic pen of one who knew him well."—*Mr. Eugene Stock in Church Missionary Intelligencer.*

Fellowship. The new Weekly Journal concerning Holiness and the possibilities of the Spiritual Life. Edited by Rev. J. Gregory Mantle. Contributions by Rev. R. W. Dale, M.A., LL.D., Rev. T. G. Selby, Professor J. Rendel Harris, M.A., Rev. George Jackson, B.A.,

Professor J. Agar Beet, D.D., the Editor, etc., etc. 1d. weekly. Monthly Parts 6d. each. Sent post free, 3 months, 1s. 8d.; 6 months, 3s. 4d.; 12 months, 6s. 8d. Single No., 1½d., post free.

Flewin.—ANGEL MINISTRIES: Being Thoughts on "Browning's Guardian Angel." By William George Flewin. Post 8vo., 6d.

<small>An appreciation of Giovanni Francesco Barbieri, better known as Guercino, the painter of the picture that so inspired Robert Browning, with the pcem in full.</small>

Gant.—FROM OUR DEAD SELVES TO HIGHER THINGS, by F. T. GANT, F.R.C.S. Crown 8vo., 2s. 6d.

<small>A capital book for young men and women.</small>

Gibbon. THE PULPIT. A Sermon. By Rev. J. Morgan Gibbon. Issued monthly, 1d.

Gospel Booklets (Torbay Series of).—No. 1. SHAKESPEARE'S DAUGHTER. A homily on her Epitaph. Oblong, 16 pages in Art Wrapper. 3d., by post 4d. Just issued.

<small>"Evangelical doctrine is clearly taught."—*Sword and Trowel.*
"Beautifully designed. Christian Endeavourers might do worse than use it instead of cards."—*Christian Endeavour.*
To be followed by: "Birds in the Pulpit; or, The Rooks of Newcastle."
"The Butler and the Baker; or, Dreams and their Sequels."</small>

Hall. — OUR SOVEREIGN FATHER. A Sermon by Rev. W. Newman Hall. Square 16mo., handsome parchment wrapper. 6d. net, by post, 7d.

<small>DR. FAIRBAIRN, Principal of Mansfield College, Oxford, says :—"What you have put so much heart into must have a message of its own."
"This is a most meritorious performance, both for spirit and execution."—*The Irish Congregational Magazine.*
"This little work, in its tasteful cover, is a thoughtful and striking exposition of the Primitive conception "Father first and King next," which grew out of the idea of the family, the nucleus of the nation. The way in which this conception is pursued so as to emphasise the side of God's benevolent sovereignty is very satisfying."—*The Rock.*
"In this brochure of about fifty pages the writer deals with the Fatherhood of God. The tone is lofty, the language elegant and forcible, and the whole subject is treated in an intelligent way from the modern evangelical standpoint, and illustrated by quotations from modern theological writers."—*The Methodist Times.*
"'Our Sovereign Father' is a thoughtful booklet."—*The Christian.*</small>

Hebblethwaite. — CASTLEHILL, A TALE OF TWO HEMISPHERES. By James Hebblethwaite. 2s. 6d. In preparation.

<small>The history of a boy who was heir to "Castlehill," his unjust treatment culminating in his being transported from his quiet north country home to the dangers and horrors of prison life in Tasmania in the early days of the Colony. His escape and meeting with his early love are related in a thrilling and artless manner.</small>

Horne. — THE SPIRIT OF DIVES : a Sermon, by Rev. C. Silvester Horne, M.A., preached to Young Men and Women in Kensington Chapel, Sunday evening, February 10th, 1895. Crown 8vo., 1d.

<small>Most valuable accompaniment to the Gospels.</small>

Kephart. — CHART OF THE PUBLIC LIFE OF CHRIST. Arranged to show at a glance the events of our Lord's Life, accompanied by a coloured diagram of a Harmony of the Four Gospels. By Rev. J. C. Kephart, M.A. 16 pages of letterpress and coloured chart printed on strong bond paper, all neatly folded into a handy book for the pocket. Cloth limp, 2s. 6d.

<small>"A pictorial harmony of the Gospels, and should be popular. An ingenious compilation."—(Am.) Congregationalist.</small>

<small>"Exceedingly helpful."—Baptist Teacher.</small>

<small>"There are evidences of great care. For many persons to whom the life of our Lord appears a historical confusion Mr. Kephart's book will be very useful."
—American Sunday School Times.</small>

<small>"It must be seen to be understood and appreciated. I do wish that every preacher, Sunday-school superintendent, and teacher could have a copy at once.'—Rev. R. Cowden, Sec. N. B. S. S. Board.</small>

Kerr. — AN INTRODUCTION TO THE STUDY OF THE BOOKS OF THE NEW TESTAMENT. By John H. Kerr, M.A. Crown 8vo., Cloth. 333 pp. 6s.

<small>"We take particular pleasure in commending this volume to students of Divinity, who will find in it a convenient summary of the facts and arguments relating to an important subject."—The Church Standard.</small>

MEDICAL MISSIONS.

Kerr. —Pioneering in Morocco. Being a Record of seven years' Medical Mission work in the Palace and the Hut. By Dr. Robert Kerr. Large Crown 8vo. 21 full-page Illustrations. 252 pp. 3s. 6d.

"Dr. Kerr's statements bear strong testimony to the great value of medical missions, he gives too, much useful information concerning mission work in general. The book is written in a pleasant, almost conversational style, contrasting favourably with some far more pretentious records of missionary work which could be named. It is also well got up—paper, type, illustration, and binding being alike good."—*The Rock*.

"Dr. Kerr has made good use of his opportunities."—*Christian World*.

"Full of interesting details of Moorish life and ways, and a large number of illustrations, taken from photographs, add much to its value.—*Evangelical Magazine*.

"An admirable record of work accomplished for Christ. Simple and gracious in its narration; picturesque and realistic in description."—*Sword and Trowel*.

Kilby. — Trips to Algeria, Holland, the North Cape, etc. Written and illustrated by Henry Kilby. Paper boards, 132 pp. 2s. 6d.
Chatty descriptions of Trips to many interesting places.

Kohaus. — Recitation Poems for Sabbath Schools, Mission Bands, etc.: Poems for Children's Day, Easter Time, Harvest Home, Christmas Festivals, Missionary Concerts, and Bands of Hope. By Hannah More Kohaus. 144 pp. 1s. 6d.

Lathrop. — Fifty Years and Beyond; or, Old Age and How to Enjoy it. Gathered Gems for the Aged. By Rev. S. S. Lathrop. With an Introduction by Rev. Arthur Edwards, D.D. 400 pp. Large crown 8vo. 3s. 6d.
"The selections are very precious."—*The Witness*.

Lewis. — The Unseen Life. Ten Sermons by Rev. F. Warburton Lewis, B.A. Contents: Part I., The Crowning of Love. Chapter 1, Love of

Friends; 2, Love and Death; 3, Love and Life; 4, Love, the first and the last. Part II., The Life Eternal. Chapter 5, Heaven; 6, Working out Salvation; 7, The Death of the Cross; 8, The Gospel of the Resurrection; 9, Sorrow and Sympathy; 10, Where there is no last night. Crown 8vo., Cloth boards. 128 pp. 2s. 6d. Now Ready.

"Mr. Lewis has the courage to say old things over again; to say them pleasantly and even impressively, and further, his work is well worth publishing, well worth our gratitude and praise."—*Expository Times.*

"Much to attract thoughtful, religious people."—*Christian Leader.*

"A volume of thoughtful and interesting sermons."—*British Weekly.*

"Much literary charm and great devotional feeling."—*Word and Work.*

A small collection of wise, simple sermons. Evangelical in the best sense of the word. The most beautiful sentence in the book: Key to the whole, is 'Loving is Life itself; being loved is life's supreme joy.' May we not hope for more from the sweetly reasonable Pen of Mr. Lewis?"—*Christian World.*

Lord.—NEW LIGHT DUMB-BELL DRILL. (Illustrated). By Charles E. Lord. Suitable for Gymnasia, Schools, and Persons of either Sex. Third Edition. Swd. 6d.

"There is a lot of valuable information to be gleaned by athletes of every class from a careful study of this neat little brochure .... more harm than good is often done in ignorance by athletes endeavouring to develop or maintain muscular power by an over-indulgence in dumb-bell practice, therefore Mr. Lord's cheerful explanation will come as a boon and a blessing to many. The book is neatly got up.—*English Sports.*

"The subject is dealt with in a terse and practical manner."—*Cycling.*

Marsh.—FAITH HEALING. A Defence; or, The Lord our Healer. By Rev. R. L. Marsh., M.A., Crown 8vo., Cloth boards. 148 pp. 2s.

"His review of objections is ingenious, and is pursued in a candid spirit."—*The Evangelist.*

Meyer.—CHRIST CHURCH MAGAZINE. Contains article each month by Rev. F. B. Meyer, M.A. One Penny.

Mills.—GOD'S WORLD; AND OTHER SERMONS. By B. Fay Mills, Author of "Victory through

Surrender," &c. Crown 8vo., Cloth. 322 pp. Just Ready. 3s. 6d.

"Mr. Mills has selected for publication in this, the first volume of his sermons ever issued, the sermons whose use has been followed by the best results in his Evangelistic work. The subjects embrace consecration, consistency, and service; sermons to those who have deserted the Master, and to those who have never confessed Him before men."

"As inspiration, as electric spark, in short as sermons, they are everything.'—*Expository Times.*

Moody in Chicago; or, the World's Fair Gospel Campaign. An account of 6 months' Evangelistic Work in Chicago and Vicinity, during the time of the World's Columbian Exposition. Cloth boards. 255 pp. 3s. 6d.

Moorehead.— OUTLINE STUDIES IN THE BOOKS OF THE OLD TESTAMENT. By M. W. G. Moorehead, D.D. Crown 8vo., Cloth. 363 pp. 6s. Just Published.

Needham.— BROKEN BREAD FOR SERVING DISCIPLES. 36 Bible Readings by the Author of "Bible Briefs." Crown 8vo., Cloth boards. 224 pp. 3s. 6d.

Otts.— AT MOTHER'S KNEE. The Mother's Holy Ministry with her Children in the Home. By J. M. P. Otts, D.D. 175 pp. Crown 8vo., Ornamental Cloth binding. 3s. Just Out.

Parkhurst.— FIRST STEPS TOWARD CHURCH UNITY. By Rev. Charles H. Parkhurst, D.D., of Brooklyn, New York. Two Studies: (1) One Body in Christ; (2) Members one of Another. Small 4to., paper cover. 32 pp. 1s.

Pentecost.— THE INVINCIBLE GOSPEL. By George F. Pentecost, D.D., Author of "Bible Studies," "In the Volume of the Book." Paper cover. 52 pp. 1s.

"Of large worth for Christian workers."

H. R. Allenson's List. 11

Perren.— REVIVAL SERMONS IN OUTLINE. With Thoughts, Themes, and Plans, by eminent Pastors and Evangelists. By Rev. C. H. Perren, Ph.D. (author of "Seed Corn for the Sower"). Crown 8vo., Cloth. 384 pp. 5s. Just Ready.

Perren.—SEED CORN FOR THE SOWER. A Book of Illustrations for the Pulpit and Platform. With Complete Indices to Subjects, Texts and Authors quoted. By Rev. C. Perren. Cloth boards. 422 pp. 5s.

Pierce and Horne.— THE PRIMER OF CHURCH FELLOWSHIP. For use in the Independent Churches. By Revs. William Pierce and C. Silvester Horne, M.A. Cheap Edition, 6d., post free, 7d. Now Ready.

This new and cheap edition has received very warm commendation by Dr. Dale, Dr. Barrett, and Dr. Brown, beside many others.

" We gladly welcome the new and cheaper edition of *The Primer of Church Fellowship*, by the Revs. William Pierce and C. Silvester Horne. Having already expressed our high opinion of it when published at 1s., we rejoice to see this cheaper edition, and trust it will be scattered broadcast over the twofold section of Christendom, known as the Churches of the Congregational order. It is an admirable handbook to the privileges and duties of Church membership."— *Word and Work.*

Porter. — SAINT MARTIN'S SUMMER. The Romance of the Cliff. By Rose Porter. Crown 8vo., Tastefully bound in Light Cloth boards. 263 pp. 2s. 6d.

"A stimulating, healthful story."—*The Golden Rule.*
" A pleasant story of English life."—*Boston Transcript.*

Powell.—CHURCH ORDER IN WORK AND WORSHIP, with an Introduction by Lieut.-Col. Henry M. Robert. By Rev. T. W. Powell. 140 pp. Cloth. 1s. net.

Young People's Society of Christian Endeavour

Pratt. — A DECADE OF CHRISTIAN ENDEAVOUR, 1881-1891. By Rev. Dwight M. Pratt. With

H. R. Allenson's List.

frontispiece portrait of Francis E. Clark, founder of the movement. Introduction by Rev. Wayland Hoyt, D.D. Crown 8vo., Cloth. 177 pp. 2s. 6d.

"Describes the origin, nature, and growth of the Society, and also explains the principles which have caused it to become so far-reaching, sturdy, attractive, and helpful. Such a book will always be wanted."—*Congregationalist (Am).*

Price.—A SYLLABUS OF OLD TESTAMENT HISTORY: Outlines and Literature, with an Introductory Treatment of Biblical Geography, interleaved with Writing Paper for Notes. Index. By Ira M. Price, Ph.D., Leipsic. Crown 8vo., Cloth. 198 pp. 5s.

"Students will find the book eminently useful."—*Am. S. S. Times.*

Pring.—THE MESSAGE OF THE INCARNATION TO THE NATION. Sermon by Rev. F. A. Pring. Crown 8vo. 16 pp. 2d., by post, 3d.

"Every social question is a moral one; and every moral question a religious one."—*Mazzini.*

Prophetic Studies, by Professor W. G. Moorehead, Rev. A. T. Pierson, D.D., Professor F. Godet, D.D., Rev. G. C. Needham, Rev. A. J. Gordon, D.D., Rev. Com. Dinwiddie, &c., &c. 216 pp. Cloth. 3s. 6d.

Putman.—HIS STAR, AND VESPER BELLS. Poems of the Inner Life. By Henry Putman. (Enamelled Paper), 6d., by post, 7d. Cloth gilt, gilt top, 1s. net.

"Putman's Vesper Bells make an admirable gift—contains twenty poems illustrative of the Christian's inner life. They are marked by tender feelings, devout insight, and a truly poetic gift."—*Methodist Times.*

"Hymns worthy of print. Seldom has so tiny a book of sacred verse been fuller of really good hymns."—*Literary World.*

"True and happy thought, the rhythm is sometimes well managed too —*Expository Times.*

Reed.—OUTLINE OF THE FUNDAMENTAL DOCTRINES OF THE BIBLE. By David Allen Reed. Crown 8vo., Cloth (interleaved with Writing Paper for Notes). 107 pp. 2s. 6d. Just Out.

H. R. Allenson's List. 13

Thew.—BROKEN IDEALS, AND OTHER SERMONS, by Rev. James Thew, Leicester. Crown 8vo., Cloth. Preparing.

Thomas.—MYRTLE STREET PULPIT SERMONS AND PRAYERS. By Rev. John Thomas, M.A., Liverpool. Large crown 8vo., Cloth boards. Each 3s. 6d. Weekly Nos., 1d. each, by post, 1½d.; 12 months, post free, 6/6; 6 months, 3/3; 3 months, 1/8. Vols. 1, 2, and 3 now Ready.

<small>Of Vol. 1, The *Expository Times* says: "This volume contains some of the finest sermons we have read for a long time. There is not a commonplace sermon in it."

Of Vol. 2, *The Presbyterian* says: "There is a fine, manly, vigorous ring about these sermons most refreshing to read. These sermons will prove tonics to every reader. His sermons display wide reading."

Replete with striking suggestive sentences in touch with present-day life, and roots the ethical in the doctrinal side of Christianity."—*Sword and Trowel.*</small>

Thompson. — THE PRAYER MEETING AND ITS IMPROVEMENT. By Lewis O. Thompson, with Introduction by Rev. A. E. Kittredge, D.D. *Seventh Edition, Revised.* Crown 8vo. 285 pp. 3s. 6d.

<small>"Most heartily do we wish this work a wide circulation, both among pastors and people, and we hope it may do much towards the lifting of the Prayer Meeting into that higher place which it ought to hold among the grand instrumentalities in the Kingdom of the Master."—*Congregationalist*, Am.</small>

Tipple. — SUNDAY MORNINGS AT NORWOOD. Sermons and Prayers by Rev. S. A. Tipple. New Edition, with additional matter. Crown 8vo., Cloth. 6s.

Towner.—HYMNS NEW AND OLD. With contributions from a very large number of well-known and popular Authors, for use in Gospel Meetings and other Religious Services. By D. B. Towner. In 2 Parts, 1s. 6d. each.

Tyndall. — OBJECT SERMONS IN OUTLINE. Illustrated Addresses for Children, for use with or without the blackboard. By Rev. C. H. Tyndall, with an Introduction by Rev. A. F. Schauffler, D.D. Crown 8vo., Cloth boards. 264 pp. Largely Illustrated. 3s. 6d.

"The lessons are well conceived and worked out with great ingenuity. We advise all who have young people's meetings in charge to examine the book."—*New York Independent.*

"Those pastors who are wrestling with the problem how to attract interest, and influence the young people, may obtain valuable suggestions from this book."—*Congregationalist*, Boston.

Tyson. — RED LETTER READINGS. By Bessie B. Tyson. A Series of Grouped Texts on such topics as "Called of God," "Confessing Christ," "Our Bodies," "Follow Jesus," etc. Paper wrapper. 366 topics. Post free, 1s. 6d.

Vance. — THE YOUNG MAN FOUR SQUARE. By James I. Vance. Contents: 1 The Young Man in Business. 2 The Young Man in Society. 3 The Young Man in Politics. 4 The Young Man in Religion. Crown 8vo., Cloth. 104 pp. 1s. 6d. Just Ready.

Weidner.—BIBLICAL THEOLOGY OF THE NEW TESTAMENT. Vol. 1, Part I. The Teaching of Jesus. Part II. The Petrine Teaching. Vol. 2, Part III. The Pauline Teaching. Part IV. The Teaching of John. By Revere Franklin Weidner. Crown 8vo., Cloth. 2 vols., each 5s.

Weidner.—BIBLICAL THEOLOGY OF THE OLD TESTAMENT. Based on Oehler. By Prof. Revere Franklin Weidner. Crown 8vo., Cloth. 212 pp. 5s.

Weidner. — STUDIES IN THE BOOK. By Prof. R. F Weidner. Old Testament, Genesis. Just Issued 2s. 6d. New Testament in 3 vols., sold separately, 2s. 6d. each. Crown 8vo., Cloth boards.
Interleaved with ruled paper for notes.

Weidner. — THEOLOGICAL ENCYCLOPÆDIA. By Weidner. Based on Hagenbach and Krauth. Vol. 1, Exegetical Theology, 3s. 6d.; Vol. 2, Historical and Systematic Theology, 5s.; Vol. 3, Practical Theology, 3s. 6d. Very extensive Bibliographical Lists of Books on the various subjects. Cloth boards. Just received.

Wells. — BUSINESS. A plain talk with Men and Women who Work. By Amos R. Wells. Ornamental boards. 1s. 6d.

West. — STUDIES IN ESCHATOLOGY. The thousand years in both Testaments. By Rev. Nathaniel West, D.D. Large crown 8vo., Cloth. 493 pp. 5s.

"We know of no work on the subject to be compared with this. We commend it to every one as a book full of warning. Students of prophecy will give it a hearty welcome." — *Methodist Review.*

Wolfe. — GOLD FROM OPHIR. A New Series of Bible Readings, edited by J. E. Wolfe. With an Introduction by Dr. James H. Brooks. Contributed to by Dr. Pentecost, Dr. A. J. Gordon, Prof. Moorehead, Rev. F. B. Meyer, &c. 8vo., Cloth boards. 302 pp. 5s.

"The owner of this fine vol. will have a warehouse of pulpit and platform furniture ready for use. Everything is condensed and analysed, so that there is not a line to spare. The doctrine is after our own heart, and the pervading spirit is one of downright earnestness." — C. H. SPURGEON, in *Sword and Trowel.*

YEAR BOOK FOR TEXTS OF SERMONS. Cloth. 3d.

H. R. Allenson's List.

Important to Sunday School Teachers.

The Sunday School Illustrator. A Commentary on the International Bible Lessons. For Teachers, Clergymen, Superintendents, and Bible Scholars. Containing Helps to Bible Study: Suggestive Questions, Bible Readings, Explanatory Notes, How to Teach Primary Lesson, Blackboard Hints, Original Illustrations, etc., etc. Monthly, 3d. Post free for 12 months for 2s. 6d. only.

Christian Evidence Gazette. — Monthly, 1d.

Friends of Foreign Missions and others are invited to inspect H. R. Allenson's Stock of Books on

MISSIONARY LIFE AND WORK.

A very large collection of the chief publishers' books in Theology, Biography, Children's Sermons, Sunday School Preparatory Work, Rewards and Prizes, and General Literature conveniently displayed for inspection.

SPECIAL FEATURE.—Almost any book not in stock will be procured in a few minutes, with the option of purchase.

H. R. ALLENSON is making a speciality of introducing many AMERICAN WORKS which have not hitherto been available easily to English readers.

CATALOGUES AND LISTS POST FREE ON APPLICATION.

30, Paternoster Row, London, E.C.

www.ingramcontent.com/pod-product-compliance
Lightning Source LLC
Chambersburg PA
CBHW031734230426
43669CB00007B/347